urban landscape transformation

urbane trans-formations-landschaften

jovis

urban landscape transformation

urbane trans-formations-landschaften

Editor Herausgeber: Internationales Doktorandenkolleg „Forschungslabor Raum"

jovis

PREFACE
VORWORT

PREFACE

Motivated by many positive experiences and proven successes with regard to the curriculum "Forschungslabor Raum" ("Spatial Research Lab") from 2007 to 2011, especially in view of the increasing number of dissertations completed as part of the first college, the second International Doctoral College "Spatial Research Lab" was set up for the period of 2013 to 2016—based on the principles of the previous program—as curriculum "2.0," with *spatial planning and design on an academic level* as a focal point, requiring initiatives for the independent exploration of uncharted territory in the form of individual doctoral theses.

The International Doctoral College is aimed at highly qualified persons from a wide range of disciplines related to spatial planning, who are keen to dedicate themselves intensely to complex spatial issues from an academic and creative point of view for their dissertation, seeking viable and innovative solutions and forward-looking methods and tools. It offers the participants the opportunity to address significant spatial issues of a high social relevance by means of interdisciplinary and cross-border exchanges. This exchange is stimulated by specific case studies and a common framework theme, promoting autonomous and original academic contributions. Accompanying lectures and guest presentations by renowned experts convey in-depth theoretical, methodological, design, and communication knowledge.

Difficult, highly complex, and convoluted spatial planning problems form the starting point for the doctoral college. These mostly involve several disciplines, different reference areas, and numerous public and private stakeholders. In this context, space comprises the entire physical environment with both *urban* and *rural* characteristics, and the possibilities it opens up for being, behaviour, and experience.

The second curriculum of the International Doctoral College "Spatial Research Lab" is also designed to foster the independent ability to identify issues relevant for spatial research. The exchange necessary for formulating individual contributions and for critical debate is developed gradually and the doctoral students take responsibility for it. The international platform of the doctoral college enables systematic comparison within the chosen topic area and critical discussion of practice-orientated concepts and strategies, in collaboration with the private and public players involved. The college not only provides excellent opportunities to engage in intense and interdisciplinary debates, but furthermore all the participating professors and lecturers are available as competent experts. In addition, guest professors are incorporated into the debate.

Motiviert durch zahlreiche positive Erfahrungen und belegbare Erfolge des Curriculums „Forschungslabor Raum" 2007 bis 2011, vor allem hinsichtlich der wachsenden Zahl der im Rahmen des Kollegs entstandenen Dissertationen, wurde das Internationale Doktorandenkolleg „Forschungslabor Raum" im Zeitraum 2013 bis 2016 – aufbauend auf den Grundsätzen des vorherigen Kollegs – als Curriculum „2.0" gestaltet: *Raumrelevantes Planen und Entwerfen auf wissenschaftlichem Niveau* stehen dabei im Mittelpunkt des Doktorandenkollegs. Dies erfordert Initiativen zur eigenständigen Erkundung von fachlichem Neuland im Rahmen individueller Doktorarbeiten.

Das Internationale Doktorandenkolleg richtet sich an besonders qualifizierte Personen aus unterschiedlichsten Fachgebieten mit Raumbezug, die sich im Rahmen ihrer Dissertation der intensiven, wissenschaftlich-kreativen Auseinandersetzung mit schwierigen raumrelevanten Fragestellungen widmen möchten, vor allem hinsichtlich der Suche nach tragfähigen und innovativen Lösungsansätzen sowie weiterführenden Methoden und Instrumenten. Es bietet den Teilnehmerinnen und Teilnehmern[1] die Möglichkeit, sich im interdisziplinären und grenzüberschreitenden Austausch mit raumbedeutsamen Fragestellungen hoher gesellschaftlicher Relevanz auseinanderzusetzen. Anhand konkreter Fallbeispiele und eines gemeinsamen Rahmenthemas wird dieser Austausch angeregt; es sollen eigenständige, originelle wissenschaftliche Beiträge gefördert werden. Begleitende Lehrveranstaltungen und Gastvorträge renommierter Fachleute vermitteln vertieftes Theorie-, Methodik-, Entwurfs- und Kommunikationswissen.

Ausgangspunkt des Doktorandenkollegs sind schwierige, äußerst komplexe und unübersichtliche Probleme der Raumentwicklung. Diese betreffen meist mehrere Sachbereiche, unterschiedliche Bezugsgebiete sowie zahlreiche öffentliche und private Akteure. Der Begriff des Raumes umfasst in diesem Zusammenhang die gesamte physische Umwelt, sowohl *städtischer* als auch *landschaftlicher* Prägung, und die dadurch eröffneten Möglichkeiten des Daseins, Verhaltens und Erlebens.

Auch im Rahmen des zweiten Curriculums des Internationalen Doktorandenkollegs „Forschungslabor Raum" soll die Fähigkeit zum eigenständigen Erkennen forschungsrelevanter und raumbedeutsamer Fragen entwickelt werden. Der zur Formulierung eigener Beiträge und zum kritischen Diskurs notwendige Austausch wird schrittweise entwickelt und in eigener Verantwortung von den Doktorandinnen und Doktoranden gepflegt. Die internationale Plattform des Doktorandenkollegs ermöglicht einen systematischen Vergleich im gewählten Themenfeld und die kritische Diskussion

While the framework theme of the first curriculum was dedicated to the development of metropolitan areas, the focus of the curriculum for the 2013–2016 doctoral college was "Urban Landscape Transformation." The wide-ranging changes in living environments with a primarily inward-looking settlement development, including changes in the areas of mobility, landscape, demography, energy, and, not least of all, climate, require integrated and clear strategies and concepts for coherent transformation. In order to explore and identify research topics, doctoral students at various universities studied significant spatial issues, specifically urban landscape transformations of national and European significance in Switzerland, Germany, and Austria. The aims were to explore the potential for cross-border concepts and strategies, to test appropriate tools and methods, and to demonstrate the effects and consequences of spatial interventions and decisions through experiments.

The core idea of the curriculum is based on simultaneous work at several university locations in a European context on central subject areas that are relevant for an academic and scientific discourse in all spatially-related planning and design disciplines. Such themes involve, for example, the management of settlement areas or cross-border tasks in spatial, infrastructure, and landscape development. In order to do so, suitable Spatial Research Labs, i. e. case studies with a common framework theme, are proposed at the participating university locations. The focal points are defined especially in the first year through a modular teaching programme: a) spatial planning methodology, b) spatial planning design, c) process development and communication, d) landscape theory. These events are carried out by various lecturers with relevant areas of focus. The doctoral college is set up so that different forms of interdisciplinary, national, and international cooperation are possible. This requires personal attendance at specified intervals at the doctoral symposia and the willingness of all those involved to cooperate using new information technologies.

A cycle of the doctoral programme takes three years. The first year serves the purposes of induction, identifying the research field, structuring the doctoral thesis, and evaluating potential case studies. The second year is dedicated in particular to more in-depth aspects of project studies, such as experiments and writing the key chapter of the thesis. The third year is reserved for evaluation, more in-depth studies of selected aspects, writing the thesis, and individual criticism.

The doctoral symposia, which are held three times a year, are an integral component of the doctoral college. These provide regular opportunities for intense exchange among the doctoral students and the participating professors. One doctoral symposium was held at each of the university locations, as well as at locations where the involved guest professors were based. They generally started on Sunday and ended on Friday and included a full programme. They were characterised by intensive exchange, excursions to the Spatial Research Labs, presentations, consultations, and

handlungsorientierter Konzepte und Strategien im Zusammenwirken mit privaten und öffentlichen Akteuren. Im Verlauf des Kollegs bieten sich nicht nur ausgezeichnete Möglichkeiten zu intensiven interdisziplinären Diskursen, sondern darüber hinaus stehen alle beteiligten Professoren und Lehrbeauftragte als kompetente Ansprechpartner zur Verfügung. Zusätzlich werden Gastprofessuren in den Diskurs eingebunden.

War das Rahmenthema des ersten Curriculums der Entwicklung metropolitaner Räume gewidmet, standen im Curriculum des Doktorandenkollegs 2013 bis 2016 nun „urbane Transformationslandschaften" im Fokus. Der vielfältige Wandel im Bereich der Lebensräume mit einer vorwiegend nach innen gerichteten Siedlungsentwicklung, Veränderungen im Bereich Mobilität, Landschaft, Demografie, Energie und nicht zuletzt Klima erfordern integrierte und anschauliche Strategien und Konzepte für eine ganzheitliche Transformation. Zur Erkundung und Eingrenzung der Forschungsthemen setzten sich die Doktorandinnen und Doktoranden an den verschiedenen Universitäten und Hochschulen exemplarisch mit bedeutsamen raumrelevanten Fragestellungen der Entwicklung urbaner Transformationslandschaften, namentlich nationaler und europäischer Bedeutung in der Schweiz, Deutschland und Österreich auseinander. Dabei sollten Möglichkeiten grenzüberschreitender Konzepte und Strategien erkundet, dafür geeignete Werkzeuge und Vorgehensweisen getestet und durch Experimente Wirkungen und Konsequenzen raumbedeutsamer Handlungen und Entscheidungen aufgezeigt werden.

Die Grundidee des Curriculums beruht auf der simultanen Bearbeitung zentraler Themenfelder, die für einen wissenschaftlichen Diskurs in allen raumbezogenen Planungs- und Entwurfsdisziplinen wesentlich sind, an mehreren Universitäts- und Hochschulstandorten im europäischen Kontext. Solche Themenfelder betreffen beispielsweise das Siedlungsflächenmanagement oder grenzüberschreitende Aufgaben der Raum-, Infrastruktur- und Landschaftsentwicklung. An den beteiligten Universitäts- und Hochschulstandorten werden dazu nach Bedarf geeignete Laborräume im Sinne von Projektgebieten mit gleichrangigen Rahmenthemen zur Verfügung gestellt.

Die Schwerpunkte werden insbesondere im ersten Jahr durch ein Lehrprogramm in Modulform vermittelt: a) Methoden der Raumplanung, b) raumplanerisches Entwerfen, c) Prozessgestaltung und Kommunikation sowie d) Landschaftstheorie. Die Veranstaltungen führen verschiedene Dozierende mit entsprechenden Schwerpunkten durch. Das Doktorandenkolleg ist so organisiert, dass unterschiedliche Formen der interdisziplinären, nationalen und internationalen Kooperation möglich sind. Das erfordert in festgelegten Zeiträumen persönliche Anwesenheit im Rahmen der Doktorandenwochen und die Bereitschaft zur Zusammenarbeit zwischen allen Beteiligten mithilfe neuer Informationstechnologien.

Ein Zyklus des Doktorandenprogramms dauert grundsätzlich drei Jahre. Das erste Jahr dient der Einarbeitung, der Eingrenzung und Ausarbeitung

shared framework events. The principles and guidelines of the International Doctoral College "Spatial Research Lab" proved to be an effective and lively framework once again the second time round. Changes compared to the 2007–2011 college were the incorporation of guest professors and guest weeks, combined with an extension of exchanges in English. The team of lecturers was also widened, in order to discuss certain key themes more intensively.

Our special thanks goes to the guest professors, lecturers, and academic coordinator of the college.

We would also especially like to thank the doctoral students, whose great enthusiasm contributed to the success of the college, and all colleagues at the host cities and universities who supported the International Doctoral College "Spatial Research Lab" on its research journey both theoretically and materially. Our special gratitude also goes to the Professor Albert Speer Foundation, which provided sponsorship for the concluding phase of selected dissertation projects.

On this basis, we were able to embark on our third journey together.

The professors at the International Doctoral College "Spatial Research Lab":
Michael Koch, Markus Neppl, Walter Schönwandt, Bernd Scholl, Andreas Voigt (speaker of the doctoral college), Udo Weilacher

des Forschungsfeldes und der Gliederung der Doktorarbeit sowie der Auswertung infrage kommender Fallbeispiele. Das zweite Jahr widmet sich insbesondere der vertieften Auseinandersetzung im Rahmen von Projektstudien wie Experimenten und der Erarbeitung der Schlüsselkapitel der Doktorarbeit. Das dritte Jahr ist der Auswertung, der Vertiefung ausgewählter Aspekte, der Abfassung der Doktorarbeit und individueller Kritik vorbehalten.

Fester Bestandteil des Doktorandenkollegs sind die dreimal jährlich stattfindenden Doktorandenwochen. Sie schaffen regelmäßig wiederkehrende Anlässe für intensiven Austausch der Doktorierenden und der beteiligten Professuren. Die Doktorandenwochen wurden wieder jeweils an einem der Universitäts- und Hochschulstandorte sowie den Standorten der einbezogenen Gastprofessuren durchgeführt. In der Regel begannen sie sonntags und endeten freitags, und beinhalteten ein durchweg gut gefülltes Programm. Sie waren geprägt durch intensiven Austausch, Exkursionen in den Laborräumen, Vorträge, Konsultationen und gemeinsame Rahmenveranstaltungen. Der Rahmen des Doktorandenkollegs konnte neuerlich mit Leben erfüllt werden. Prinzipien und Grundsätze des Internationalen Doktorandenkollegs „Forschungslabor Raum" haben sich auch im zweiten Durchgang bewährt. Die wesentlichen Veränderungen zum Kolleg 2007 bis 2011 umfassten die Einbindung von Gastprofessorinnen und die Gestaltung von Gastwochen, verbunden mit der Erweiterung des Sprachraumes und des Austausches in englischer Sprache. Zudem wurde das Team der Lehrbeauftragten vergrößert, um bestimmte Schlüsselthemen intensiver erörtern zu können.

Unser besonderer Dank gilt den Gastprofessorinnen, Lehrbeauftragten und dem wissenschaftlichen Koordinator des Kollegs.

Wir danken vor allem aber auch den Doktorierenden, die mit großer Begeisterung zum Gelingen des Kollegs beigetragen haben, und allen Kolleginnen und Kollegen der gastgebenden Städte und Universitäten, die mit besonderem Engagement ideell und materiell das Internationale Doktorandenkolleg „Forschungslabor Raum" auf unserer Forschungsreise unterstützt haben.

Besonders möchten wir auch der Professor Albert Speer Stiftung danken, die für die Abschlussphase ausgewählter Dissertationsvorhaben Stipendien zur Verfügung gestellt hat.

Auf dieser Basis konnte die gemeinsame Reise zum zweiten Mal beginnen.

Die Professoren des Internationalen Doktorandenkollegs „Forschungslabor Raum":
Michael Koch, Markus Neppl, Walter Schönwandt, Bernd Scholl, Andreas Voigt (Sprecher des Doktorandenkollegs), Udo Weilacher

METHODOLOGY OF THE DOCTORAL COLLEGE

METHODIK IM DOKTORANDENKOLLEG

ENABLING LEARNING, SETTING UP TRANSFORMATION PROCESSES
The organisation and culture of the International Doctoral College

WERNER TSCHIRK

Writing a dissertation means leaving well-trodden paths behind and venturing down a new one. It is an exceptional achievement, which requires both enormous motivation and freeing up time and financial resources for a period of several years. This article is based on the notion that, apart from personal factors, general conditions, that is the university and private surroundings, play a central role in the successful completion of a dissertation. Doctoral students in the field of planning had a second opportunity to master this challenge as part of the International Doctoral College "Spatial Research Lab."

The framework conditions and principles that define the organisational core of the doctoral research college will be documented here. How can independent research and the writing of a dissertation be supported by a doctoral programme? How can one improve the success of a doctoral programme, measured by the number of graduates on the one hand and the quality of work on the other?[1] How can one ensure successful "learning" and thereby enable a "transformation process?"

Organisational framework and scheduling of the International Doctoral College[2]

The core concept of a doctoral college is parallel work on research projects about central subject areas in spatial and landscape planning and urban development. The projects are orientated towards the college's framework topic in the respective curriculum.

The cycle of a curriculum lasts three years. Induction takes place in the first year, and serves the purpose of identifying topics, mapping out the field of research, and setting up a research plan. The second year is dedicated to the preparation of a key chapter of the doctoral thesis and more in-depth work on key research aspects, e.g. carrying out case studies in laboratories or conducting interviews. If everything goes according to plan, then, in the third year, the focus is on evaluating empirical data, presenting first results, and compiling a comprehensive draft of the work. ▶ 1

1 *The cycle of a doctoral programme*

LERNEN ERMÖGLICHEN, TRANSFORMATIONSPROZESSE GESTALTEN
Organisation und Kultur des Internationalen Doktorandenkollegs

WERNER TSCHIRK

Eine Dissertation zu verfassen bedeutet, bereits bekannte Pfade zu verlassen und Neues in die Welt zu bringen. Es setzt voraus, eine außerordentliche Leistung zu vollbringen, eine enorme Motivation aufzubringen und nebenbei zeitliche und finanzielle Ressourcen für einen Zeitraum von mehreren Jahren freizuschaufeln. Neben persönlichen Faktoren – so die These, die diesem Artikel zugrunde liegt – spielen vor allem die Rahmenbedingungen bzw. das universitäre und private Umfeld eine zentrale Rolle für einen erfolgreichen Abschluss einer Dissertation. Bereits zum zweiten Mal hatten Doktoranden der Planungsdisziplinen die Möglichkeit, diese Herausforderung im Rahmen des Internationalen Doktorandenkollegs „Forschungslabor Raum" zu meistern.

Die Rahmenbedingungen und Prinzipien, welche den organisatorischen Kern des Internationalen Doktorandenkollegs definieren, sollen hier dokumentiert werden. Wie können freies Forschen und das Verfassen einer Dissertation durch ein Doktorandenprogramm unterstützt werden? Wie kann der Erfolg eines Doktorandenprogramms, gemessen an der Zahl der Absolventen einerseits und an der Qualität der Arbeiten andererseits, gesteigert werden?[1] Wie kann „Lernen" gelingen und so ein „Transformationsprozess" ermöglicht werden?

Organisatorischer Rahmen und zeitlicher Ablauf des Internationalen Doktorandenkollegs[2]

Die Kernidee des Doktorandenkollegs beruht auf der parallelen Bearbeitung von Forschungsarbeiten zu zentralen Themenfeldern der Raum- und Landschaftsplanung und der Stadtentwicklung. Die Arbeiten orientieren sich dabei am Rahmenthema des Kollegs im jeweiligen Curriculum.

Der Zyklus eines Curriculums dauert drei Jahre. Im ersten Jahr findet die Einarbeitung statt. Es dient vor allem der Themenfindung, der Eingrenzung des Forschungsfeldes und der Erstellung des Forschungsplans. Das zweite Jahr widmet sich der Erstellung eines Schlüsselkapitels der Doktorarbeit sowie der vertiefenden Bearbeitung der Forschungsschwerpunkte wie zum Beispiel der Durchführung von Fallstudien in Laborräumen oder von Interviews. Verläuft alles nach Plan, liegt im dritten Jahr der Schwerpunkt auf der Auswertung der empirischen Daten, der Präsen-

Doctoral symposia are held three times per year to provide individual appraisals of the doctoral projects and to exchange additional assessments. They are carried out at one of the participating universities and colleges, or in locations where the guest professors involved are based. The doctoral week is set up by the host professor, in consultation with the council, doctoral students, and the coordinator. In the 2013–2016 curriculum, the symposia comprised a total of ten weeks in different locations.[3]

As a rule, the doctoral symposia start on Sunday afternoons with a "welcome aperitif" and end on Fridays with a shared review and a look into the future. The first half of the week is dedicated to in-depth exchanges about the dissertations in the form of presentations and discussions. In addition, there are usually educational events and guest presentations. The second half of the week is for exploring the respective "laboratories" and working on assignments in smaller workshops. The programme is interspersed with bilateral or trilateral individual consultations (doctoral students with professors and/or lecturers). As work progresses, the time allocated to mutual exchange about the dissertations is increasingly used for work with the laboratories and for topical inputs.

Learning paradigms and insights from research into cognition

Cognitive science deals with the processing of information in human thought and decision-making processes. Subjects such as perception, thinking, evaluation, learning, etc. are the focus of this discipline. Notions of how we learn and generate new knowledge have taken a significant new turn in recent decades. Originally, the brain was viewed as a type of black box that was stimulated by "external" stimuli and reacted to them (behaviourism); since the 1960s and 1970s, the focus has been on the "internal" processes of human thought (cognitivism). It was no longer a case of producing the right response to certain stimuli, but about learning the right methods and procedures for solving problems. Contrary to the two aforementioned theories, the constructivist learning model is based on the notion that knowledge cannot simply be funnelled into the learner. Knowledge is not a "thing" that exists externally and is transported to the learner, but an active process that is significantly influenced by the learning environment and the learners themselves. Learners should be faced not with answers, but with questions. They should be stimulated by means of complex, practice-related, and authentic tasks and should solve problems independently. In learning practice, these models are not mutually exclusive, but complement each other, playing different and important roles depending on the task and requirement.

The doctoral college promotes scientific and creative approaches to difficult, space-related issues by means of selected laboratories and associated tasks. Starting points for mutual exchanges are provided by concrete and highly complex spatial development problems requiring independent and original academic contributions. The necessary critical discourse is

tation erster Ergebnisse sowie der Erstellung eines durchgeschriebenen Entwurfs der Arbeit.

Zur individuellen Kritik der Doktorarbeiten sowie zum Austausch und zum Erwerb von zusätzlichen Qualifikationen finden dreimal pro Jahr Doktorandenwochen statt. Sie werden jeweils an einem der teilnehmenden Universitäts- und Hochschulstandorte oder an den Standorten der einbezogenen Gastprofessuren durchgeführt. Die Gestaltung einer Doktorandenwoche erfolgt durch die gastgebende Professur in Abstimmung mit dem Kollegium, den Doktoranden sowie mit dem Koordinator. Im Curriculum 2013–2016 waren es insgesamt zehn Wochen an unterschiedlichen Standorten[3].

In der Regel beginnen die Doktorandenwochen sonntags nachmittags mit einem „Willkommens-Apéro" und enden freitags mit dem gemeinsamen Rückblick und Ausblick. Die erste Wochenhälfte steht dem vertiefenden Austausch zu den Dissertationen im Rahmen von Präsentationen und Diskussionen zur Verfügung. Zudem finden meist Lehrveranstaltungen und Gastvorträge statt. Die zweite Hälfte der Woche dient der Erkundung der jeweiligen Laborräume und der Bearbeitung von Aufgabenstellungen in kleineren Workshops. Bi- oder trilaterale Einzelkonsultationen (Doktoranden mit Professoren und/oder Lehrbeauftragen) akzentuieren das Programm. Die Zeiträume für den gemeinsamen Austausch über die Dissertationen nehmen mit Fortschreiten der Arbeiten zugunsten der Beschäftigung mit den Laborräumen bzw. zugunsten von Inputs zu den Lehrthemen zu.

Lernparadigmen und Erkenntnisse der Kognitionsforschung

Die Kognitionswissenschaft beschäftigt sich mit der Verarbeitung von Informationen bei menschlichen Denk- und Entscheidungsprozessen. Themen wie Wahrnehmung, Denken, Urteilen, Lernen etc. stehen im Fokus dieser Disziplin. Die Vorstellung über die Art und Weise, wie wir lernen und neues Wissen generieren, hat sich in den letzten Jahrzehnten entscheidend gewandelt: Wurde ursprünglich das Gehirn als eine Art Blackbox verstanden, die durch „äußere" Reize stimuliert wird und auf diese reagiert (Behaviorismus), wurde ab den 1960er und 1970er Jahren der Fokus auf die „inneren" Prozesse des menschlichen Denkens gelegt (Kognitivismus). Es ging schließlich nicht mehr darum, auf gewisse Stimuli die richtige Antwort zu produzieren, sondern richtige Methoden und Verfahren zur Problemlösung zu lernen. Im Gegensatz zu den beiden zuvor genannten Theorien geht das konstruktivistische Lernmodell davon aus,

developed step by step and the doctoral students take responsibility for elaborating it.

Like the writing of a doctoral thesis, learning by means of complex problems has more to do with questioning, reflection, and observation than with accumulating further knowledge. It is especially important to take alternative perspectives on board, to view one's own thoughts "from the outside," to reflect, and to question knowledge critically. The doctoral college provides a safe environment for failing or rejecting theories—a basic precondition for learning and academic progress.

The significance of emotional factors in learning processes

Learning processes are dependent on many factors, most of which are influenced by the limbic system.[4] The limbic system thus plays an important role with regard to perception, emotions, feelings and motivation, contributing to successful learning. As early as the 1970s, the psychologist and psychotherapist Carl R. Rogers[5] recognised that learning can be improved if the learner perceives subject matter as relevant for their own purposes and that learning processes are understood and assimilated more easily if "external threats" are seen as minimal.

Traditionally, in science, we are used to thinking and arguing on a rational level guided by reason. There is increasing awareness of the role that emotional, cultural, or artistic aspects, as well as interpersonal relations, play in learning processes. This should be more firmly anchored in traditional scientific understanding. At the same time, the freedom of learning and research is increasingly under pressure due to financial restrictions and uncertain employment situations. The independent setting of focal points and interest-led research have become a rare occurrence in everyday university life.

The framework of the International Doctoral College "Spatial Research Lab" takes the aforementioned aspects into special consideration. Examples of this include the following factors:

- The doctoral college promotes the ability to identify issues relevant to research and space independently. The core of the International Doctoral College is a common framework topic, within which the research focuses can be developed according to the abilities and interests of the doctoral students, in consultation with the professor in charge.
- The meetings during the doctoral symposia provide a safe environment. Guests are only permitted to attend presentations and discussions about the research work in exceptional cases. This creates an open attitude and creates the preconditions for an in-depth academic discourse.
- The interdisciplinary exchange in the respective laboratories, which is based on concrete problems, enables one to see beyond one's own discipline, helps to qualify specialist discourse, and, at the same time, creates opportunities for networking among participants researching similar subjects.

dass dem Lernenden Wissen nicht einfach wie mit einem Trichter einge-gossen werden kann. Wissen ist kein „Ding", das außerhalb existiert und zum Lernenden transportiert wird, sondern ein aktiver Prozess, der von der Lernumgebung sowie vom Lernenden selbst maßgeblich beeinflusst wird. Der Lernende sollte nicht mit Antworten, sondern mit Fragen kon-frontiert werden. Er sollte durch komplexe, praxisrelevante und authen-tische Aufgabenstellungen angeregt werden und eigenständig Probleme generieren. In der Praxis des Lernens stehen diese Modelle nicht nebenei-nander, sondern ergänzen sich und spielen je nach Aufgabenstellung und Anforderung eine unterschiedlich bedeutende Rolle.

Das Internationale Doktorandenkolleg fördert durch ausgewählte La-borräume und die damit verbundenen Aufgabenstellungen die wissen-schaftlich-kreative Auseinandersetzung mit schwierigen raumrelevanten Fragestellungen. Anhand konkreter und äußerst komplexer Probleme der Raumentwicklung werden Anlässe zum gemeinsamen Austausch gegeben und eigenständige, originelle wissenschaftliche Beiträge gefördert. Der notwendige kritische Diskurs wird schrittweise entwickelt und in eigener Verantwortung von den Doktorierenden gepflegt.

Lernen anhand von komplexen Problemen hat – wie das Verfassen einer Doktorarbeit – viel mehr mit Hinterfragen, mit Reflexion und mit Beob-achten zu tun als mit der Ansammlung von weiterem Wissen. Eine fremde Perspektive einzunehmen, die eigenen Gedanken „von außen" zu betrach-ten, zu reflektieren und Wissen kritisch zu hinterfragen, scheinen dabei von besonderer Bedeutung. Durch das geschützte Umfeld des Internatio-nalen Doktorandenkollegs ist die Möglichkeit des Scheiterns und des Ver-werfens von Thesen gegeben – eine Grundvoraussetzung für Lernen und wissenschaftlichen Fortschritt.

Die Bedeutung emotionaler Faktoren in Lernprozessen

Lernprozesse sind darüber hinaus von vielen Faktoren abhängig, von de-nen die meisten durch das limbische System[4] beeinflusst werden. Dieses spielt hinsichtlich Aufmerksamkeit, Emotionen, Gefühlen und Motivation eine große Rolle und ist auf diese Weise am Lernerfolg beteiligt. Bereits in den 1970er Jahren erkannte der Psychologe und Psychotherapeut Carl R. Rogers[5], dass Lernen gefördert werden kann, wenn Lerninhalte vom Ler-nenden für seine eigenen Zwecke als relevant wahrgenommen werden und dass Lernprozesse leichter verstanden und assimiliert werden, wenn „äußere Bedrohungen" minimal erscheinen.

Traditionell sind wir in der Wissenschaft gewohnt, in der rationalen, ver-nunftgeleiteten Ebene zu denken und zu argumentieren. Welche Rolle emo-tionale, kulturelle oder künstlerische Aspekte sowie die zwischenmensch-liche Ebene besonders in Lernprozessen spielen, wird zunehmend bewusst und sollte im traditionellen Wissenschaftsverständnis stärker verankert werden. Gleichzeitig gerät die Freiheit von Lehre und Forschung durch fi-nanzielle Restriktionen und prekäre Dienstverhältnisse zunehmend unter

- A targeted framework programme with shared experiences (attending events, a conference dinner in special venues, etc.) also provides the opportunity to get to know others personally and to engage in exchanges beyond the formal agenda.
- The host professors take care of providing the infrastructure and technical equipment for the duration of the doctoral symposia, as well as financial support. Almost all the costs (accommodation, catering, etc.) incurred during the doctoral symposia could be covered through subsidies, the respective professors, and the respective higher education establishments. In addition, in the 2013–2016 curriculum, several participants received funding in the final year for the particularly intense finalisation phase.
- Between physical meetings, the doctoral students have the opportunity to share views via an Internet-based platform. The internal area of this platform provides access to various documents. The participants themselves are required to record their personal insights in log books.
- The accompanying coaching, available both for individual discussions and as part of educational assignments for the whole group over the course of the curriculum, is also worth mentioning in this context. Apart from training communication and presentation skills, the coaching also includes topics such as self-management and the organisation of one's own work process.[6]

Creating transformation processes consciously

The term "transformation"/"to transform" originates from Latin (from *transformare*) and means "to change shape," or, in current language usage, also "to modify," "to change." Compared to the notion of "learning"—understood as the individual or collective acquisition of mental, physical, or social knowledge, skills, and abilities—the term "transformation" also implies the aspect of conscious behaviour and action in itself. Furthermore, "learning" is an ability exclusive to living creatures. "Transformation," on the other hand, can involve both mental processes (for example value systems), as well as physical space or the built-up world. Creating transformation processes consciously is therefore the core task of planning disciplines. Planning either involves changing physical space or creating formal and organisational conditions for solving spatial problems. To do so, plans are drawn up and instructions are developed. As problems per se do not exist, but are a social construct based on value systems and the requirements of individuals, the connection between learning and transformation becomes clear. Consciously set–up transformation processes are based on corresponding learning processes. Changes—both in physical space and in the thinking of individuals—can therefore be particularly successful if suitable conditions for learning can be created. This applies to the core aspects of planning disciplines, as well as to the particularly

Druck. Freie Schwerpunktsetzung und interessengeleitete Forschung sind im universitären Alltag zum seltenen Glücksfall geworden.

Das Umfeld des Internationalen Doktorandenkollegs „Forschungslabor Raum" trägt den zuvor genannten Aspekten in besonderer Weise Rechnung. Beispielgebend dafür sind unter anderem folgende Faktoren:

- Im Rahmen des Doktorandenkollegs wird die Fähigkeit zum eigenständigen Erkennen forschungsrelevanter und raumbedeutsamer Fragen entwickelt. Kern des Doktorandenkollegs ist ein gemeinsames Rahmenthema, innerhalb dessen die Forschungsschwerpunkte je nach Fähigkeiten und Neigungen der Doktoranden und in Absprache mit der jeweils betreuenden Professur entwickelt werden können.

- Die gemeinsamen Treffen im Rahmen der Doktorandenwochen bieten einen geschützten Ort. Gäste sind nur in Ausnahmefällen bei Präsentationen und Diskussionen über die Forschungsarbeiten zugelassen. Dies erzeugt eine offene Haltung und schafft die Voraussetzung für einen tiefergehenden, wissenschaftlichen Diskurs.

- Der interdisziplinäre Austausch anhand konkreter Probleme in den jeweiligen Laborräumen ermöglicht den Blick über den Tellerrand der eigenen Disziplin hinaus, trägt zur Qualifikation des fachlichen Diskurses bei und schafft gleichzeitig Möglichkeiten zum Vernetzen mit Teilnehmern, die zu ähnlichen Themen forschen.

- Ein bewusst gestaltetes Rahmenprogramm mit Elementen des gemeinsamen Erlebens (Besuch von Veranstaltungen, Conference-Dinner an besonderen Orten etc.) bietet zudem Gelegenheit für persönliches Kennenlernen und Austausch abseits der formalen Agenda.

- Die jeweiligen gastgebenden Professuren bemühen sich sowohl um Bereitstellung der Infrastruktur und des technischen Equipments über den Zeitraum der Doktorandenwochen als auch um die finanzielle Unterstützung. So ist es stets gelungen, dass nahezu alle Kosten (Unterkunft, Verpflegung etc.) während den Doktorandenwochen durch Förderungen bzw. über die jeweiligen Professuren und Hochschulstandorte getragen wurden. Darüber hinaus standen beispielsweise im Curriculum 2013–2016 mehreren Teilnehmern im Abschlussjahr Stipendien für die besonders zeitintensive Finalisierungsphase zur Verfügung.

- Auch zwischen den physischen Treffen haben die Doktoranden über eine internetbasierte Plattform die Möglichkeit zum Austausch und können über den internen Bereich dieser Plattform auf sämtliche Unterlagen zugreifen. Die Teilnehmer selbst sind aufgefordert, in Logbüchern ihren persönlichen Erkenntnisgewinn festzuhalten.

- In diesem Zusammenhang erwähnenswert ist auch das begleitende Coaching, das sowohl für Einzelgespräche als auch im Rahmen von Lehraufträgen für die gesamte Gruppe über den Zeitraum des Curriculums zur Verfügung steht. Neben der Schulung der kommunikativen und präsentationstechnischen Fähigkeiten sind auch Themen wie Selbstmanagement und Organisation des eigenen Arbeitsprozesses Teil des Coachingangebots[6].

creative process involved in writing a dissertation. Both in professional practice and at a university level, it is about asking repeatedly: how can one enable learning in order to create transformation processes?

Transformationsprozesse bewusst gestalten

Der Begriff „Transformation" stammt aus dem Lateinischen (von *transformare*) und bedeutet „umformen" oder im heutigen Sprachgebrauch auch „modifizieren", „verändern". Im Vergleich zum Begriff des „Lernens" – verstanden als individueller oder kollektiver Erwerb von geistigen, körperlichen oder sozialen Kenntnissen, Fähigkeiten und Fertigkeiten – beinhaltet der Terminus „Transformation" auch den Aspekt des bewussten Handelns, der Aktion in sich. Zudem ist „Lernen" eine Fähigkeit, die Lebewesen vorbehalten ist. „Transformation" hingegen kann sowohl geistige Prozesse (zum Beispiel Werthaltung) als auch den physischen Raum, die gebaute Umwelt, betreffen.

Transformationsprozesse bewusst zu gestalten ist somit Kernaufgabe der planenden Disziplinen. Beim Planen geht es entweder darum, den physischen Raum zu verändern oder formale und organisatorische Voraussetzungen zu schaffen, um Probleme im Raum zu lösen. Dazu werden Pläne verfasst und Handlungsanleitungen entwickelt. Da Probleme per se nicht existieren, sondern aufgrund von Werthaltungen und Bedürfnissen von Individuen sozial konstruiert sind, wird der Zusammenhang zwischen Lernen und Transformation deutlich. Bewusst gestaltete Transformationsprozesse setzen dementsprechende Lernprozesse voraus. Veränderungen – sowohl im physischen Raum als auch im Denken von Individuen – können daher besonders dann gelingen, wenn es möglich ist, geeignete Voraussetzungen für das Lernen bereitzustellen. Dies trifft auf das Kerngeschäft der planenden Disziplinen genauso zu wie für den besonders kreativen Schaffensprozess beim Verfassen einer Dissertation. Sowohl in der beruflichen Praxis als auch auf universitärer Ebene gilt es stets aufs Neue zu fragen: Wie kann Lernen ermöglicht werden, um Transformationsprozesse zu gestalten?

INTERNATIONALES
DOKTORANDENKOLLEG
FORSCHUNGSLABOR RAUM
CuriticAum 2013 – 2016
Urbane Transformationslandschaften

INFORMATIONEN ZUR DOKTORANDENWOCHE

IN : FORMATION

2. Woche Doktorandenkolleg vom 11.08. – 16.08.2013 in München

THE BELGRADE—ZURICH—MILAN TRILOGY
Exploring space means interaction with the locality!

ROLF SIGNER

Confronting real problematic situations is one of the focal points of the doctoral symposia, as was already the case in the first doctoral college.[1] In the context of the framework topic "Urban Landscape Transformation," the local organisers each chose a Spatial Research Lab to which a whole-day excursion was respectively dedicated. The Spatial Research Labs were prepared with an introduction and rounded off by a workshop. The basic idea was to gain a visual impression of the current and conceivable problems in a relatively unknown and complicated situation within a short period of time, in other words: to learn. This text initially reports about important aspects of learning. Impressions of the encounters with three selected Spatial Research Labs, in Belgrade, Zurich, and Milan, conclude this contribution.

Modes of knowledge

Before we take a look at various aspects of learning, we will adopt a system of forms of knowledge put forward by Bunge;[2] he makes a distinction between *sensory-motor, perceptual,* and *conceptual knowledge.* Examples of sensory-motor knowledge include the ability to use a computer or to drive a car. Examples of perceptual knowledge are the identification of a plane flying past (e.g. as an Airbus A340) or the song of a lark. Examples of conceptual knowledge are the theory of central places, the concept of the degree of motorisation, or the knowledge that traffic lights can be operated by detector signals.[3]

These three forms of knowledge are interconnected, for example conceptual knowledge can improve motor skills or perception. An aircraft can be piloted better if the pilot has knowledge of aerodynamics and meteorology for example— also because a trained pilot pays particular attention to special display units in certain situations. All three forms of knowledge are involved simultaneously in many cognitive activities such as drawing, writing, or piloting.

Knowledge of a conceptual nature may be in the foreground for many clarification processes in spatial planning, but the other forms are by no

> ### Belgrade
> "Framing is [...] always a process of delimitation and exclusion that structures, individuates, and differentiates material configurations." Alloa calls the frame a "border control." It closes off outwardly and inwardly. A frame therefore helps the viewer to carry out their exploratory activities in a more targeted manner.
>
> Cf. Alloa, Emmanuel: Das durchscheinende Bild. Zurich 2011, p. 288

DIE TRILOGIE BELGRAD – ZÜRICH – MAILAND
Den Raum erkunden heißt Berührungen mit der Örtlichkeit!

ROLF SIGNER

Die Auseinandersetzung mit realen Problemsituationen bildet wie bereits im ersten Doktorandenkolleg[1] einen Schwerpunkt während der Doktorandenwochen. Die lokalen Organisatoren wählten im Kontext des Rahmenthemas „Urbane Transformationslandschaften" jeweils einen Laborraum aus, dem eine ganztägige Exkursion gewidmet war. Diese wurde durch eine Einführung vorbereitet und mit einem Workshop abgeschlossen. Die grundlegende Idee dabei war, sich in kurzer Zeit ein Bild über die aktuellen und absehbaren Probleme in einer relativ unbekannten, verworrenen Situation verschaffen zu können, also zu lernen. Hier wird zunächst über einige wichtige Aspekte des Lernens berichtet. Impressionen über die Auseinandersetzungen mit drei dieser ausgewählten Laborräume in Belgrad, Zürich und Mailand schließen diesen Beitrag.

Formen des Wissens

Bevor wir uns einigen Aspekten des Lernens zuwenden, übernehmen wir eine Systematik der Wissensformen von Bunge[2]: Er unterscheidet in *sensor-motorisches*, *perzeptuelles* und *konzeptuelles* Wissen. Beispiele für sensor-motorisches Wissen sind die Fertigkeiten, einen Computer bedienen oder ein Auto lenken zu können. Beispiele für perzeptuelles Wissen sind das Identifizieren eines vorbeifliegenden Flugzeuges (zum Beispiel als Airbus A340) oder des Gesangs einer Lerche. Beispiele für konzeptuelles Wissen sind die Theorie der zentralen Orte, das Konzept des Motorisierungsgrades oder das Wissen, dass die Steuerung einer Lichtsignalanlage in Abhängigkeit von Detektormeldungen erfolgen kann.[3]

Diese drei Wissensformen sind miteinander verbunden: Konzeptuelles Wissen kann die motorischen Fertigkeiten oder die Wahrnehmung verbessern. Ein Flugapparat lässt sich zum Beispiel bei Kenntnis von Aerodynamik und Meteorologie besser steuern – unter anderem weil der geschulte Pilot in bestimmten Situationen spezielle Anzeigegeräte besonders beachtet. Alle drei Wissensformen sind bei vielen kognitiven Aktivitäten simultan beteiligt, wie beim Zeichnen, beim Schreiben oder beim Fliegen.

> ### Belgrad
> „Rahmung ist [...] stets ein Ein- und Ausgrenzungsgeschehen, das materielle Konfigurationen ordnet, individuiert und differenziert." Alloa nennt den Rahmen einen „Grenzhüter". Er schließt nach außen und nach innen ab. Somit hilft ein Rahmen dem Betrachtenden, seine Erkundungsaktivitäten gezielter durchzuführen.
>
> Vgl. Alloa, Emmanuel: Das durchscheinende Bild. Zürich 2011, S. 288

means irrelevant. To be able to recognise that somebody is suffering from a participation deficit in a meeting may be important for the success of the meeting. "And whoever has spent a number of hours by a busy urban road may judge parameters such as average daily traffic or noise emissions to be what we should really be using them for, namely as indications of living environments, in other words of situational entities, to which countless additional characteristics can be attributed, such as noise, stench, danger, damage and dirty façades, social segregation, dilapidation, higher crime rates etc. Inspections, on-site viewings and so on are especially important when dealing with complex problem situations, because it enables an interplay or opposition between different points of view [...], which is usually a means of ensuring that nothing important is forgotten."[4,5]

Learning—Acquisition of knowledge

According to Bunge, knowledge can be acquired in three ways, namely through ideation, action, and perception.[6]

Under the title "inferring,"[7] which involves reasoning, he writes about two ways to develop conceptual knowledge: firstly, new insights can be gained from non-propositional material (i. e. perceptions), for example if the observer of a river landscape tries to imagine the scenery during a flood. Secondly, new insights can be gained from those already known, for example when calculating an employment rate using empirical sources, such as counting employed people and the overall population of a certain area at a given point in time.

The second way of learning is by doing. In order to gain more reliable information about the geological structure of a mountain for example, an exploratory shaft is often bored before the definitive location of a tunnel is determined or the drift method has been selected. If a problem that cannot be solved in a routine manner has to be tackled then a pilot project is often chosen as the way forward.[8] If the task is to get to

Belgrade

Mario Schneider: "When I move through an unknown city, I always have my sketchpad at the ready. If I encounter situations that are interesting, or reflect the character of the place, or if I am standing in front of significant landmarks, I whip out my pen and take a bit of time. There is often no time limit for a drawing, unless I'm out and about with my wife and the weather is rather British. On our boat tour on the Sava and Danube, however, I became acquainted with a more intense form of time limit. Owing to the continuous movement, the view of the banks was changing constantly, which left me with little time to draw individual situations. I then had the brilliant idea of capturing the whole trip. If it was difficult to capture small-scale spatial situations on account of the travelling speed, then I would dedicate myself to the whole. This resulted in a continuous panorama of the banks we passed. With this type of spatial exploration, it was particularly interesting to capture the changing landscape on the banks."

Für viele raumplanerische Klärungsprozesse mag das Wissen konzeptueller Art im Vordergrund stehen, die anderen Arten sind aber keineswegs unbedeutend. In einer Sitzung erkennen zu können, dass jemand unter einem Beteiligungsdefizit leidet, kann dem Erfolg des Treffens förderlich sein. „Und wer sich einmal einige Stunden an einer stark befahrenen städtischen Hochleistungsstraße aufgehalten hat, vermag in Zukunft Kenngrößen wie den durchschnittlichen täglichen Verkehr oder die Lärmemissionen eher als das beurteilen, als was wir sie sinnvollerweise verwenden sollten, nämlich als Hinweise auf Lebensräume, auf situative Gebilde also, zu denen zahllose weitere Merkmale gehören können wie: Lärm, Gestank, Gefahr, beschädigte und verschmutzte Fassaden; soziale Entmischung, Verwahrlosung, erhöhte Kriminalität etc. Augenscheine, also Begehungen, Exkursionen etc. sind bei der Behandlung verworrener Problemsituationen besonders wichtig, weil dadurch ein Wechselspiel oder eine Konkurrenz zwischen verschiedenen Sichtweisen […] stattfinden kann, was üblicherweise eine Bedingung dafür ist, dass nichts Wichtiges vergessen wird."[4,5]

Belgrad

Mario Schneider: „Wenn ich mich durch eine fremde Stadt bewege, habe ich immer das Skizzenbuch parat. Entdecke ich Situationen, die interessant sind, den Charakter des Ortes wiedergeben, oder stehe ich vor bedeutenden Landmarks, zücke ich den Stift und nehme mir etwas Zeit. Oft gibt es kein Zeitlimit für eine Zeichnung, es sei denn ich bin mit meiner Frau unterwegs und das Wetter ist eher britisch. Auf unserer Bootstour auf Save und Donau schloss ich aber noch Bekanntschaft mit einer verschärfteren Form des Zeitlimits. Durch die kontinuierliche Fahrt veränderte sich der Blick auf das Ufer ständig, was mir nur wenig Zeit zum Zeichnen einzelner Situationen ließ. Ich kam dann auf den genialen Gedanken, die ganze Fahrt festzuhalten. Wenn ich aufgrund der Fahrtgeschwindigkeit kleine räumliche Situationen nur schwer erfassen kann, dann widme ich mich eben dem großen Ganzen. So entstand ein kontinuierliches Panorama der von uns abgefahrenen Ufer. Bei dieser Art der Raumerkundung war es besonders spannend, den Wandel der Uferlandschaft festzuhalten."

Lernen – Wissenserwerb

Wissen kann gemäß Bunge auf drei Arten erworben werden, nämlich durch Nachdenken, Handeln und Wahrnehmen.[6]

Er schreibt unter dem Titel „Inferring"[7], wo das Räsonieren behandelt wird, über zwei Arten, wie man konzeptuelles Wissen ausbaut: Zum einen lassen sich neue Aussagen aus nichtpropositionellem Material (zum Beispiel Wahrnehmungen) gewinnen, etwa wenn der Betrachter einer Flusslandschaft sich die Szenerie bei einem Hochwasser vorzustellen versucht. Zum anderen können unter Verwendung bekannter Aussagen neue erzeugt werden, etwa die Berechnung einer Erwerbsquote unter Benützung empirischer Gegenstände wie die Zählungen der erwerbstätigen Personen sowie der Gesamtbevölkerung eines bestimmten Gebietes zu einem bestimmten Zeitpunkt.

Die zweite Möglichkeit des Lernens ist Handeln. Um zuverlässigere Informationen etwa zur geologischen Beschaffenheit eines Gebirges zu erhalten, wird oft ein Sondierstollen gebohrt, ehe die definitive Lage eines Tunnels festgelegt sowie die Vortriebsmethode gewählt

1 *Green shaft cover on the bottom left at the Zurich Bellevue*
1 *Grüner Schachtdeckel links unten am Zürcher Bellevue*

know a particular space, then it is necessary to walk around it, to inspect it, which is what happened at each case in our trilogy.

The third way of acquiring knowledge is through perception. Perception is an activity that relates the perceiver to their environment at a given moment. It provides numerous stimuli for the sensory system of the person, who can see, hear, feel, smell, and taste, as well as watch, listen, touch, sniff, and savour—if he or she is curious. In this case, the perceiver directs their attention towards a particular aspect of their environment, notices it, and explores it. In this context, I like to report about an experiment carried out for many years with students attending my lecture "Planning Methodology" at the Swiss Federal Institute of Technology Zurich (ETH). These students used the tram and bus daily. The question "what is there between the Zurich tram tracks?" was commonly answered with "asphalt" or "paving with grass," but practically never with "colourful shaft covers." However, there are many of these, both in green and in yellow. The students had never noticed these objects which have been part of the urban streetscape for many years, before that point. ▶1

In this context one should mention the perceptual cycle described by Neisser.[9] This concept links perceivable objects with the perceiver; schemata within the perceiver guide and change perceptions.[10] ▶2

Guski formulates it like this: "the perception process basically runs continuously and as a cycle: perception takes place in the constant shift between expectations (which he [Neisser; note by the author] called anticipatory schemata), awareness of object characteristics, potential changes to ex-

wird. Wenn ein Problem angegangen werden soll, das nicht routinemäßig gelöst werden kann, wird häufig der Weg des Pilotvorhabens eingeschlagen.[8] Wenn es darum geht, einen bestimmten Raum kennenzulernen, ist es nötig, ihn zu begehen, wie dies in unserer Trilogie jeweils geschehen ist. Die dritte Möglichkeit des Wissenserwerbs ist schließlich das Wahrnehmen. Wahrnehmung ist eine Betätigung in der Zeit, die den Wahrnehmenden mit seiner Umgebung in Beziehung bringt. Sie bietet zahlreiche Reize für das sensorische System des Menschen. Er kann sehen, hören, fühlen, riechen und schmecken; er kann aber auch – wenn er neugierig ist – betrachten, lauschen, tasten, wittern und kosten. In diesem Fall richtet der Wahrnehmende seine Aufmerksamkeit auf einen bestimmten Teil seiner Umgebung, er schenkt ihm Beachtung, er erkundet ihn. Ich berichte in diesem Zusammenhang gerne von einem während vielen Jahren durchgeführten Experiment mit Studierenden meiner Vorlesung „Planungsmethodik" an der ETH Zürich, die täglich Tram und Bus benutzten. Auf die Frage „Was gibt es zwischen den Zürcher Tramschienen?" sind Antworten wie „Asphalt" oder „Rasenziegel" gängig, praktisch aber nie „farbige Schachtdeckel". Solche gibt es aber zuhauf, sowohl in grüner als auch in gelber Farbe. Die Studierenden hatten bisher noch nie ihre Aufmerksamkeit auf diese Objekte gerichtet, die seit vielen Jahren Bestandteil der städtischen Möblierung sind. ▶1

In diesem Zusammenhang ist der Wahrnehmungszyklus von Neisser[9] zu erwähnen. Dieses Konzept bringt die wahrnehmbaren Objekte mit dem Wahrnehmenden zusammen, indem Schemata im Innern des Wahrnehmenden die Wahrnehmung leiten und dadurch verändert werden.[10] ▶2

Guski formuliert das so: „Im Wesentlichen läuft der Wahrnehmungspro-

2 *Perceptual cycle according to Neisser*[11] *(The terms "external" and "internal" were added by the author)*
2 *Wahrnehmungszyklus nach Neisser*[11] *(Die Begriffe „draußen" bzw. „drinnen" wurden durch den Autor hinzugefügt.)*

Objekt
wahrnehmbare Reize
«draußen»

verändert / wählt aus

Schema
«drinnen»   leitet   Erkundungsaktivitäten

zess kontinuierlich und zyklisch ab: Im ständigen Wechsel zwischen Erwartungen (die er [Neisser; Anmerkung des Autors] antizipierende Schemata nennt), Aufnahme von Objektmerkmalen, eventueller Veränderung der Erwartungen aufgrund objektiver Information, neuer Erwartung, weiterer Aufnahme von Objektmerkmalen usw. findet Wahrnehmung statt."[11] Ein Schema wird also während des Erkundungsprozesses möglicherweise verändert, etwa indem man auf Neues stößt: Man wird zum Beispiel

pectations due to objective information, new expectations, further noticing of object characteristics, etc."[11]

Schemata may therefore be modified during the exploration process, i. e. through encountering something new. For example, one will notice that there are colourful shaft covers between the Zurich tram tracks, of which some are green and others are yellow. The perceiving person is therefore not only informed, but also transformed, because from now on they will distinguish the shaft covers by colour. The ability to make distinctions (to notice differences) increases with the accumulation of background knowledge (for example about how something functions). Green shaft covers indicate an induction loop, which can detect a tram driving over it, while yellow shaft covers control the track switches. Neisser speaks of perceptual learning.[12]

Green and yellow covers between the tram tracks are now recognised as something ("sense & identify"). Through learning, they have become familiar units to the viewer, and, what's more, one cannot avoid recognising these objects as something — "You can't help recognising it!"[13] When encountering the Spatial Research Labs, all these forms of knowledge acquisition came into play. Thinking may have been predominant while being introduced to the Spatial Research Labs, but during the explorations on site, as well as at the concluding workshop, there was an interplay of doing, perceiving, and inferring.

About the Belgrade | Zurich | Milan trilogy of Spatial Research Labs

All the Spatial Research Labs chosen were so large that they could not be grasped all at once. Only parts of the Spatial Research Labs were available for immediate inspection. Owing to this difficulty, the maxim[14] of three

Belgrade

Anita Grams: "When I am exploring, a simultaneous perception of time and space is important to me. As text alone is not suitable to represent the simultaneity of the perception of atmosphere, smells, sounds, or associations, owing to the necessarily chronological sequence of words, our group decided to capture the perceptions during the boat trip on a continuous exploration grid. For me, the acoustic backdrop emerged as a suitable focal point and individual approach. The types of sound convey a variety of spatial situations: the humming of other boot engines at a widening of the river like a lake, the laughing of swimming children on an easily accessible stretch of shore, or the droning of a jet plane as the boat was approaching the airport area. This "spatial soundtrack," captured in words and pictures, was amalgamated with the exploration grids of my colleagues who also captured aspects such as borders/barriers, accessibility to the banks, or eye-catchers on a time axis. Like with a musical score, individual voices can thus be layered and linked in time and space by synchronous bar lines. Those viewing the musical score are given a continuous impression of the happenings in space. It is only through the synchronous interplay of the individual and different exploration grids that the space reveals something new or unexpected, enabling us to think together about what had been explored."

Anita Grams: „Beim Erkunden ist mir eine simultane Wahrnehmung von Zeit und Raum wichtig. Weil Text allein wegen der zwingend chronologischen Abfolge von Worten nicht geeignet ist, um die Gleichzeitigkeit der Wahrnehmung von Atmosphäre, Gerüchen, Geräuschen oder Assoziationen darzustellen, hat sich unsere Gruppe entschlossen, das während der Bootsfahrt Wahrgenommene an einem zeitlich fortlaufenden Erkundungsraster festzumachen. Als ‚Brille' und individuellen Zugang hat sich für mich die Geräuschkulisse als geeignet herausgestellt. Die Art der Geräusche transportiert unterschiedliche räumliche Bedingungen: das Brummen von anderen Bootsmotoren bei einer seeähnlichen Ausweitung des Flusses, das Lachen von badenden Kindern an einem gut zugänglichen Ufer oder das Dröhnen eines Düsenflugzeugs, als das Boot sich dem Flughafengebiet näherte. Diese ‚Raum-Tonspur', festgehalten in Wort und Bild, habe ich mit den Erkundungsrastern meiner Kolleginnen und Kollegen überlagert, die Themen wie Grenzen/Barrieren, Uferzugänglichkeit oder Eyecatcher ebenfalls auf einer Zeitachse festgehalten haben. Wie bei einer Partitur in der Musik können so einzelne Stimmen (oder ‚Brillen') übereinander angeordnet und mit zeitlich und räumlich synchronen Taktstrichen verbunden werden. So entsteht für den Betrachter der Partitur ein zeitlich fortlaufender Eindruck über das Geschehen im Raum. Erst im synchronen Zusammenspiel der individuellen und unterschiedlichen Erkundungsraster gibt der Raum Neues oder Unerwartetes preis und das gemeinsame Nachdenken über das Erkundete wird möglich."

merken, dass sich zwischen den Zürcher Tramgleisen farbige Schachtdeckel befinden, von denen einige grün, andere gelb sind. Die wahrnehmende Person wird also nicht nur informiert, sondern auch transformiert, indem sie von nun an die Schachtdeckel nach Farbe unterscheiden wird. Die Fähigkeit zur Unterscheidung (Unterschiede bemerken) steigt mit der Zunahme des Hintergrundwissens (zum Beispiel zur Funktionsweise). Grüne Schachtdeckel deuten auf eine Induktionsschleife hin, mit deren Hilfe ein darüberfahrender Tramzug erfasst werden kann, der gelbe Schachtdeckel dient der Weichensteuerung. Neisser spricht von Wahrnehmungslernen.[12]

Grüne und gelbe Deckel zwischen den Tramschienen werden jetzt als *etwas* erkannt („*sense & identify*"), sie sind für den Betrachter durch Lernen zu vertrauten Einheiten geworden, ja, mehr noch: Es lässt sich nicht vermeiden, diese Objekte als *etwas* zu erkennen – „You can't help recognizing it!".[13] Bei der Auseinandersetzung mit den Laborräumen kamen alle diese Arten des Wissenserwerbs zum Einsatz: Bei der Einführung in den Laborraum mag das Nachdenken im Vordergrund gestanden haben, bei den Erkundungen im Raum wurde jedoch das Zusammenspiel von Handeln, Wahrnehmen und Nachdenken gepflegt, ebenso beim abschließenden Workshop.

Zur Trilogie der Laborräume Belgrad | Zürich | Mailand

Alle Laborräume waren so groß gewählt, dass sie nicht auf einmal erfassbar waren. Nur Teile der Laborräume waren einer unmittelbaren Inspektion zugänglich. Wegen dieser Schwierigkeit kam die Maxime[14] der drei Durchgänge zum Tragen. Damit sollten die Teilnehmenden die Gelegenheit erhalten, die eigenen Erfahrungen reflektieren zu können und später davon zu profitieren.

Mit der Örtlichkeit in Berührung zu geraten, heißt im Rahmen der höheren Ausbildung auch, sich darüber im Klaren zu sein, mit welcher „Brille" man dies tun will, denn: Was auch

walkthroughs applied. This was designed to give the participants the opportunity to reflect on their own experiences and to benefit from this later on. In the context of higher education, interacting with the locality also means being clear about with which "glasses" one wishes to do this. Seeing always occurs from a particular viewpoint.[15,16] The first task for the participants was therefore always to explain their particular *approach*,[17] namely on the basis of the subject area groups of the doctoral college (the so-called connect groups).[18]

The individual Spatial Research Labs, which we could call part of the preparatory stage of the interaction with the locality, were introduced by the local organisers.[19] This included the setting of tasks for the tour around the research labs. The interactions with the localities each took one day.

Impressions from the Spatial Research Labs

Belgrade (June 2014)

The participants initially set out their own exploration parameters for the tour, with a focus on the following questions:

- What can you see? Describe the current problematic situation.
- What is behind it that you cannot see?
- Can you see traces of past problems?
- Can you see indications of conceivable problems or where do you suspect they might occur?
- Use words, images, and numbers for your notes.[20]

The participants were given some key words as prompts for the spatial explorations:[21] borders/barriers, transitions, guiding structures, disturbances, connecting elements, contrasts between inner and outer appearances, traces of use and abuse (e.g. beaten paths, rubbish, graffiti, an abundance of geocaches, etc.), visual axes, eye catchers, orientation providers, sounds, smells, temperature changes, inner attitude, associations, atmosphere, etc. The exploration took place by boat according to the motto "slow down."

Zurich

Extract from "Stadt statt Güterwagen?" (City instead of freight wagons?), p. 129:

"Is the right place for a freight railway station between Killwangen and Spreitenbach, in the midst of the agglomeration and wedged between two chains of hills? [...] Politicians and planners have swept it under the carpet that the population in the Limmat Valley is growing rapidly and therefore needs more space, that already now 60,000 people a day commute from the Aargau to other cantons, most of them through the Limmat Valley to Zurich, because they cannot find affordable housing in the city. Furthermore, in future even more people from Zurich will move westwards [...]. Would it not make more sense to unbundle housing and logistics in densely populated Switzerland? So that the resulting transport distances could be minimised? [...] However, who should be in charge of such overarching considerations in federal Switzerland? Who in our country is responsible for optimising the use of space, transport routes, and energy consumption?"

Zürich

Leseprobe „Stadt statt Güterwagen?",
S. 129: „Ist zwischen Killwangen und Spreitenbach, mitten in der Agglomeration und eingeklemmt zwischen zwei Hügelzügen, noch der richtige Ort für einen Güterbahnhof? [...] Unter den Tisch kehren Politiker und Planer, dass die Bevölkerung im Limmattal rasant wächst und also mehr Platz braucht. Dass schon heute täglich 60.000 Menschen aus dem Aargau in andere Kantone pendeln – die meisten davon durch das Limmattal nach Zürich, weil sie dort keine bezahlbaren Wohnungen mehr finden. Und dass in Zukunft noch mehr Zürcher nach Westen ziehen werden [...]. Wäre es nicht sinnvoller, in der dicht besiedelten Schweiz das Wohnen und die Logistik zu entflechten? So, dass sich die daraus entstehenden Transportdistanzen minimieren lassen? [...] Nur, wer sollte solche übergeordneten Überlegungen in der föderalistischen Schweiz überhaupt anstellen? Wer ist in unserem Land dafür zuständig, dass Raumnutzung, Verkehrswege und Energieverbrauch gleichzeitig optimiert werden?"

gesehen wird, es geschieht immer von einem bestimmten Standpunkt aus.[15,16] Die erste Aufgabe für die Teilnehmenden war deshalb immer, den jeweiligen *Approach*[17] zu klären, und zwar auf der Basis der Themenbereichsgruppen des Doktorandenkollegs (der sogenannten Connect-Gruppen).[18]

Die einzelnen Laborräume wurden durch die lokalen Organisatoren vorgestellt, was wir mit Lucius Burckhardt Teil der Vorinszenierung[19] nennen können. Dazu gehörte auch die Aufgabenstellung für die Tour im Laborraum. Die Berührungen mit der Örtlichkeit nahmen dabei einen Tag in Anspruch.

Impressionen aus den Laborräumen

Belgrad (Juni 2014)

Die Teilnehmenden konzipierten in Belgrad zunächst ihr individuelles Erkundungsraster für die Tour mit Schwerpunkt auf folgenden Fragen:
- Was sehen Sie: Beschreiben Sie die aktuelle Problemlage.
- Was liegt dahinter, was Sie nicht sehen können?
- Sehen Sie Spuren vergangener Probleme?
- Sehen Sie Hinweise auf absehbare Probleme oder wo vermuten Sie sie?
- Benutzen Sie für Ihre Notizen Wort, Bild und Zahl.[20]

Den Teilnehmenden wurden für die Raumerkundung einige Stichworte zur Anregung mitgegeben:[21] Grenzen/Barrieren, Übergänge, richtungsgebende Strukturen, Störungen, verbindende Elemente, Widersprüche zwischen inneren und äußeren Bildern, Nutzungsspuren (zum Beispiel Trampelpfad, Müll, Graffiti, Häufung von Geocaches, etc.), Sichtachsen, Eyecatcher, Orientierung stiftend, Geräusche, Gerüche, Temperaturwechsel, innere Haltung, Assoziationen, Atmosphäre/Stimmung etc.

Die Erkundung fand per Boot unter dem Motto „slow down" statt. Aus logistischen Gründen war es nicht möglich, an Land zu gehen.[22] Die Inspektion der Örtlichkeit beschränkte sich somit auf jene Reize, die vom Boot aus wahrnehmbar waren. Umso wichtiger waren die im Vorfeld gegebenen Hinweise, die es erlaubten, über das direkt Wahrnehmbare hinaus zu räsonieren. Als wichtige Orientierungshilfe dienten die Brücken über Save und Donau. Die Präsentation der Resultate fand noch auf dem Boot statt.

For logistical reasons, it was not possible to go ashore.[22] The inspection of the locality was therefore limited to the stimuli that could be perceived from the boat. The indications given in advance were all the more important, enabling reasoning beyond what was immediately perceivable. The bridges over the Sava and the Danube served as important orientation guides. The presentation of the results took place while still on the boat.

Zurich (November 2014)

The Zurich Spatial Research Lab encompassed the Limmat Valley, one of the most densely populated areas of Switzerland to the west of the city of Zurich. The local organisers set out the tasks for the respective subject area groups.[23]

An extract from the tasks for public spaces:
- What might a future strategy—a guiding principle for the future—for the public spaces in Spreitenbach look like?
- What immediate measures can be taken?
- What measures are connected to the opening of the Limmat Valley railway (Limmattalbahn)?
- What long-term options should be ensured?

In accordance with the prescribed script, the groups moved around by train, bus, or on foot. In between there were readings outdoors from the book *Daheim. Eine Reise durch die Agglomeration* (At home. A journey through the agglomeration).[24] The processing of the materials and the concluding workshop were carried out and presented at the Fahr monastery within the Spatial Research Lab. Notes about the presentation: what significant insights were gained from the explorations and the prepared documentation? What tasks should be pursued by those involved for the Limmat Valley as a whole? What conclusions can be drawn for one's own dissertation topics? This point was a thread running through all the doctoral symposia, encouraging making use of the gained insights for one's own work.

> ### Zurich
> *The Swiss sociologist Lucius Burckhardt developed the method of 'strollology' (the science of strolling) in the 1980s: "an aim of what we call strollology must be to define our forms of perception at the same time as we are perceiving, enabling new and unfamiliar evaluations of well-known situations. [...] What results from this is the image of a stroll as a composition of routes and distinctive places, like a string of pearls."*
>
> Cf. Burckhardt, Lucius: Warum ist Landschaft schön? Die Spaziergangswissenschaft. Berlin 2006, p. 263

Milan (March 2015)

The Milan Spatial Research Lab comprised the Bovisa area of around 90 hectares,[25] which is about five kilometres to the northwest of the town centre. Until the 1980s, gas was produced here and the ground is contaminated accordingly. Now, research and innovation establishments are to be set up here, as is the new university campus (a section has already

Zürich (November 2014)

Der Zürcher Laborraum umfasste das Limmattal, einen der am dichtest besiedelten Räume der Schweiz westlich der Stadt Zürich. Die lokalen Organisatoren konzipierten die Aufgabenstellungen für die jeweiligen Themenbereichsgruppen.[23]

Aus der Aufgabenstellung für die öffentlichen Räume:

- Wie könnte eine zukünftige Strategie – ein leitender Gedanke in die Zukunft – für die öffentlichen Räume Spreitenbachs aussehen?
- Wie sehen Sofortmaßnahmen aus?
- Welche Maßnahmen stehen im Zusammenhang mit der Eröffnung der Limmattalbahn?
- Welche langfristigen Optionen sind zu sichern?

Die Gruppen bewegten sich gemäß den vorgegebenen Drehbüchern per Bahn, Bus oder zu Fuß. Zwischendurch erfolgten im Freien Lesungen aus dem Buch *Daheim. Eine Reise durch die Agglomeration*.[24] Die Aufarbeitung der Materialien und der abschließende Workshop wurden im Kloster Fahr innerhalb des Laborraums selbst durchgeführt und präsentiert. Hinweise zur Präsentation:

- Was sind bedeutsame Erkenntnisse aus den Erkundungen und den vorbereitenden Unterlagen?
- Welche Aufgaben sollten für das Limmattal als Gesamtraum von den Akteuren weiterverfolgt werden?
- Welche Schlussfolgerungen lassen sich für die eigenen Dissertationsthemen ziehen? Dieser Punkt zog sich als roter Faden durch alle Doktorandenwochen, um die gewonnenen Erkenntnisse für die eigene Arbeit nutzbar zu machen.

Zürich

Der Schweizer Soziologe Lucius Burckhardt entwickelte die Methode der Spaziergangswissenschaft in den 1980er Jahren: „Ein Anliegen der von uns so genannten Spaziergangswissenschaft muss es also sein, gleichzeitig mit der Wahrnehmung auch die Determiniertheit unserer Wahrnehmungsformen aufzuzeigen, so dass auch neue und ungewohnte Beurteilungen altbekannter Situationen möglich werden. [...] Es ergab sich jeweils das Bild des Spaziergangs als einer Zusammensetzung von Strecken und von ausgezeichneten Orten, also einer Perlenkette."

Vgl. Burckhardt, Lucius: Warum ist Landschaft schön? Die Spaziergangswissenschaft. Berlin 2006, S. 263

Mailand (März 2015)

Der Mailänder Laborraum umfasste das rund 90 Hektar große Bovisa-Areal,[25] das circa fünf Kilometer nordwestlich des Stadtzentrums liegt. Bis in die 1980er Jahre wurde hier Gas produziert; der Boden ist entsprechend belastet. Auf dem Gelände sollen nun Forschungs- und Innovationsbetriebe angesiedelt werden sowie der neue Campus der Universität (ein Teil wird bereits seit 1995 von der Universität genutzt).[26]

Auch hier bestand das Ziel der Erkundung des Laborbereichs darin, in einer kurzen Zeit eine Lagebeurteilung vorzunehmen und in kleinen Gruppen Ideen für die Weiterentwicklung des Areals zu entwickeln. Diese Ideenfindung sollte wiederum durch die spezielle „Brille" der einzelnen Gruppen geleitet werden.

been used by the university since 1995).[26] The aims of the exploration of the research lab here also included carrying out an evaluation of the locality in a short space of time and coming up with ideas in small groups for the further development of the area. This brainstorming was also guided by the particular "glasses" of the individual groups. The whole group took part in the exploration. Starting at the Bovisa-Politecnico FN train station, the route continued on foot through the Bovisa area, then past the Farini area to the Fondazione Riccardo Catella by Porta Nuova, where the evaluation and presentation of the results were held.

Conclusion

Interaction with the locality is an integral component of spatial planning. Perception, as an activity at a given moment in time, brings the perceiver into contact with the environment and enables learning. New insights can be gained by doing and by actions, for example by seeking and adopting new perspectives, as well as by exchanging thoughts and reasoning. This makes it possible to direct attention towards particular objects if it is deemed necessary. The better one has been introduced to the locality beforehand, and therefore the more developed one's expectations/schemata are, the more likely one is to discern certain aspects, even if they are not directly visible. The exchange of thoughts can be promoted not only by talking, but also by showing and the use of graphic elements like ad hoc sketches. The Belgrade, Zurich, and Milan trilogy, conceived as part of the International Doctoral College, created opportunities for the participants to familiarise themselves with unknown situations in a relatively short period of time, based on a few walkthroughs, and to use the insights gained for their own work.

<u>Milan</u>

"Every eye that scans surfaces and probes them is comparing. Comparison sharpens and shapes what one sees. One can train the eye to compare and increase its attentiveness. [...] What is even more fundamental than comparison is the identification of contexts and the illumination of connections. [...] It is a real nuisance to walk through town with people who do not see, whilst one's own alarm bells are constantly ringing. [...] Of course it's only those who know something who actually see. Those who know nothing do not see anything either. One has to know something about mastery, building forms, craftsmanship, styles. However, none of this is of any use if one distrusts one's eye, if one does not attribute any meaning to the form."

Cf. Schlögel, Karl: Im Raume lesen wir die Zeit. Über Zivilisationsgeschichte und Geopolitik. Frankfurt 2006, p. 272f.

Mailand

*„Jedes Auge, das über Oberflächen hinglei-
tet und sie abtastet, vergleicht. Vergleichen
schärft und bildet den Blick. Man kann das
Auge im Vergleichen schulen, zu erhöhter
Aufmerksamkeit bringen. [...] Grundle-
gender als Vergleichen ist das Aufspüren
von Kontexten und das Aufhellen von
Zusammenhängen. [...] Es ist eine wahre
Plage, mit Leuten durch die Stadt zu gehen,
die nicht sehen, während bei einem selbst
ständig die Alarmsignale schrillen. [...]
Freilich sieht nur, wer etwas weiß. Wer
nichts weiß, sieht auch nichts. Man muss
etwas von Meisterschaft, von Bauformen,
von Handwerk, von Stilen wissen. Aber
all das nützt nichts, wenn man dem Auge
selbst misstraut, wenn man der Form keine
Bedeutung beimisst."*

Vgl. Schlögel, Karl: Im Raume lesen wir die Zeit. Über
Zivilisationsgeschichte und Geopolitik. Frankfurt
2006, S. 272f.

Die Erkundung fand in der gesamten Gruppe statt. Mit Start am Bahnhof Bovisa-Politecnico FN ging es zu Fuß durch das Bovisa-Areal, dann am Farini-Areal vorbei zur Fondazione Riccardo Catella bei der Porta Nuova, wo auch die Auswertung und die Präsentation der Resultate stattfanden.

Fazit

Berührungen mit der Örtlichkeit sind ein fester Bestandteil der Raumplanung. Die Wahrnehmung als Betätigung in der Zeit bringt die Wahrnehmenden mit ihrer Umgebung in Beziehung und lässt sie gemeinsam lernen. Durch Handeln, zum Beispiel indem neue Perspektiven gesucht und eingenommen werden, können ebenso neue Einsichten gewonnen werden wie durch den Austausch von Gedanken, also durch Räsonieren. Dies erlaubt es, die Aufmerksamkeit dann auf bestimmte Gegenstände zu richten, wenn man es für erforderlich hält. Je besser man vorher in die Örtlichkeit eingeführt worden ist, je besser ausgebildet also die Erwartungen/Schemata sind, desto eher wird man bestimmte Gegenstände vermuten, auch wenn sie nicht direkt sichtbar sind. Der Austausch von Gedanken kann neben der gesprochenen Sprache auch durch Zeigen und den Einsatz von grafischen Elementen wie ad hoc erstellten Skizzen gefördert werden. Mit der im Rahmen des Doktorandenkollegs konzipierten Trilogie Belgrad, Zürich und Mailand wurden für die Teilnehmenden Möglichkeiten geschaffen, sich in mehreren Durchgängen in relativ kurzer Zeit mit unbekannten Situationen vertraut zu machen und die Erkenntnisse für die eigene Arbeit zu nutzen.

Belgrade, June 2014
Belgrad, Juni 2014

The locality is viewed through the frame.
Die Örtlichkeit wird durch den Rahmen betrachtet.

Rolf Signer during preparations for the tour at the Architecture Faculty at Belgrade University: a yardstick is converted to a frame.
Rolf Signer anlässlich der Vorbereitung auf die Tour an der Architektur-Fakultät der Universität in Belgrad: Ein Zollstock wird zu einem Rahmen umfunktioniert.

Mario Schneider draws continuously.
Mario Schneider zeichnet am laufenden Meter.

Belgrade at the confluence of the Sava and Danube. The boat trip started at the Beton Hala (1), led upstream along the Sava to the bridge Most na Adi (2), then to point 3 and 4 (Zemun), down the Danube to the harbour (5) and ended at point 1.
Belgrad am Zusammenfluss von Save und Donau. Die Bootsfahrt begann bei der Beton Hala (1), führte saveaufwärts zur Brücke Most na Adi (2), dann zu Punkt 3 und 4 (Zemun), donauabwärts zum Hafen (5) und endete bei Punkt 1.

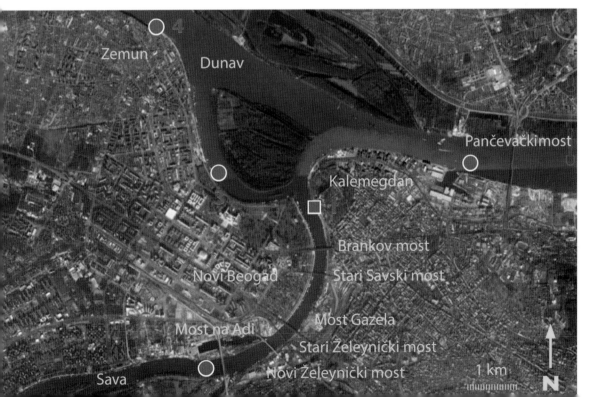

Anita Grams records the
acoustic backdrop as a "spatial
soundtrack."
Anita Grams zeichnet die
Geräuschkulisse als „Raum-
Tonspur" auf.

The subject area groups present the insights gained on the tour whilst still on the boat.
Die Themenbereichsgruppen stellen noch auf dem Boot ihre auf der Tour gewonnenen Erkenntnisse vor.

Measuring and comparing
Maß nehmen und vergleichen

Zurich, November 2014
Zürich, November 2014

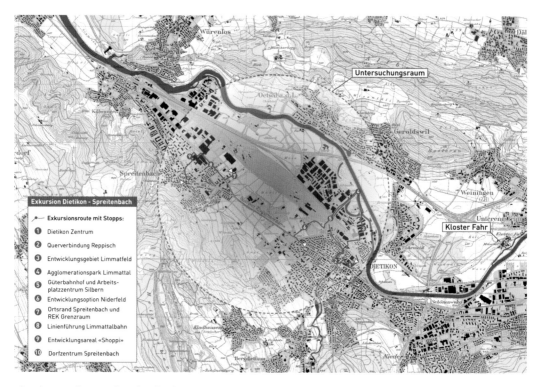

Untersuchungsraum

Exkursion Dietikon - Spreitenbach

Exkursionsroute mit Stopps:

1. Dietikon Zentrum
2. Querverbindung Reppisch
3. Entwicklungsgebiet Limmatfeld
4. Agglomerationspark Limmattal
5. Güterbahnhof und Arbeitsplatzzentrum Silbern
6. Entwicklungsoption Niderfeld
7. Ortsrand Spreitenbach und REK Grenzraum
8. Linienführung Limmattalbahn
9. Entwicklungsareal «Shoppi»
10. Dorfzentrum Spreitenbach

The Limmattal. Excursion plan for the group "Integrated Development Concept Dietikon-Killwangen-Spreitenbach"
Das Limmattal. Exkursionsplan für die Gruppe „Integriertes Entwicklungskonzept Dietikon-Killwangen-Spreitenbach"

The actor Bodo Krummwiede reads on the bridge (Furttalstrasse) about the Limmattal railway yard from the book Daheim. Eine Reise durch die Agglomeration by Matthias Daum and Paul Schneeberger (Zurich 2013): "Stadt statt Güterwagen?"
Der Schauspieler Bodo Krummwiede liest auf der Brücke (Furttalstrasse) über den Rangierbahnhof Limmattal aus dem Buch Daheim. Eine Reise durch die Agglomeration von Matthias Daum und Paul Schneeberger (Zürich 2013): „Stadt statt Güterwagen?"

The processing of the materials and the concluding workshop were carried out in the Spatial Research Lab itself, at Fahr Monastery. The further development of the Limmattal railway yard is being discussed here.

Die Aufarbeitung der Materialien und der abschließende Workshop wurden im Laborraum selbst durchgeführt, und zwar im Kloster Fahr. Hier kommt gerade die Weiterentwicklung des Rangierbahnhofs Limmattal zur Sprache.

The group in Spreitenbach in the Limmattal. The Limmattal railway yard is in the background.
Die Gruppe zu den öffentlichen Räumen im Limmattal ist in Spreitenbach. Im Rücken der Rangierbahnhof Limmattal

Milan, March 2015
Mailand, März 2015

Introduction at Aula Magna Rettorato at the Politecnico di Milano
Einführung in der Aula Magna Rettorato des Politecnico di Milano

In Bovisa. The remains of gas containers in the background.
In Bovisa. Im Hintergrund die Überreste der Gasbehälter

The Bovisa area (red)
Das Bovisa-Areal (rot)

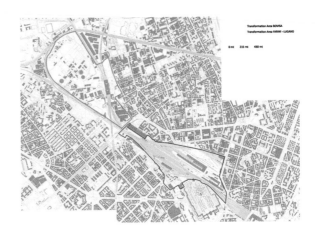

Ideas for financial flows
Ideen für Finanzströme

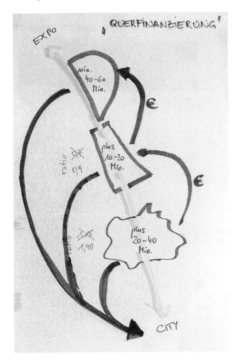

Final adjustments before the presentation
Letzte Retuschen vor der Präsentation

*Workshop at the Fondazione
Riccardo Catella at Porta Nova*
**Workshop in der Fondazione
Riccardo Catella bei der Porta
Nova**

*First designs are
discussed intensely
in Bovisa.*
*Erste Entwürfe
werden in Bovisa
intensiv diskutiert.*

*Presentation of the results
at the Fondazione Riccardo
Catella at Porta Nova
Präsentation der Ergebnisse
in der Fondazione Riccardo
Catella bei der Porta Nova*

APPROACHING TRANSFORMATION
Four questions about the transformation of a landscape

NICOLE UHRIG

Landscapes change. We have known that for a long time. We know from experience that our settlements and economy leave traces, that our living environment is continuously changing and developing further. These developments usually take place over longer periods of time and occur so incidentally that we scarcely notice them. We are even hardly aware of the associated small and gradual changes to our everyday and perceived worlds. "Cultural landscapes are a system of signs. Each era has left its hieroglyphs behind. Each generation has bequeathed a pool of symbols significant to them. It is a history of the recording and deleting of signs [...]."[1] Especially in the cultural landscapes shaped lastingly by people, there are repeated shifts in the signs left behind by civilisation and their meanings. For example, the characteristics that we associate today with what we consider to be a "typical Mediterranean landscape" have shifted considerably over time, as the French historian Lucien Febvre described in 1940 from the fictional perspective of the Greek history writer and geographer Herodotus of Halicarnassus. Herodotus was familiar with the Mediterranean landscape of the ancient world around 450 BC. What would he say today?

"Imagine old Herodotus sailing around the Eastern Mediterranean again today. He would be amazed! Golden fruits on dark green trees, said to be 'characteristic of the whole Mediterranean area:' orange, lemon, and mandarin trees – he doesn't remember ever having seen them in his life.... Of course! They are from the Far East, imported by the Arabs. These weird plants with unusual shapes, spines and flowering branches, and strange names: cactus, agave, aloe – how they have spread! He has never ever seen them in his lifetime.... Of course! They are American. These great trees with pale leaves that, however, have a Greek name: eucalyptus – the Father of History has never seen anything like them in the known world.... Of course! They are Australian. And these palms? Herodotus has seen them in the past, in oases, in Egypt; but never on the European shores of the Mediterranean. Never, nor the cypresses, unless they were Persian."[2]

It has therefore not always been the case that a Lawson's cypress is immediately associated with Tuscany in Italy, especially within the European cultural space. Over the course of our cultural history, the appearance of the landscape in the Mediterranean has changed so significantly that Herodotus would not have recognised it at the end of his imaginary journey in time.

APPROACHING TRANSFORMATION
Vier Fragen an die Transformationslandschaft

NICOLE UHRIG

Landschaften verändern sich. Das wissen wir längst. Wir haben die Erfahrung gemacht, dass unser Siedeln und Wirtschaften Spuren hinterlässt, dass sich unsere Lebensumwelt kontinuierlich verändert und weiterentwickelt. Meist finden diese Entwicklungen über längere Zeiträume statt und geschehen so beiläufig, dass wir sie kaum wahrnehmen. Auch die damit verbundenen kleinen, schrittweisen Veränderungen unserer gewohnten Bildwelten sind uns dann kaum bewusst.

„Kulturlandschaften sind Zeichensysteme. Jede Epoche hat ihre Hieroglyphe hinterlassen. Jede Generation hat einen Fundus an für sie bedeutsamen Symbolen hinterlassen. Es ist eine Geschichte der Einschreibung und Löschung von Zeichen [...]."[1] Insbesondere in den dauerhaft von Menschen geprägten Kulturlandschaften kommt es immer wieder zu Verschiebungen der von der Zivilisation hinterlassenen Zeichen und ihrer Bedeutungen. So haben sich beispielsweise die Zeichen, die wir heute mit einer für uns „typischen Mittelmeerlandschaft" verbinden, im Laufe der Zeit weit verschoben, wie es der französische Historiker Lucien Febvre im Jahr 1940 aus der fiktiven Perspektive des griechischen Geschichtsschreibers und Geografen Herodot von Halikarnassos beschreibt. Herodot war vertraut mit einer Mittelmeerlandschaft der antiken Welt um 450 v. Chr. Was würde er heute sagen?

„Imagine old Herodotus sailing around the Eastern Mediterranean again today. He would be amazed! Golden fruits on dark green trees, said to be ‚characteristic of the whole Mediterranean area': orange, lemon, and mandarin trees – he doesn't remember ever having seen them in his life.... Of course! They are from the Far East, imported by the Arabs. These weird plants with unusual shapes, spines and flowering branches, and strange names: cactus, agave, aloe – how they have spread! He has never ever seen them in his lifetime.... Of course! They are American. These great trees with pale leafs that, however, have a Greek name: eucalyptus – the Father of History has never seen anything like them in the known world.... Of course! They are Australian. And these palms? Herodotus has seen them in the past, in oases, in Egypt; but never on the European shores of the Mediterranean. Never, nor the cypresses, unless they were Persian."[2] Dass man eine Säulen-Zypresse ohne zu zögern mit der italienischen Toskana konnotiert (insbesondere im europäischen Kulturraum), war also nicht immer so. Im Laufe unserer Kulturgeschichte hat sich das Landschaftsbild des Mittelmeerraumes so stark verändert, dass sie für Hero-

Changing style eras have also brought the transformation of landscapes. Following on from the baroque era, when garden art was at its zenith as a highly regarded art genre, there was a particularly fundamental change, breaking with tradition and signifying a change of aesthetic paradigm. The emergence of the English landscape garden usurped the dominance of the formal–geometric baroque garden, in favour of a new, seemingly naturally–grown landscape ideal. However, this transformation did not occur inconspicuously, instead it was discussed in society and was part of a wider debate about values among educated circles. The "redesigning" of countless castle parks, from a previously mathematically ordered nature to a natural appearance with free and curvaceous forms, proceeded very quickly compared to the gradual, large-scale developments in the Mediterranean region.

1 *By reinterpreting existing features, the former bunkers in the Duisburg-Nord landscape park have become the "Monte Thysso" climbing trail.*
1 *Durch die Uminterpretation vorhandener Zeichen wurden die ehemaligen Bunkeranlagen des Landschaftsparks Duisburg-Nord zum Klettersteig „Monte Thysso".*

2 *Segments of the Berlin Wall, memorial site at Bernauer Strasse, Berlin*
2 *Segmente der Berliner Mauer, Gedenkstätte Bernauer Straße, Berlin*

dot am Ende seiner gedachten Zeitreise nicht mehr wiederzuerkennen wäre.

Auch im Wechsel der Stilepochen fanden landschaftsgestalterische Transformationen statt. Ausgehend von der Epoche des Barock, in der die Gartenkunst als hoch angesehene Kunstgattung am Zenit ihrer Wertschätzung stand, kam es zu einer besonders tiefgreifenden Veränderung, die einem Traditionsbruch und ästhetischen Paradigmenwechsel gleichkam. Das Aufkommen des Englischen Landschaftsgartens stürzte die Vorherrschaft des formal-geometrischen barocken Gartens zugunsten eines neuen scheinbar natürlich gewachsenen Landschaftsideals. Jene Transformation geschah jedoch ganz und gar nicht beiläufig, die Diskussion war gesellschaftlich präsent und Teil einer breiten Wertediskussion in den gebildeten Schichten. Auch ging das „Redesign" zahlloser Schlossparks von einer bislang mathematisch geordneten Natur hin zu einem Naturbild der frei geschwungenen Form im Vergleich zu den schrittweisen, großmaßstäblichen Entwicklungen im Mittelmeerraum recht zügig vonstatten.

Heute kommt dem Phänomen der Landschaftstransformation wieder Aufmerksamkeit zu, jedoch vor einem anderen Hintergrund: der anhaltenden Diskussion um Nachhaltigkeit und Resilienz. Das Wachstum der Siedlungsräume in den Metropolregionen, der damit einhergehende steigende Flächenverbrauch, die zunehmende Knappheit an Rohstof-

Today the phenomenon of the transformation of landscapes is once again drawing attention, but against a different background: the ongoing discussion about sustainability and resilience. The growth of settlement areas in the metropolitan regions, the associated expanding land usage, the increasing shortage of raw materials, and advancing climate change are showing us their spatial consequences and therefore the finiteness of landscape resources, which is ultimately culminating in the demand for more sustainable development. "Reduce/reuse/recycle" was postulated by the German contribution to the International Architecture Exhibition La Biennale di Venezia back in 2012. However, even mundane and simple reasons, such as a lack of space or money, have allowed exceptional repurposing projects to spring up on old and disused airport, railway, and industrial sites. Compared to the transformation processes outlined at the beginning of the text, many transformation and conversion projects today are carried out very quickly, propelled and directed by political and economic interests. In accompanying the implementation of such projects, the development of solutions and viable concepts with the aim of giving the planning area a new spatial organisation, a new function, and a new use can present a considerable challenge to planners. Given that the transformation of landscapes and settlement areas is characterised by so many interdependences and complex interactions within society, one has to reckon with an open-ended development process. Any planning solution can therefore ultimately only be approximate.

Transformation

What questions are raised when something is to be transformed? The definition and the Latin origins of the word "transformation" could open up one of many approaches to handling the planning of a transformation landscape:

transformare = to change, to convert

trans (Lat.): across, cross over, beyond, through

formare (Lat.): to form, shape, create, instruct[3]

Thus the meaning of *trans* (cross over) leads to the first and second question: *from what* and *to what* is something being formed? The questions require a decisive definition of the starting situation and end situation and require an attempt to plan with a before and after scenario.

From what? —The starting situation

The process of shifting signs or features and their meanings described by Karl Schlögel at the beginning opens up a variety of potential design approaches. When converting a landscape, the existing traces of the history of the locality are often explicitly highlighted—especially in the case of memorial landscapes and at remembrance sites ▶2—or else they undergo a reinterpretation. ▶1

The landscape can gain further contentual dimensions through the asso-

fen und ein fortschreitender Klimawandel führen uns die räumlichen Folgen und damit die Endlichkeit von Landschaftsressourcen deutlich vor Augen, was schließlich in der Forderung nach einer nachhaltigeren Entwicklung mündet. „Reduce/Reuse/Recycle" postulierte der deutsche Beitrag auf der Internationalen Architekturausstellung La Biennale di Venezia bereits im Jahr 2012. Doch auch profane, einfache Notwendigkeiten wie Platz- oder Geldmangel ließen außergewöhnliche Umnutzungsprojekte auf alten Flughafen-, Bahn- oder Industriebrachen entstehen. Im Vergleich mit den zu Beginn des Textes skizzierten Transformationsprozessen geht heute so manches Transformationsprojekt, forciert und geleitet von politischen und ökonomischen Interessen, rasend schnell vonstatten. Die Umwandlung eines solchen Projektes planerisch zu begleiten, Lösungsstrategien und tragfähige Konzepte zu entwickeln, mit dem Ziel das Planungsgebiet neuen Ordnungsstrukturen, einer neuen Funktion und Nutzung zuzuführen, stellt uns Planer vor große Herausforderungen. Weil die Landschafts- und Siedlungstransformation von so vielen Interdependenzen und komplexen Wechselwirkungen mit der Gesellschaft geprägt ist, muss man von einem entwicklungsoffenen Prozess ausgehen. Deshalb kann jede planerische Lösung letztlich nur eine Annäherung sein.

Transformation

Welche Fragen stellen sich, wenn etwas transformiert werden soll? Die Definition und die lateinische Herkunft des Begriffes „Transformation" könnte einen von vielen möglichen Zugängen zum Umgang mit dem Planungsobjekt Transformationslandschaft eröffnen:

transformare = umwandeln, verwandeln

trans (lat.): über, über…hin, über…hinaus; jenseits

formare (lat.): formen, bilden, schaffen, gestalten, ausbilden, unterweisen[3]

So führt die Bedeutung von *trans* (über…hin) bereits zur ersten und zur zweiten Frage: *Woher* und *wohin* wird etwas formiert? Die Fragen fordern eine dezidierte Definition von Ausgangs- und Endsituation und legen eine planerische Annäherung durch ein Vorher-nachher-Szenario nahe.

Woher? – Die Ausgangslage

Jener von Karl Schlögel eingangs beschriebene Vorgang der Verschiebung der Zeichen und ihrer Bedeutungen eröffnet verschiedene Möglichkeiten des entwurflichen Arbeitens. Bei der Umwidmung einer Landschaft werden häufig die noch vorhandenen, von der Geschichte des Ortes zeugenden Zeichen explizit herausgestellt – besonders zu finden in Erinnerungslandschaften und an Gedenkorten ▶2 – oder sie erfahren eine Um- oder Neuinterpretation ▶1.

Mit der damit einhergehenden Konnotationsverschiebung kann die Landschaft weitere inhaltliche Dimensionen hinzugewinnen. Ein weiterer interessanter Aspekt in jener „Geschichte der Einschreibung und Löschung

ciated shift in connotations. A further interesting aspect of this "history of the recording and deleting of signs" is the effect of layering and multiple coding. Transformations of landscapes are characterised in particular by sign systems with multiple codes.

The Duisburg-Nord landscape is a frequently cited reference project and a prime example of multiple coding, multifacetedness, and ambiguity. The landscape with industrial ruins at Duisburg-Nord, which previously had negative connotations, was reinterpreted within a relatively short space of time. The well-marketed International Building Exhibition (IBA) Emscher Park succeeded in giving the neglected old industrial landscapes, which were perceived primarily as a symbol of economic decline, a new value and interpretation, in other words a positive image, by means of high-quality architecture, art, and landscape architecture. The IBA Fürst-Pückler-Land also invested heavily into the abandoned surface mining landscapes of Lausitz; there are first reports of a positive image shift about the newly-created aquatic and recreational landscape.

To what? —The planning aim

What is the aim and in what direction should the landscape be transformed? The planning aims are not always clearly defined and they rarely set out definitively which direction the development of an industrial wasteland or an abandoned military site next to an airport should take. The uncertain prognoses of major planning projects are changing faster than ever today. Sometimes it is too difficult to gage the future development of the political, economic, and administrative framework conditions to be able to work out an appropriate long-term development scenario with certainty and a sense of responsibility. Planners handle this by thinking increasingly in terms of flexible concepts and phased plans, having the courage to define certain variables as uncertain, or by initially leaving the final scenario of the planning open-ended.

For example, the exact final status of the Hugo Biomass Park pilot project [4] was deliberately not conclusively defined. The mining area of the former Hugo 2/5/8 mine in Gelsenkirchen-Buer is to be converted as part of the climate metropolis RUHR 2022, with the prime objective of promoting the development of regenerative energy. The abandoned site is to be transformed and regenerated by means of a 22-hectare biomass park. The planning envisages a double use: on the one hand as an economically-used short-rotation plantation, on the other hand as a publicly-accessible park for leisure and recreational purposes. Eight tons of wood are to be felled each year from classical types of energy wood such as poplar and willows. ▶3

It has not yet been determined what mix of trees and other plants will best meet the requirements of the unusual usage mix. The plan is to make observations, learn, and try out new things during operation. The project embarked on this learning process in spring 2016, without having defined

von Zeichen" ist der Effekt der Schichtung und Mehrfachkodierung. Transformationslandschaften zeichnen sich ganz besonders durch mehrfach codierte Zeichensysteme aus.

Der Landschaftspark Duisburg-Nord ist ein häufig zitiertes Referenzprojekt und ein Paradebeispiel für den Umgang mit Mehrfachkodierung, Vielstimmigkeit und Vieldeutigkeit. Innerhalb relativ kurzer Zeit erfuhr die zuvor negativ konnotierte Landschaft der Industrieruinen am Standort Duisburg-Nord eine Umdeutung. Die gut vermarktete Internationale Bauausstellung (IBA) Emscher Park vermochte mithilfe hochwertiger Architektur, Kunst und Landschaftsarchitektur, den vernachlässigten, altindustriellen Landschaften, die vor allem als Zeichen des wirtschaftlichen Niedergangs wahrgenommen wurden, einen neuen Wert und damit eine neue Deutung, das heißt ein positives Image abzuringen. Auch die IBA Fürst-Pückler-Land investierte massiv in die verlassenen Tagebaulandschaften der Lausitz und es gibt in der neu entstehenden Wasser- und Freizeitlandschaft erste Meldungen in Richtung eines positiven Imagewechsels.

Wohin? – Das Planungsziel

Was ist das Ziel, in welche Richtung soll die Landschaft transformiert werden? Nicht immer sind die Planungsziele klar definiert und selten steht fest, wohin die Entwicklung einer Industriebrache oder eines verlassenen Militärstandortes nebst Flughafen gehen soll. Die Unwägbarkeiten und Vorzeichen großer Planungsvorhaben ändern sich heute schneller denn je. Mitunter fällt es zu schwer, die künftige Entwicklung der politischen, ökonomischen und administrativen Rahmenbedingungen so einzuschätzen, als dass mit Gewissheit und Verantwortungsbewusstsein ein sinnvolles und nachhaltiges Entwicklungsszenario entworfen werden könnte. Dem begegnen Planer, indem sie zunehmend in flexiblen Konzepten und Stufenplänen denken, den Mut haben, gewisse Variablen als unbestimmt zu definieren, oder indem sie das finale Szenario der Planung zunächst noch offen lassen. So wurde zum Beispiel der genaue Endzustand des Pilotprojektes Biomassepark Hugo[4] bewusst nicht abschließend definiert. Mit dem obersten Ziel, den Ausbau regenerativer Energien zu fördern, soll im Rahmen der klimametropole RUHR 2022 das Zechenareal des ehemaligen Bergwerks Hugo 2/5/8 in Gelsenkirchen-Buer saniert werden. Die brach gefallene Fläche soll mithilfe eines 22 Hektar großen Biomasseparks transformiert und revitalisiert werden. Die Planung sieht eine Doppelnutzung vor: einerseits als wirtschaftlich genutzte Kurzumtriebsplantage, andererseits als öffentlich nutzbare Parkanlage, die der Freizeit- und Erholungsnutzung zur Verfügung steht. Aus klassischen Energieholzarten wie Pappeln und Weiden sollen pro Hektar acht Tonnen Holz im Jahr gewonnen werden. ▶3

Welche Gehölzmischung und Zupflanzungen den Anforderungen der ungewöhnlichen Nutzungsmischung am besten gerecht wird, steht noch nicht fest. Man wird im laufenden Betrieb beobachten, lernen und neue Dinge ausprobieren. Das Projekt hat sich seit Frühjahr 2016 in diesen Lern-

the precise end situation in advance. The question of whether the project will be economically viable, alongside its undoubted social and ecological benefits, can also not yet be definitively answered. Here once again one must have the courage to face an open ending.

How? —Models, maxims, methods

How will the transformation be carried out? Which models, maxims, and methods guide the development of design strategies?

The handling of large-scale infrastructure projects has been discussed for a number of years in the field of landscape architecture. Up until now, it is mostly the rational aspect of functionality that has appeared to be in the foreground. However, nowadays there is also an emergence of dialogue-orientated, interdisciplinary approaches and new models for planning infrastructures, which adds a tentative aesthetic discourse to the previous viewpoint. Is it possible, for example, to integrate infrastructures into the landscape in such a way that they are orientated towards the natural geographical and cultural features of the locality, in order to appear as a complementary, harmonious, and inconspicuous part of the landscape as much as possible? Or should infrastructures be staged more as contrasting and confident elements? Should infrastructural peripheries be upgraded spatially? Does this counteract acceptance problems among users? Can infrastructure design be adapted to the landscape?

At the department of landscape architecture for regional open spaces at TU Munich, Sören Schöbel defines basic rules for the organisation of infrastructural elements in the city: ensure functionality, establish connections, integrate structures, show collective goodwill, preserve individuality, enable diversity, extend leeway.[5] He is therefore clearly bringing a design-orientated, conceptual, and creative perspective into the discussion, which may enable new models to generate new forms of landscape in future.

Who? —The involved parties

The parties involved in transformation have an influence on the setting of goals and therefore on the outcome of the development. Politics and the economy are also influential powers in the transformation process, as are the planners with their individual understanding of planning and ideal models. Last but not least, there is the influence of the stakeholders and other parties involved in a project, such as investors, users, residents, local societies, etc. The particular dynamics of the "who is transforming?" aspect are evident in the many changes of planning direction for the Tempelhof site in Berlin. ▶4

The first civic participation in the future of the Tempelhof site in Berlin took place in 2007. Bus tours, exhibitions, presentations, expert discussions, guided debates, and an online dialogue were organised. "What does Berlin need in this location?" was the central question of the online di-

3 The Hugo biomass
park is to be planted
initially with a wide
range of different trees
as a trial area in order
to gather experience
about the optimal types
of wood for this location.
3 Im Sinne einer
Versuchsfläche wird der
Biomassepark Hugo zu-
nächst mit einer breiten
Palette verschiedener
Gehölzsorten bepflanzt,
um Erfahrungen über
die für den Standort
optimalen Sorten sam-
meln zu können.

prozess begeben, ohne den genauen Endzustand vorab definiert zu haben.
Zur Frage, ob sich das Projekt neben seinem zweifellos sozialen und ökologischen Mehrwert wirtschaftlich selbst tragen wird, kann derzeit ebenfalls
noch keine abschließende Aussage getroffen werden. Mut zum offenen
Ende auch hier.

Wie? – Leitbilder, Maximen, Methoden

Auf welche Art und Weise wird transformiert? Nach welchen Leitbildern,
Handlungsmaximen und Methoden werden Entwurfsstrategien entwickelt?
Vonseiten der Landschaftsarchitektur wird seit geraumer Zeit der Umgang mit großräumigen Infrastrukturprojekten diskutiert. Bislang schien
hier meist der rationale Aspekt der Funktionalität im Vordergrund zu
stehen. Doch zeigen sich heute dialogorientiertere, interdisziplinäre Her-
angehensweisen und neue Leitbilder zum planerischen Umgang mit Infrastrukturen, welche die bisherige Sichtweise um einen zaghaften ästhetischen Diskurs erweitern. Kann man beispielsweise Infrastrukturen so in
die Landschaft integrieren, dass sie sich an den natürlich-geografischen
und kulturellen Gegebenheiten des Ortes orientieren, um als ergänzender,
möglichst harmonischer, unauffälliger Teil der Landschaft zu erscheinen?
Oder sollten Infrastrukturen eher als kontrastierende, selbstbewusste Ele-

164 FEET
FIELD ELEVATION

BERLIN-TEMPELHOF

Hold for
FOLLOW ME
or
RTF
Instructions

alogue. About 33,000 participants put forward around 900 ideas for the reuse of the Tempelhof site. The ideas were commented on, processed, and evaluated in a concluding guided discussion. Then the models were substantiated together with political and economic decision-makers, with the specialist public, with the local residents, and with the citizens of Berlin, forming the basis for the ensuing call for tenders. The winning design by Gross May was conceived as a flexible construct and design framework, which enables changes over the course of the transformation process. The partial "pilot projects" initiated by private persons, societies, or companies (mostly intermediary usages set up with limited financial resources, but with a high level of personal involvement) could also open up a range of usage options. They were integrated into the overall concept in such a way that they could be kept and developed further if they proved successful, or else could be removed again.

In the meantime, the coordination of interest groups intended by the participatory procedure, which appeared to be a success, has been shown to have failed. The group "100% Tempelhofer Feld," which is strongly interest-

4 *The hitherto largest civic participation in the future of the Tempelhof site took place in 2007 in Berlin.*
4 *Im Jahr 2007 fand in Berlin die bis dahin größte Bürgerbeteiligung zur Zukunft des Tempelhofer Feldes statt.*

mente inszeniert werden? Muss man Infrastrukturränder räumlich aufwerten? Wirkt dies Akzeptanzproblemen bei Nutzern entgegen? Gibt es ein landschaftsgerechtes Entwerfen von Infrastrukturen?

An der Professur für Landschaftsarchitektur regionaler Freiräume der TU München definiert zum Beispiel Sören Schöbel Grundregeln für die Anordnung von Infrastrukturanlagen in der Stadt: Sinn stiften, Zusammenhänge herstellen, strukturell einfügen, Gemeinwillen zeigen, Eigenart erhalten, Vielfalt ermöglichen, Spielräume erweitern.[5] Damit bezieht er die entwurflich-konzeptionelle und gestalterische Perspektive deutlich in den Diskurs mit ein, wodurch zukünftig vielleicht die neuen Leitbilder auch neue Landschaftsbilder generieren könnten.

Wer? – Die Akteure

Die Akteure der Transformation haben Einfluss auf die Zielformulierung und damit auf das Ergebnis der Entwicklung. Politik und Wirtschaft sind ebenso wirkungsvolle Größen im Transformationsprozess wie der Planer mit seinem individuellen Selbstverständnis von Planung und seinen Leitbildern. Hinzu kommt nicht zuletzt der Einfluss der Stakeholder und Akteure eines Projektes, wie Investoren, Nutzer, Anwohner, ansässige Vereine etc. An den vielfältigen Kurswechseln des Planungsgeschehens zum Tempelhofer Feld in Berlin kann man die Eigendynamik des Aspektes „wer transformiert?" gut ablesen. ▶4

Im Jahr 2007 fand die erste Bürgerbeteiligung zur Zukunft des Tempelhofer Feldes statt. Es wurden Busrundfahrten, Ausstellungen, Vorträge, Expertengespräche, moderierte Gespräche und ein Online-Dialog organisiert. „Was braucht Berlin an diesem Ort?" war die zentrale Frage des Online-Dialogs. Etwa 33.000 Teilnehmer brachten rund 900 Ideen zur Nachnutzung des Tempelhofer Feldes ein. In einer abschließenden moderierten Diskussion wurden die Ideen kommentiert, bearbeitet und bewertet. Daraufhin wurden die Leitbilder gemeinsam mit politischen und wirtschaftlichen Entscheidungsträgern, mit der Fachöffentlichkeit, mit den Anwohnern und Berliner Bürgern konkretisiert und somit zur Grundlage der darauffolgenden Wettbewerbsausschreibung. Der Siegerentwurf von Gross Max war als flexibles Konstrukt und gestalterischer Rahmen gedacht, der Veränderungen im Laufe des Transformationsprozesses erlaubt. Die in Teilbereichen von Privatpersonen, Vereinen oder Unternehmen initiierten „Pionierprojekte" (meist mit geringen finanziellen Mitteln, aber hohem persönlichen Engagement entstandene Zwischennutzungen) konnten zudem Handlungsspielräume für viele Akteure schaffen. Sie wurden so in das Gesamtkonzept integriert, dass sie bei Erfolg bestehen bleiben und weiterentwickelt oder aber wieder entfernt werden können. Inzwischen hat sich gezeigt, dass der im Partizipationsverfahren angestrebte und scheinbar erfolgreich verlaufene Ausgleich zwischen den Interessengruppen missglückt ist. Die stark am Erhalt des Status Quo interessierte Gruppe „100% Tempelhofer Feld" wurde nach Abschluss der

ed in maintaining the status quo, became active again after the conclusion of the civic participation process and over the course of further planning negotiations. It instigated a referendum on 25 May 2014, which overthrew the outcome of the previous civic participation and planning. This example shows how inconsistent social consensus can be and how difficult it is to filter out a "valid civic opinion" as a planning basis. It especially shows the great influence of the involved parties on planning and not least how strong social reservations towards change and landscape transformation can be. In the same way that social changes cause landscape changes, the reverse also applies: "these physical-spatial consequences of the transformation process have a reverse effect on people's notions of landscape. Consequently, physical objects become symbols of belonging and well-being, in short of the homeland."[6] The transformation of physical objects in the landscape is therefore linked to social notions of landscape, which also makes social resistance possible whenever the change goes too much against these notions of landscape or appears inappropriate. The experience of mass demonstrations and riots surrounding major building projects such as "Stuttgart 21" or in the Gezi Park in Istanbul testifies very clearly to this. Society is becoming more active and is demanding more information and greater decision-making power for its own environment. The geographer and sociologist Olaf Kühne is convinced that transformation processes can be guided.[7] We planners will also assume this role more often in future, in order to accompany the transformation of landscapes as decisively and at the same time as flexibly, cleverly, and sustainably as necessary.

Bürgerbeteiligung und im Laufe der weiteren Planungsverhandlungen erneut aktiv. Sie führte am 25. Mai 2014 einen Volksentscheid herbei, der die Ergebnisse der vorangegangenen Bürgerbeteiligung und die Planung stürzte. Das Beispiel zeigt, wie unbeständig ein gesellschaftlicher Konsens sein kann und wie schwierig es ist, eine „gültige Bürgermeinung" als Planungsgrundlage herauszufiltern. Vor allem zeigt es den großen Einfluss von Akteuren auf Planung und legt nicht zuletzt dar, wie stark gesellschaftliche Vorbehalte gegen Wandel und Landschaftstransformation sein können. So wie gesellschaftliche Veränderungen einen Wandel von Landschaft verursachen, gilt auch der umgekehrte Fall: „Diese physisch-räumlichen Auswirkungen des Transformationsprozesses wirken wieder zurück auf die landschaftliche Vorstellung der Menschen, schließlich erfolgt werden physische Objekte zu Symbolen der Zugehörigkeit und des Wohlbefindens, kurz, für Heimat."[6] Der Wandel von physischen Objekten in der Landschaft ist also mit gesellschaftlichen Vorstellungen von Landschaft verbunden, und damit ist auch gesellschaftlicher Widerstand möglich, sobald der Wandel den Vorstellungen von Landschaft zu sehr widerspricht beziehungsweise nicht nachvollziehbar erscheint. Auch die Erfahrung massiver Demonstrationen und Ausschreitungen im Vorfeld großer Bauvorhaben wie „Stuttgart 21" oder im Gezi-Park in Istanbul belegen diesen Umstand nachdrücklich. Die Gesellschaft wird aktiver und fordert mehr Information, mehr Entscheidungs- und Gestaltungsmöglichkeiten für das eigene Lebensumfeld ein. Der Geograf und Soziologe Olaf Kühne geht davon aus, dass man Transformationsprozesse moderieren kann.[7] Auch in diese Rolle werden wir Planer in Zukunft häufiger schlüpfen, um den Wandel von Landschaften künftig so determiniert und gleichsam flexibel wie nötig, und so klug und nachhaltig wie möglich begleiten zu können.

LANDSCAPE TRANS-
FORMATION

TRANSFORMATIONS-
LANDSCHAFTEN

URBAN LANDSCAPE TRANSFORMATION

With the chosen framework theme of "Urban Landscape Transformation," the International Doctoral College "Spatial Research Lab" further pursued significant issues between 2013 and 2016 that had already been formulated for the 2007–2011 curriculum entitled "Perspectives on the Spatial Development of European Metropolitan Regions." "Sustainable development [...] demands that high priority is given to the renewal and expansion of existing settlements and infrastructures. The expansion of settlement areas needs to take a back seat. Here, special significance is attributed to the integration of landscape areas and their knowing design. Such tasks place increased demands on cooperation and communication across subject-specific and political boundaries; and this is against a background of national, European, and global competition; changes in demography and climate; and the continuing worldwide trend towards bigger and bigger metropolises."[1] At the same time, the new framework theme put forward a different spatiotemporal context, with a focus on the "urban," on "transformation" (and therefore the scheduling and organisational aspects of planning), and especially on the notion of "landscape." This resulted in numerous further issues and themes that are the subject of this logbook 2.0 and in particular of the dissertations that are presented as brief portraits in this book. The "Spatial Research Labs" explored together allowed extensive insights into the multitude of complex problems presented by the new framework theme and comprise many still unanswered questions that are the focal tasks of current and especially future planning and spatial development. The exchanges with key parties involved in urban and spatial involvement in the Spatial Research Labs that were visited also opened up access to disciplinary and transdisciplinary background knowledge, which can only be gained comprehensively through personal dialogue. Spatial Research Labs are shared "exploratory spaces" in which "urgent tasks for our societies and communities"[2] come together. By exploring these spaces, insights can be gained into "similarities" and "differences"[3]—with regard to problems, methods, tools for solving problems, exemplary approaches, and underlying planning methods. The direct reference to the Spatial Research Labs is, in our opinion, essential for research and teaching in spatial planning disciplines. The doctoral symposia "have proved to be a central stage for exchange, discourse, and the critical feedback that is so important in research."[4] The Spatial Research Labs at the locations of the network partners within the International Doctoral College, namely Hamburg, Karlsruhe, Munich, Stuttgart, Vienna, and Zurich-Limmattal, were sources of a wealth of insights, especially in relation to the specified framework theme of "Urban Landscape Transformation." The additional case studies in Bel-

URBANE TRANSFORMATIONS-
LANDSCHAFTEN

Mit dem gewählten Rahmenthema „Urbane Transformationslandschaften"
verfolgte das Internationale Doktorandenkolleg „Forschungslabor Raum"
2013 bis 2016 wesentliche Fragestellungen weiter, die bereits anlässlich des
Curriculums 2007 bis 2011 unter dem Titel „Perspektiven zur räumlichen
Entwicklung europäischer Metropolregionen" formuliert wurden: „Nachhaltige Entwicklung [...] verlangt mit hoher Priorität, bestehende Siedlungen und Infrastrukturen zu erneuern und zu ergänzen. Siedlungsflächen-
erweiterung muss zur Ausnahme werden. Dabei kommt der Integration
von Landschaftsräumen und ihrer bewussten Gestaltung eine besondere
Bedeutung zu. Solche Aufgaben stellen erhöhte Anforderungen an die Kooperation und Kommunikation über Fach- und politische Grenzen hinweg;
dies vor dem Hintergrund nationaler, europäischer und globaler Konkurrenz, dem Wandel von Demografie und Klima und der weltweit anhaltenden Metropolisierung."[1] Gleichzeitig entstand mit dem neuen Rahmenthema ein veränderter raum-zeitlicher Kontext, der das Augenmerk auf
das „Urbane", die „Transformation" (und somit die zeitlichen und organisatorischen Aspekte der Planung), aber vor allem auf den Begriff „Landschaft"
lenkte. Daraus ergaben sich zahlreiche weitere Fragen und Themen, die
Gegenstand des vorliegenden Logbuches 2.0 und insbesondere der Dissertationen sind, die im Buch als Kurzportraits vorgestellt werden.
Die gemeinsam erkundeten Forschungslaborräume erlaubten intensive
Einblicke in die Vielfalt der komplexen Probleme, die sich aus dem neuen
Rahmenthema ergaben und beinhalteten als Schwerpunktaufgaben der-
zeitiger und vor allem künftiger Planung und Raumentwicklung zahlreiche
noch unbeantwortete Fragestellungen. Der Austausch mit Schlüsselakteu-
ren der Stadt- und Raumentwicklung der bereisten Laborräume eröffnete
überdies Zugang zu disziplinärem und transdisziplinärem Hintergrundwissen, das sich erst im persönlichen Dialog in vollem Umfang erkennt-
nisgewinnend erschließen lässt. Forschungslaborräume sind gemeinsame
„Erkundungsräume", in denen „drängende Aufgaben unserer Gesellschaften und Gemeinwesen"[2] zusammen kommen. Bei der Erkundung dieser
Räume konnten Erkenntnisse gewonnen werden zu „Gemeinsamkeiten"
und „Unterschieden"[3] – bezogen auf Problemstellungen, Methoden und
Instrumente zur Problemlösung, Lösungsrichtungen, beispielhafte Lösungsansätze und zugrunde liegende Planungsansätze. Der direkte Bezug zu den Laborräumen ist unseres Erachtens unverzichtbar für Forschung und Lehre in raum- und handlungsbezogenen Disziplinen und
Wissenschaften. Die Doktorandenwochen („Vor-Ort-Kollegwochen")„haben sich als zentrale Bühne des Austausches, des Diskurses und der bei
Forschung so wichtigen kritischen Begleitung erwiesen und bewährt."[4]

grade and Milan, as locations where the guest professors were based, also provided access to issues surrounding the theory that planning is closely linked to language and culture, to paradigm-based ways of thinking and acting, and consequently to planning culture.[5]

Concepts are the framework for our knowledge and therefore for content, sense, and meaning. They structure our knowledge base and therefore objects and events in the real world, even if they cannot be defined conclusively. However, as a basis for academic exchange, concepts require appropriate clarification, in order to enable and promote understanding and the transparency of thought processes.[6] The framework title of the college, "Urban Landscape Transformation," opens up a wide field of experimentation in terms of interpretation and definition—as shown by the dissertation briefs. The focuses of attention below are the three core aspects relating to the chosen framework theme, namely "Urbanity," "Transformation," and "Landscape."[7]

Focus on urbanity

The future of humanity will be an urban, future, because, according to current prognoses, around 75 per cent of the world population will live in urban areas by 2050. This future is set within the context of the potential "futures" of those people who live in differently structured areas with differing development perspectives, for example in rural and alpine areas, peripheral areas, recreational areas attractive to tourists, functional settlement areas, or areas close to nature, in which man's usage of space is supposed to be secondary. The development perspectives of the various spatial typologies are interrelated and influence each other. Enabling a sustainable and resilient co-existence of the aforementioned areas is an essential precondition for safeguarding human existence, especially with regard to the long-term securing of the essentials of life such as water and air, food and energy, free access to education and recreation.

What is "urbanity?" What is "urban?" These questions lead to the roots of the human invention of "city" and to a wide range of interpretations and constant reinterpretations of the concept of "city," in the form of a built reality experienced through specific actions. The following key attributes and interpretations are often associated with "urbanity" and "urban," with "city" and "municipal:" dense spatial properties, wide-ranging usage possibilities, opportunities for personal development, exchanges, engaging in dialogue, acquiring knowledge, trading information, goods and services, cultivated mobility and "short routes," the stimulating juxtaposition of wide-ranging spatial usages, cultures, and languages, and the "familiar" and the "foreign." The questions also lead to the roots of Europe, to the concepts of "agora" and "polis," which are a precondition for viable direct democracy, for a thriving social, legal, and economic development, and consequently for freedom, social justice, and peace. These qualities mentioned as examples are in the context of various global, regional, and local

Die Forschungslaborräume an den Standorten der Netzwerkpartner des Internationalen Doktorandenkollegs, namentlich Hamburg, Karlsruhe, München, Stuttgart, Wien und Zürich-Limmattal, boten Quellen für einen reichhaltigen Erkenntnisgewinn, vor allem auch hinsichtlich des gestellten Rahmenthemas „Urbane Transformationslandschaften". Die weiteren Laborräume in Belgrad und Mailand, Standorte der Gastprofessorinnen, ermöglichten überdies Zutritt zu Fragestellungen, die mit der These verbunden sind, dass Planung eng mit Sprache und Kultur, mit paradigmatisch begründeten Denk- und Handlungsweisen und darauf aufbauend mit Planungskultur verknüpft sind.[5]

„Begriffe", verstanden als Konstrukte oder Konzepte, sind die Träger unseres Wissens und damit von Inhalt, Sinn und Bedeutung. Sie beleuchten die Kerne unseres Erkenntnisinteresses, somit Gegenstände und Ereignisse der realen Welt, auch wenn sie nicht abschließend definiert werden können. Als Grundlage für den wissenschaftlichen Austausch bedürfen Begriffe jedoch einer angemessenen Klärung („kernprägnant", nicht „randscharf"), sodass darauf aufbauend Verständigung und Nachvollziehbarkeit der Denkprozesse ermöglicht und befördert werden können.[6] Der Rahmentitel des Kollegs „Urbane Transformationslandschaften" spannt ein erkenntnisreiches Experimentierfeld für Interpretation und Definition auf – das zeigen die vorliegenden Dissertationsportraits.

Im Zentrum der Betrachtung stehen nachfolgend jene drei mit dem gewählten Rahmenthema verbundene Fokusse, namentlich „Urbanität", „Transformation" und „Landschaft"[7]:

Fokus Urbanität

Die Zukunft der Menschheit wird in besonderer Weise eine urbane Zukunft sein, denn nach aktuellen Prognosen werden 2050 etwa 75 Prozent der Weltbevölkerung in Städten leben. Diese Zukunft steht im Kontext der möglichen „Zukünfte" jener Menschen, die in teils gänzlich anders strukturierten Räumen mit anderen Entwicklungsperspektiven leben, beispielhaft in ländlichen und alpinen Räumen, peripheren Räumen, touristisch attraktiven Erholungsräumen, in funktionalen Ausgleichsräumen oder in naturnahen Räumen, in denen menschliche Raumnutzung Nachrang haben soll. Die Entwicklungsperspektiven der verschiedenen Raumtypen stehen in Beziehung und beeinflussen einander. Die Ermöglichung einer nachhaltigen und resilienten Koexistenz der beispielhaft benannten Räume ist unverzichtbare Voraussetzung für die Existenzsicherung der Menschen, insbesondere hinsichtlich der dauerhaften Sicherung ihrer Lebensgrundlagen wie Wasser und Luft, Nahrungsmittel und Energie, freier Zugang zu Bildung und Erholungsmöglichkeiten.

Was ist „Urbanität"? Was ist „urban"? Diese Fragen führen zu den Wurzeln der menschlichen Erfindung „Stadt" und zu vielfältiger Interpretation und ständiger Neuinterpretation des Konzeptes „Stadt" in Form gebauter und durch konkrete Handlungen gelebter Wirklichkeit. Häufig werden nach-

tendencies and events: climate change and demographic change (including dramatic migrations caused by socio-economic disasters), natural disasters, and drastic changes in energy supply. Many other aspects flow into specialist discourse.

Focus on transformation

The central theme of "transformation" applies to a wide range of spatial structures and spatial usage processes. It comprises both physical spatial structures (including settlement and development structures, spatial infrastructures, open space structures) that are, in some cases, an object of direct perception, as well as system structures[8] that need to be developed. The required transformation therefore refers to the "appearance"[9] of the space that we gain through perception, and to the determining "structures" and the "resources" of the space with its material and energy supplies, of which we need to gain an understanding. From a temporal perspective, we recognise changes to these structures and processes if we observe them over time and can even watch the transformation as it unfolds. In planning, it is necessary to employ suitable planning processes in a conscious and transparent, problem-based and solution-oriented manner, so that the creation of spatial structures and usage processes is also a social learning process. The focus of planning considerations must be problems[10] that are already present and problems that may occur in future if the attitude to space does not change. At the start of planning processes there must always be a shared awareness among the parties involved in both planning and the day–to–day reality; this shared awareness could and should lead to a common understanding of the problem through dialogue.

We are of the view that today—especially in a European context—there should be a primary focus on continuously redeveloping and regenerating existing urban living spaces, in other words transforming what is there, instead of driving land usage forwards unchecked by appropriating new areas for the development of urban space.

Focus on landscape

Using terms such as "in-between city," "urban cultural landscape," and similar neologisms, expert circles have attempted for a long time to provide an apt description of the spatially disparate conglomerates of city and countryside in Central Europe. These new concepts were also intended to provide conceptual indications of potential development strategies designed to transform the complex meshes of naturally created and anthropogenically-transformed structures into the best possible living environments. The historic-cultural term "landscape" is used at the International Doctoral College because it refers to the totality of the spatial structure at the centre of our joint research activity. However, "landscape" has to be defined differently today than about half a century ago. The traditional understanding of landscape is reflected in a conceptual definition that was

folgende Schlüsselattribute und Interpretationen mit „Urbanität" und „urban", mit „Stadt" und „städtisch" verknüpft: Dichte räumlicher Qualitäten, vielfältige Nutzungsmöglichkeiten; Möglichkeiten sich frei zu entfalten, sich auszutauschen, den Dialog zu führen, Wissen zu erwerben, Informationen, Güter und Dienstleistungen zu tauschen; kultivierte Mobilität und „kurze Wege"; das anregende Nebeneinander verschiedenster Raumnutzungen, Kulturen und Sprachen, das „Vertraute" und das „Fremde". Die Fragen führen auch zu den Wurzeln Europas, zu den Konzepten „agora" und „polis", die eine Voraussetzung für gelebte direkte Demokratie, gedeihliche gesellschaftliche, rechtliche und wirtschaftliche Entwicklung und in weiterer Folge für Freiheit, soziale Gerechtigkeit und Frieden bilden. Diese beispielhaft benannten Qualitäten stehen im Kontext verschiedener globaler, regionaler und lokaler Tendenzen und Ereignisse: Klimawandel und demografischer Wandel (einschließlich dramatischer Wanderungsbewegungen verursacht durch sozio-ökonomische Katastrophen), Naturkatastrophen, drastische Veränderungen in der Bereitstellung der Energie. Viele weitere Aspekte prägen den fachlichen Diskurs.

Fokus Transformation

Der leitende Gedanke „Transformation" bezieht sich auf vielfältige räumliche Strukturen und Prozesse der Raumnutzung. Diese Betrachtung umschließt sowohl physische räumliche Strukturen (unter anderem Siedlungs- und Bebauungsstrukturen, räumliche Infrastrukturen, Freiraumstrukturen), die teils Gegenstand direkter Anschauung sind, als auch Systemstrukturen[8], die es zu erschließen gilt. Die erforderliche Transformation bezieht sich somit auf das „Bild"[9] des Raumes, das wir durch Wahrnehmung gewinnen, auf die Gestalt bestimmenden „Strukturen" und den „Haushalt" des Raumes mit seinen Stoff- und Energieströmen, dessen Verständnis wir erschließen müssen. Im zeitlichen Kontext erkennen wir bei längerer Betrachtung Veränderungen dieser Strukturen und Prozesse, wir können die Transformation und den Wandel gleichsam beobachten; im planerischen Sinn gilt es, in bewusster und nachvollziehbarer Weise, problembasiert und lösungsorientiert Raumstrukturen und Nutzungsprozesse mittels geeigneter Planungsprozesse als gesellschaftliche Lernprozesse zu gestalten. Dabei müssen sowohl Probleme[10], die bereits anliegen, als auch Probleme, die vermutlich in der Zukunft auftreten werden, falls das Raumverhalten nicht verändert wird, im Mittelpunkt planerischer Überlegungen stehen. Zu Beginn der Planungsprozesse muss stets eine gemeinsame Bewusstseinsbildung aller Beteiligten und zu beteiligender Akteure der Planungs- und Alltagswelt stattfinden, die im Dialog zu einem gemeinsamen Problemverständnis führen könnte und sollte.

Wir vertreten die Ansicht, dass es heute – insbesondere im europäischen Kontext – in erster Linie darum gehen muss, vorhandene urbane Lebensräume kontinuierlich umzubauen und zu erneuern, also Bestände zu transformieren, anstatt den Landverbrauch hemmungslos voranzutrei-

formulated in 1963 by the German philosopher Joachim Ritter, which was considered universally valid for a long time: "Landscape is nature, becoming aesthetically present in the gaze of a sensitive and sentient observer. Not the fields outside the city, not the river as a 'boundary,' 'channel of trade,' and 'problem for bridge-builders,' not mountains and plains of the shepherds and caravans (or the searcher of oil) are as such 'landscape.' They only become landscape if man 'freely' enjoys the sight without any practical interest, to be in nature as himself."[11] A view of landscape that focuses one-sidedly on aesthetics and Kantian "disinterested pleasure" is no longer appropriate today for overcoming the complex and convoluted problems of spatial development. At the doctoral college we therefore base our research activities on a different definition of landscape.

"A landscape is not a natural feature of the environment but a synthetic space, a man-made system of spaces superimposed on the face of the land, functioning and evolving not according to natural laws but to serve a community."[12] This definition proposed in 1984 by one of the founding fathers of American Landscape Studies, the American historian and literary scholar John Brinckerhoff Jackson, is considered a guiding principle in expert circles and contrasts with the frequently cited view of Joachim Ritter. Landscape is defined by J.B. Jackson as the entire human environment, both built and unbuilt, city and countryside, and the organisers of the International Doctoral College subscribe to this view.

Jackson's notion of landscape is very advantageous as an anchor point for planning and design disciplines, especially with regard to the new challenges presented by spatial and environmental planning, as well as by transformation. If one accepts the conceptually significant aspect that landscape is not nature, not even a natural phenomenon of the environment, but a system created by man, then the obvious consequence is that man has to assume responsibility for the landscape as a complex whole. The permanent pressure to distinguish between natural and artificial components, between city and countryside, no longer applies. For example, one no longer needs to discuss whether infrastructure can in fact generate landscape, instead infrastructure is landscape.

In Jackson's definition, the conceptual strength of the term landscape is highlighted once again when he writes: "Landscape is not a scenery, it is not a political unit; [...] Whatever its shape or size, it is never simply a natural space, a feature of the natural environment; it is always artificial, always synthetic, always subject to sudden or unpredictable change."[14]

Non-linearity, emergence, and surprise are the primary characteristics of complexity. This finding leads to an understanding of landscape as a complex and vibrant system that can never be harnessed in a finished and ideal state. Landscape is no longer the ideal, compensatory counterpart with which humankind—like once in the Romantic period—can console itself over the loss of the closeness of nature. A central theory derived from what has been said is therefore: "landscape" is a fundamental plan-

ben, indem ausschließlich neue Flächen für die Entwicklung urbaner Räume in Anspruch genommen werden.

Fokus Landschaft

Mit Begriffen wie „Zwischenstadt", „urbane Kulturlandschaft" und ähnlichen Neologismen versuchte man in der Fachwelt lange Zeit, die räumlich dispersen Konglomerate aus Stadt und Land in Mitteleuropa treffend zu beschreiben. Diese neuen Begriffe sollten aber auch konzeptionelle Hinweise liefern auf mögliche Entwicklungsstrategien, um die komplexen Gefüge aus natürlich entstandenen und anthropogen stark überformten Strukturen in möglichst gute Lebensumwelten zu verwandeln. Der kulturgeschichtlich etablierte Begriff „Landschaft" wird im Kolleg gebraucht, weil er die Gesamtheit jenes Raumgefüges bezeichnet, welches im Zentrum unserer gemeinsamen Forschungstätigkeiten steht. Dabei ist jedoch „Landschaft" heute anders zu definieren als noch vor etwa einem halben Jahrhundert.

Das traditionell geprägte Verständnis von Landschaft spiegelt sich in einer Begriffsdefinition wider, die 1963 von dem deutschen Philosophen Joachim Ritter formuliert wurde. Sie galt lange Zeit als allein gültig: „Landschaft ist Natur, die im Anblick für einen fühlenden und empfindenden Betrachter ästhetisch gegenwärtig ist: Nicht die Felder vor der Stadt, der Strom als ‚Grenze', ‚Handelsweg' und ‚Problem für Brückenbauer', nicht die Gebirge und Steppen der Hirten und Karawanen (oder der Ölsucher) sind als solche schon ‚Landschaft'. Sie werden dies erst, wenn sich der Mensch ihnen ohne praktischen Zweck in ‚freier' genießender Anschauung zuwendet, um als er selbst in der Natur zu sein."[11] Eine einseitig auf Ästhetik und „interesseloses Wohlgefallen" im Kant'schen Sinne fokussierte Betrachtung von Landschaft ist für die Bewältigung komplexer und unübersichtlicher Probleme der Raumentwicklung heute nicht mehr angemessen. Deshalb legen wir im Doktorandenkolleg eine andere Definition von Landschaft unserer Forschungstätigkeit zugrunde.

„Landschaft ist kein natürliches Phänomen der Umwelt, sondern ein synthetischer Raum, ein von Menschen gemachtes System von Räumen, welches ins Gesicht des Landes übertragen wurde und sich in Funktion und Entwicklung nicht nach natürlichen Gesetzen richtet, sondern der Gemeinschaft dient."[12] Diese Definition, 1984 verfasst von einem der Gründerväter der American Landscape Studies, dem amerikanischen Historiker und Literaturwissenschaftler John Brinckerhoff Jackson, gilt heute in Fachkreisen als richtungsweisend und steht in einem gewissen Gegensatz zur immer wieder zitierten Auffassung von Joachim Ritter. Landschaft wird von J. B. Jackson als gesamte menschliche Umwelt definiert, die sowohl Gebautes als auch Ungebautes, also Stadt und Land umfasst, und dieser Auffassung schließen sich auch die Träger des Internationalen Doktorandenkollegs an. Jacksons Landschaftsbegriff ist als Ankerpunkt für die planerischen und entwerferischen Disziplinen gerade im Hinblick auf die neuen Herausforderungen der Raum- und Umweltgestaltung, der Transformation von

ning concept and design strategy in which important basic rules and laws for the development of viable spatial and environmental systems of high complexity are already embedded. One could also say that landscape is a model for viable spatial and environmental systems that are highly complex. Many of the immanent rules of "landscape" have established themselves over the course of the long development history of landscape, and other principles and laws must be readjusted to do justice to current natural and social environmental conditions. The International Doctoral College provides far-reaching contributions to this.

Conclusion

The many changes within living environments that have and should have a primarily inward-looking settlement development, including changes in the areas of mobility, landscape, demography, energy, and, not least of all, the climate, require integrated and transparent strategies and concepts for integrative transformation.

The professors at the International Doctoral College "Spatial Research Lab":
Michael Koch, Markus Neppl, Walter Schönwandt, Bernd Scholl, Andreas Voigt, Udo Weilacher

großem Vorteil. Akzeptiert man nämlich den konzeptionell bedeutenden Aspekt, dass Landschaft nicht Natur, ja noch nicht einmal ein natürliches Phänomen der Umwelt ist, sondern ein von Menschen gemachtes System, dann hat das zur Folge, dass der Mensch selbstverständlich die Verantwortung für die Landschaft als komplexe Gesamtheit zu übernehmen hat. Der permanente Zwang zur Unterscheidung zwischen natürlichen und künstlichen Komponenten, zwischen Stadt und Land wird damit hinfällig. So muss man beispielsweise nicht mehr darüber diskutieren, ob Infrastruktur tatsächlich Landschaft erzeugen kann, sondern Infrastruktur ist selbstverständlich Landschaft.

In Jacksons Definition wird die konzeptionelle Stärke des Begriffs Landschaft nochmals besonders deutlich, wenn er schreibt: „Landschaft ist nicht einfach Szenerie, sie ist auch keine politische Kategorie; [...] Egal, wie groß sie ist oder welche Form sie hat, Landschaft lässt sich nicht allein als natürlicher Raum, als Merkmal der natürlichen Umwelt verstehen. Sie ist stets künstlich, stets synthetisch, stets plötzlichen und unvorhersehbaren Veränderungen ausgesetzt."[13] Nichtlinearität, Emergenz und Überraschung sind die wesentlichen Kennzeichen von Komplexität. Was in dieser Feststellung zum Tragen kommt, ist das Verständnis von Landschaft als ein komplexes lebendiges System, das niemals in einen fertigen Idealzustand überführt werden kann. Landschaft ist nicht mehr das ideale kompensatorische Gegenüber, mit dem sich der Mensch – wie einst in der Romantik – über den Verlust der Nähe zur Natur hinwegtrösten kann. Eine zentrale These, die sich aus dem Gesagten ableitet, lautet also: „Landschaft" ist ein grundlegendes planungs- und entwurfsstrategisches Konzept, in das wichtige Grundregeln und Gesetzmäßigkeiten zur Entwicklung tragfähiger Raum- und Umweltsysteme von hoher Komplexität bereits eingebettet sind. Man könnte auch sagen, Landschaft ist ein Modell für tragfähige Raum- und Umweltsysteme von hoher Komplexität. Viele der systemimmanenten Regeln von „Landschaft" haben sich im Laufe der langen Entwicklungsgeschichte von Landschaft etabliert und andere Grundsätze und Gesetze müssen neu justiert werden, um aktuellen natürlichen und gesellschaftlichen Umweltbedingungen gerecht zu werden. Dazu liefert das Internationale Doktorandenkolleg weitreichende Ansätze.

Fazit

Der vielfältige Wandel im Bereich der Lebensräume mit einer vorwiegend nach innen gerichteten und zu richtenden Siedlungsentwicklung, Veränderungen im Bereich Mobilität, Landschaft, Demografie, Energie und nicht zuletzt Klima, erfordern integrierte und veranschaulichbare Strategien und Konzepte für die ganzheitliche Transformation.

Die Professoren des Doktorandenkollegs „Forschungslabor Raum":
Michael Koch, Markus Neppl, Walter Schönwandt, Bernd Scholl, Andreas Voigt, Udo Weilacher

THE KEY QUESTION: WHAT IS PLANNING?

DIE GRUNDFRAGE: WAS IST PLANUNG?

THE KEY QUESTION: WHAT IS PLANNING?

WALTER SCHÖNWANDT

What content should be included in the central, key topics of a doctoral college on the subject of spatial planning? A number of subject areas can be considered. However, one topic should definitely be included, namely the question: what is (spatial) planning? After all, this is the fundamental question about the contentual core of the entire profession.

Some readers may respond at this point with the comment: "well, that should really be quite clear." However, those who are familiar with such fundamental matters know or suspect that this question does not have an easy answer, not only because there are many different views on "what planning actually is," but also because these views have been changing constantly over time and will probably continue to do so.

Addressing the question of "what is planning?" and answering it are necessary to ensure an on-going process of self-reflection and self-monitoring as to whether one is on the right and expedient path, or whether one is making mistakes during planning. This means that it is not merely an academic exercise, it is about more than that. If this process of self-reflection and self-monitoring does not work, then the profession stagnates as a self-learning system. It is therefore necessary to compare what one is thinking and doing during the planning process with one's own standards, with what one has intended to think and do, in other words with one's own concept of "what planning is." To do so, one must be sufficiently aware of both.

If one translates the question "what is planning?" into scientific language, then it can be formulated as: which planning concept are the relevant thoughts and actions based on? *Planning concept* means the corresponding "understanding of planning." In other words: the planning concept specifies what content and procedures are to be taken account of or omitted in planning. Those who look into the general subject area can find other expressions which are used in this context instead of the term *planning concept*, such as *planning theory, planning model,* etc. In this chapter, however, the term *planning concept* is used throughout for this topic.

What should such a planning concept entail? It should have a structure that shows (i) which elements/components play a role in planning, (ii) how they are linked structurally and how they interrelate, (iii) how planning unfolds, and (iv) how all this relates to the relevant context.

This simple example is designed to illustrate what type of planning tasks this involves: "There is an area of unused urban land, requiring the development of proposals for the future development of this area." In more gen-

DIE GRUNDFRAGE: WAS IST PLANUNG?

WALTER SCHÖNWANDT

Welche Inhalte gehören zu den zentralen Grundlagenthemen eines Doktorandenkollegs in der räumlichen Planung? Sicher, hier kommen etliche Themenfelder in Betracht. Doch ein Thema dürfte in jedem Fall dazugehören – nämlich die Frage: Was ist (räumliche) Planung? Schließlich ist dies die grundlegende Frage nach dem inhaltlichen Kern der gesamten Profession.

Mancher Leser dürfte an dieser Stelle mit der Bemerkung reagieren: „Na, das müsste doch eigentlich klar sein." Wer sich indes mit derartig grundlegenden Themen auskennt, weiß oder ahnt, dass dies keine einfach zu beantwortende Frage ist, nicht nur, weil es viele verschiedene Ansichten darüber gibt, „was Planung eigentlich ist", sondern auch, weil sich diese Ansichten über die Zeit ständig verändert haben und wohl immer verändern werden.

Die Beschäftigung mit und die Antwort auf die Frage „Was ist Planung?" sind notwendig, um sich in einem fortwährenden Prozess der Selbstreflexion und Selbstüberprüfung zu vergewissern, ob man auf einem richtigen, sachdienlichen Weg ist oder ob man beim Planen Fehler macht. Das heißt, hier geht es nicht um eine rein akademische Übung – es geht um mehr: Wenn dieser Prozess der Selbstreflexion und Selbstüberprüfung nicht funktioniert, stockt die Profession als selbstlernendes System. Deshalb ist es nötig, das, was man beim Planen denkt und tut, mit den eigenen Ansprüchen zu vergleichen, also dem, was man zu denken und zu tun beabsichtigt hat, eben den eigenen Vorstellungen davon, „was Planung ist", und dazu muss man beides hinreichend genau kennen.

Wenn man die Frage „Was ist Planung?" in die Wissenschaftssprache übersetzt, so lautet sie: Welcher Planungsbegriff liegt (dem jeweiligen Denken und Handeln) zugrunde? Mit *Planungsbegriff* ist dabei das jeweilige „Verständnis von Planung" gemeint. Anders ausgedrückt: Der Planungsbegriff spezifiziert, welche Inhalte sowie Abläufe beim Planen zu beachten und zu bearbeiten sind und welche nicht. Wer sich mit diesem gesamten Themenbereich befasst, findet weitere Ausdrücke, die in diesem Zusammenhang zuweilen anstelle des Wortes *Planungsbegriff* benutzt werden, wie zum Beispiel *Planungstheorie*, *Planungsmodell* etc. Im vorliegenden Kapitel wird jedoch für dieses gesamte Themenfeld der Terminus *Planungsbegriff* verwendet.

Was sollte ein solcher Planungsbegriff enthalten? Er sollte eine Struktur haben, indem er aufzeigt, (i) welche Elemente/Komponenten beim Planen eine Rolle spielen, (ii) wie sie strukturell zusammenhängen sowie welche

eral terms, it is about setting out relevant, effective, and justifiable proposals for action, namely in the fields of architecture and urban development, as well as spatial and regional planning.

What has to be emphasized in this context is that this self-reflection and self-monitoring is only possible if there is an *explicit* answer to the question "what is planning?", which means if the parties involved in the discussion are able to provide an *explicit* description of their specific answers to this question, in other words their respective *planning concept*. The purpose of this explicitness becomes clear if one considers that what is implicit—and that is the decisive point—can scarcely be analysed, compared, tested, improved, or communicated. This means that planning concepts that are only used intuitively, but are not formulated clearly, are not accessible for analysis or an ensuing further development and improvement, precisely because they are applied subconsciously.

This leads to the core focus of this chapter: in discussions among experts about planning theory, what is the situation with regard to structured, explicit planning concepts? In anticipation of the answer: this is a difficult debate that is faced more with hurdles than with success. To formulate it pointedly: planning theory has little regard for "what planning is"—in other words, for reflection about what forms the core of the planning profession. The consequences of this are a low self-learning rate within the profession, more planning errors, and a waste of resources and time, therefore anything other than marginal.

If attention is drawn to this conceptual deficit, then one can observe very differing reactions. Some colleagues say: "yes, there is a gap in content here, which should be worked on more thoroughly." This is often followed by interjections such as: "…but that is rather difficult." However, there are also other reactions. Some say: "that's impossible," others say "we don't need that," while others say "we've already had that for a long time." The following takes a closer look at the latter three reactions.

"That's impossible"

Those who say "formulate planning concepts explicitly? That's impossible" are mostly evoking a debate that took place in the 1970s. An article by Mandelbaum from the year 1979 is often cited as a reference in this context, with the indicative title "A complete general theory of planning is impossible."[1]

Some have concluded from this that one does not need to pay any further heed to the topic of planning concepts. However, if one subscribed to this attitude, what would the consequences be? They would be considerable. A profession that is incapable of reflecting on the content and therefore the substance of its own field of work—however difficult that may be in terms of content—is pulling the carpet out from under its own feet and side-lining itself. In other words, this way of thinking cannot be a solution. It is helpful to clarify at this point what the definition of a planning con-

Wechselwirkungen zwischen ihnen bestehen, (iii) wie Planung abläuft und (iv) wie all dies in Beziehung zum jeweiligen Umfeld steht.

Ein einfaches Beispiel soll illustrieren, um welche Art planerischer Aufgabenstellungen es dabei geht: „Gegeben ist eine städtische Brachfläche, zu erarbeiten sind Handlungsvorschläge, wie diese Fläche zukünftig entwickelt werden soll." Allgemeiner ausgedrückt geht es darum, zweckdienliche, wirksame sowie verantwortbare Handlungsvorschläge zu erarbeiten, und zwar in den Themenfeldern von Architektur und Städtebau bis zur Raum- und Landesplanung.

Wesentlich ist in diesem Zusammenhang hervorzuheben, dass diese Selbstreflexion und Selbstüberprüfung nur dann möglich ist, wenn es eine *explizite* Antwort auf die Frage „Was ist Planung?" gibt. Das heißt, wenn die beteiligten Diskutanten in der Lage sind, ihre spezifischen Antworten auf die Frage „Was ist Planung?", also ihren jeweiligen *Planungsbegriff* (wobei es auch mehrere sein können) *explizit* zu beschreiben. Der Nutzen dieses Explizitmachens wird klar, wenn man sich vergegenwärtigt, dass Implizites – und das ist der entscheidende Punkt – kaum analysiert, verglichen, getestet, verbessert oder kommuniziert werden kann. Das heißt, Planungsbegriffe, die nur intuitiv benutzt, aber nicht nachvollziehbar formuliert werden, sind – eben weil sie nur unbewusst angewandt werden – für eine Analyse und in der Folge für eine Weiterentwicklung und Verbesserung nicht zugänglich.

Damit lässt sich die Kernfrage fokussieren, um die es in diesem Kapitel geht: Wie steht es in der planungstheoretischen Fachdiskussion um strukturierte, explizite Planungsbegriffe? Um die Antwort vorwegzunehmen: Dies ist eine schwierige Debatte, die eher mit Holprigkeiten zu kämpfen als Erfolge vorzuweisen hat. Zugespitzt formuliert: Die Planungstheorie kümmert sich wenig darum, „was Planung ist" – also um die Reflexion dessen, was den Kern der Planungsprofession ausmacht. Die Folgen sind eine geringe Selbstlerngeschwindigkeit der Profession, mehr Planungsfehler sowie Ressourcen- und Zeitverschwendung, also alles andere als marginal.

Bringt man dieses konzeptuelle Defizit zur Sprache, so lassen sich höchst unterschiedliche Reaktionen beobachten. Manche Kolleginnen und Kollegen sagen: „Ja, hier haben wir eine inhaltliche Lücke, daran sollte intensiver gearbeitet werden." Nicht selten werden dabei Ergänzungen nachgeschoben, wie: „Das ist aber schwierig." Doch es gibt auch andere Reaktionen. Einige sagen: „Das geht nicht", andere sagen: „Das brauchen wir nicht", und wieder andere sagen: „Das haben wir doch schon längst." Nachfolgend sollen die drei letztgenannten Reaktionen etwas ausführlicher betrachtet werden.

„Das geht nicht"

Diejenigen, die sagen: „Planungsbegriffe explizit formulieren? Das geht nicht", verweisen meist auf eine Debatte, die in den 1970er Jahren geführt wurde. Als Referenz wird dabei oft ein Artikel von Mandelbaum aus dem

cept is *not* about. It is not about formulating a conclusive, all-encompassing, indisputable, eternally valid and applicable, general planning concept. After all, concepts are always temporary and fragmentary in principle, at best with some core relevance, but never sharp at the edges. They have *acuities* and *blind spots*. They change, are never true or false, but at best useful or helpful, and consequently can always be criticised.[2] There can therefore never be a truly conclusive planning concept, instead we are always dealing with a "temporary concept" mostly relating to the particular assignment and context. However, if we want to make use of the aforementioned advantages of explicit planning concepts (namely in order to analyse and improve our working basis) we cannot avoid setting out corresponding concept definitions.

"We don't need that"

Some of those who have already understood and digested the aforementioned point say: "planning concepts? Of course they exist, but they are not my concern. After all, I am a practitioner and my project successes show that I can do my job, even without having to give thought to such fundamental matters." Indeed, a planning practitioner who does not make mistakes can avoid reflecting on their own planning concept (for the time being we will leave aside the question of how and who defines what a "planning mistake" is). However, this much is clear: upon closer examination, there are few planning projects that do not experience some form of mistake. The public media in Germany have been full of it in recent years. The premise "don't make a mistake" is undoubtedly simply illusory.

Another relevant aspect is teaching. The problem is: how can one teach something if one is not capable of describing and explaining what one intends to teach? One might ask: is there not some way of teaching planning to a large extent without explicit planning concepts? A propagated and practiced route in relation to this is the principle of *learning by doing*. This principle undoubtedly has unsurpassable advantages and is an integral aspect of education in planning, for example when preparing students for real tasks in practice. However, difficulties arise if this method seeks to get by without explanations of the underlying planning concept. Such a teaching concept leaves the discovery and definition of what can be applied to the next planning case—namely the planning concept—up to the student and therefore the one with least specialist knowledge. Such an educational concept costs a lot of time, owing to the trials and errors of the student, and is therefore neither efficient nor effective. Richard Sennett formulates the problem that arises as a result as follows, that this educational concept "places the burden on the student."[3] Furthermore, the teacher does not know at all what—exactly—the students have actually learnt through the principle of *learning by doing*. Adopting an attitude of "we don't need that" is therefore not very helpful either in this context.

Jahre 1979 angeführt, mit dem bezeichnenden Titel „A complete general theory of planning is impossible".[1]

Manche haben daraus abgeleitet, dass man sich um das Thema Planungsbegriffe nicht weiter zu kümmern braucht. Doch würde man dieser Auffassung folgen, was wären die Konsequenzen? Sie wären erheblich. Eine Profession, die unfähig ist, über die Inhalte und damit die Substanz ihres eigenen Arbeitsfeldes zu reflektieren – wie schwierig das inhaltlich auch immer sein mag –, entzieht sich selbst den Boden und manövriert sich damit ins Abseits. Das heißt, diese Denkrichtung kann keine Lösung sein.

Hilfreich ist, an dieser Stelle klarzustellen, worum es bei der Erarbeitung eines Planungsbegriffes *nicht* geht. Es geht nicht darum, einen abschließenden, allumfassenden, unstrittigen, für alle Zeiten, für jede Anwendung gültigen allgemeinen Planungsbegriff zu formulieren. Begriffe sind schließlich *prinzipiell und immer* vorläufig und fragmentarisch, sie sind bestenfalls kernprägnant, nie jedoch randscharf, haben *Sehschärfen* und *tote Winkel*, sie wandeln sich, sind nie wahr oder falsch, sondern allenfalls nützlich/ hilfreich und folglich immer kritisierbar.[2] Einen wirklich abschließenden Planungsbegriff kann es also nicht geben, wir haben es stattdessen immer mit zumeist aufgaben- und kontextbezogenen „Begriffsdauerbaustellen" zu tun. Doch wenn wir die oben beschriebenen Vorteile expliziter Planungsbegriffe nutzen wollen (nämlich, unsere Arbeitsgrundlage analysieren und verbessern zu können), kommen wir um das Erarbeiten entsprechender Begriffsdefinitionen nicht herum.

„Das brauchen wir nicht"

Manche, die den oben genannten Punkt bereits verstanden und verdaut haben, sagen: „Planungsbegriffe? Sicher, so etwas gibt es, aber ich brauch' mich darum nicht zu kümmern. Schließlich bin ich Praktiker und meine Projekterfolge zeigen, dass ich meinen Job kann, und zwar auch ohne dass ich mich mit derart grundlegenden Themen beschäftigen müsste." In der Tat, ein Planungspraktiker, der keine Fehler macht, kann auf die Beschäftigung mit dem eigenen Planungsbegriff verzichten. (Für den Moment sei die Frage beiseite gelassen, wie und von wem definiert wird, was ein „Planungsfehler" ist.) Doch so viel ist klar: Bei genauerer Betrachtung dürfte es kaum Planungsprojekte geben, bei denen nicht doch irgendwelche Fehler passieren; die öffentlichen Medien sind gerade in Deutschland in den letzten Jahren voll davon. Die Prämisse „keine Fehler machen" ist mit ziemlicher Sicherheit schlicht illusorisch.

Ein weiterer relevanter Bereich ist die Lehre. Das Problem: Wie will man etwas lehren, wenn man nicht in der Lage ist, das, was man zu lehren beabsichtigt, zu beschreiben und zu erklären? Man könnte fragen: Gibt es nicht doch irgendwelche Möglichkeiten, Planung weitgehend ohne explizite Planungsbegriffe zu lehren? Ein in diesem Zusammenhang mitunter propagierter und praktizierter Weg ist die Lehre nach dem Prinzip *Learning by Doing*. Fest steht, dieses Lehrprinzip hat ohne jeden Zweifel unschlag-

"We've already had that for a long time"

Some react to the idea of needing to work more thoroughly on fundamental planning concepts with: "why? We've already had that for a long time." Their argument is that there are already many explicit and structured planning concepts.

This chapter represents a different argument, namely that not many explicit, structures planning concepts remain after examining the three groups of planning concepts described below in terms of their viability. These are (i) the rational planning concept, (ii) sub-concepts of planning, and (iii) so-called one-word definitions of planning, i. e. planning is *communication* or planning is *strategy*.

The rational planning concept

Although the rational planning concept, which is also referred to as the *rational planning model*, has been the subject of criticism at the latest since the essay by Lindblom in 1959 with the title "The Science of Muddling Through,"[4]— and increasingly since the beginning of the 1970s—, and should therefore have become obsolete, it actually appears to be highly persistent and undefeatable.[5]

Two points to be noted: (a) a short version of the rational planning concept is "speaking truth to power," (b) how does one recognise the rational planning concept? If the relevant description bears no reference to the fact that planning also depends on the planning approach or the professional "glasses" of the planner, it is a clear indication that one is dealing with the rational planning concept.

A study in the USA, for example, showed that more than half of all planning schools continue to teach the rational planning concept.[6] In other words, even though it has been known for a long time that the rational planning concept, as a description of planning, has long been obsolete and can therefore no longer be considered a viable planning concept, it is still used—in many cases unconsciously.

Sub-concepts of planning

A second group only considers so-called sub-concepts of planning, in other words individual partial aspects. What is lacking is a comprehensive conceptual framework into which these partial aspects are integrated. Examples of this are focusing on dealing with prognosis or evaluation processes, with creative methods, with aims (as goals), with participatory processes, with individual conflicts of value, with the topic of power, etc. Of course all these individual topics are significant for planning, but, even taken together, they do not lead to a conclusive planning concept. What conclusions can be drawn from this? These sub-concepts are not viable as planning concepts in the aforementioned sense either.

bare Vorteile und ist aus der Planungslehre nicht wegzudenken, wenn es darum geht, Studierende auf reale Praxisaufgaben vorzubereiten. Schwierig wird die Sache jedoch, wenn bei dieser Lehre versucht wird, im Wesentlichen ohne Erläuterungen des zugrunde liegenden Planungsbegriffs auszukommen. Ein so verstandenes Lehrkonzept überlässt das Entdecken und Herausarbeiten des auf den nächsten Planungsfall Übertragbaren – eben des jeweiligen Planungsbegriffs – den Studierenden und damit den fachlich Schwächsten. Ein solches Lehrkonzept kostet wegen der vielen Irrwege und Fehlversuche der Studierenden viel Zeit und ist folglich weder effizient noch effektiv. Richard Sennett formuliert das sich dadurch auftuende Problem so: Bei diesem Lehrkonzept „[…] fällt die Last dem Lernenden zu".[3] Hinzu kommt, dass der Lehrende überhaupt nicht weiß, was – genau – die Lernenden bei einer Lehre nach dem Prinzip *Learning by Doing* eigentlich gelernt haben.

Die These „Das brauchen wir nicht" ist im hiesigen Zusammenhang also ebenfalls wenig hilfreich.

„Das haben wir schon längst"

Manche reagieren auf den Hinweis, man müsse intensiver an den zugrunde liegenden Planungsbegriffen arbeiten, mit dem Satz: „Wieso? Das haben wir doch schon längst." Ihre These lautet, dass es bereits zahlreiche explizite, strukturierte Planungsbegriffe gibt.

Das Resultat vorweg: In diesem Kapitel wird eine andere These vertreten. Nämlich, dass nicht viele explizite, strukturierte Planungsbegriffe übrig bleiben, nachdem man die drei nachfolgend beschriebenen Gruppen von Planungsbegriffen auf ihre Tauglichkeit hin überprüft hat. Dies sind (i) der rationale Planungsbegriff, (ii) Sub-Begriffe der Planung sowie (iii) sogenannte Ein-Wort-Definitionen von Planung wie: Planung ist *Kommunikation* oder Planung ist *Strategie*.

Der rationale Planungsbegriff

Obwohl der rationale Planungsbegriff, der auch als das *rationale Planungsmodell* bezeichnet wird, spätestens seit dem Aufsatz von Lindblom 1959 mit dem Titel „The Science of ‚Muddling Through'"[4] – sowie deutlich verstärkt ab Anfang der 1970er Jahre – in die Kritik geraten ist und deshalb eigentlich ausgedient haben sollte, scheint er höchst zählebig und kaum totzukriegen zu sein.[5]

Zwei Anmerkungen: (a) Die Kurzversion des rationalen Planungsbegriffs lautet „Speaking truth to power". (b) Woran erkennt man den rationalen Planungsbegriff? Wenn in der entsprechenden Beschreibung kein Hinweis darauf zu finden ist, dass Planungen auch vom jeweiligen Planungsansatz, das heißt der professionellen „Brille" des Planers abhängig sind, so ist dies ein deutliches Indiz dafür, dass man es mit dem rationalen Planungsbegriff zu tun hat.

One-word planning concepts

A third group uses abstract one-word concept definitions to describe the subject area of planning, such as: planning is *communication* or planning is *strategy*, without offering any further adequate structuring of the topic. What differs from the sub-theories (see above) is the scope: it is not about partial planning aspects, but about planning "as a whole."

The content of these one-word definitions mostly only describes a few partial aspects, as is the case with the sub-theories, in a little more detail. If one asks about other partial aspects, one almost always receives the answer: "yes, of course, that topic is *also* part of it." However, this does not constitute a structured planning concept.

Those who are content with such one-word definitions are heading towards a methodological problem that can be summarised by the following maxim: "sense or content is inversely related to extension or truth domain."[7] This means: the more comprehensive the (reality) domain is (or should be) that the definition refers to, the smaller the content and substance of what is said. The relevant tenet is: *dictum de omni, dictum de nullo.* To put it differently: an extremely general (meaning: too general) concept can only cover the characteristics that all the members it refers to have in common, consequently all peculiarities and most effective mechanisms, which are usually system-specific anyway, are overlooked.

What are the consequences of this? Ultimately, such one-word definitions basically do not substantiate or structure anything. Any descriptions of content remain largely nebulous. Sometimes this nebulousness is noticed and is commented on critically. An example of this is the essay by Luigi Mazza: "If Strategic 'Planning Is Everything, Maybe It's Nothing.'"[8]

An example of how concepts that are too generalised fail when it comes to applying them to real (and therefore specific) contexts is provided by a book on the subject of strategy.[9] This book with the title *Strategic Planning. An International Perspective*[10] describes and analyses more than a dozen cases of strategic planning from around the world. However, with regard to specifying the term *strategic planning*, in other words the theoretical umbrella that is supposed to bring the various contributions together, one can only find the following text passage about it (apart from a very brief, highly abstract, and therefore too general definition): "strategic planning [...] has been defined in many different ways and has been called many different things {p 1} [...] the meaning which has been attributed to the term strategic has often been unclear and sometimes even contradictory. As strategic planning will be influenced by the available and effective policy levers and by past patterns of spatial and institutional development it is unlikely that it means the same thing when it has been translated into a different cultural setting, political system, policy context, and planning tradition."[11] With this statement, the authors concede are no overarching definitions of the term *strategy* available that are suitable for describing the various planning cases compiled in the book. This shows the aforementioned

Eine Untersuchung in den USA beispielsweise ergab, dass mehr als die Hälfte aller Planerschulen nach wie vor den rationalen Planungsbegriff lehren.[6] Das heißt, auch wenn man schon lange weiß, dass der rationale Planungsbegriff als Beschreibung von Planungen überholt ist und somit als tauglicher Planungsbegriff ausfällt, wird er trotzdem – oft unbewusst – benutzt.

Sub-Begriffe der Planung

In einer zweiten Gruppe beschäftigt man sich nur mit sogenannten Sub-Begriffen des Planens, also einzelnen Teilaspekten. Was fehlt, ist ein umfassenderer Begriffsrahmen, in den diese Teilaspekte eingeordnet werden. Beispiele hierzu sind die Fokussierung auf die Beschäftigung mit Prognose- oder Bewertungsverfahren, mit Kreativitätstechniken, mit Leitbildern (als Ziele), mit Partizipationsverfahren, mit einzelnen Wertkonflikten, mit dem Thema Macht und so fort. Selbstverständlich sind all diese Einzelthemen für das Planen bedeutsam. Trotzdem ergibt sich daraus auch in der Zusammenschau kein schlüssiger Planungsbegriff. Was folgt daraus? Auch diese Sub-Begriffe taugen nicht als Planungsbegriffe im oben beschriebenen Sinne.

Ein-Wort-Planungsbegriffe

In einer dritten Gruppe werden abstrakte Ein-Wort-Begriffsdefinitionen verwendet, um das Themenfeld der Planung zu fassen, wie zum Beispiel: Planung ist *Kommunikation* oder Planung ist *Strategie*, und zwar ohne eine weitergehende, hinreichende Strukturierung des Themenfeldes anzubieten. Der Unterschied zu den Subtheorien (siehe oben) liegt im Anspruch: Hier geht es nicht um planerische Teilthemen, sondern um Planung „als Ganzes".

Zur inhaltlichen Ausfüllung dieser Ein-Wort-Definitionen werden meist nur einige wenige Teilthemen, wie bei den Subtheorien, etwas ausführlicher beschrieben. Fragt man bezüglich weiterer Teilthemen nach, so erhält man fast immer die Antwort: „Ja, klar, dieses Thema ist *auch* damit eingeschlossen." Ein strukturierter Planungsbegriff wird damit jedoch nicht angeboten.

Wer sich mit solchen Ein-Wort-Definitionen begnügt, steuert nicht zuletzt auf ein methodisches Problem zu, welches sich in folgendem Satz verdichten lässt: „Sense or content is inversely related to extension or truth domain."[7] Das bedeutet: Je umfassender der (Realitäts-)Bereich ist (oder sein soll), auf den sich eine Definition bezieht, desto geringer wird der Inhalt, die Substanz des Gesagten. Der Lehrsatz dazu lautet: *Dictum de omni, dictum de nullo*. Anders ausgedrückt: Ein extrem allgemeiner (das heißt: zu allgemeiner) Begriff kann nur solche Merkmale abdecken, die alle Mitglieder, auf die er sich bezieht, gemeinsam haben, folglich werden alle Besonderheiten und die meisten Wirkungsmechanismen, die ohnehin in der Regel systemspezifisch sind, übersehen. Was folgt daraus? Am Ende

methodological trap: a definition that is overarching and is at the same time applicable to specific contexts is not possible with such one-word definitions.

Conclusion

Thinking about and working on our planning concepts is helpful, especially because it provides the opportunity to analyse and improve our planning. However, those who thus assume that this topic is being worked on fervently will be disappointed. On the contrary, one might even get the impression that this subject is deliberately ignored by some colleagues. It is time to change this. After all, no profession can afford not to make use of opportunities for self-reflection, for self-monitoring, and consequently for improving one's own thoughts and actions—and this also applies to the planning profession.

substanziieren und strukturieren solche Ein-Wort-Definitionen im Grunde nichts. Was inhaltlich beschrieben werden soll, bleibt weitgehend im Nebel. Zuweilen fällt dieses Im-Nebel-Bleiben auf und wird entsprechend kritisch kommentiert. Ein Beispiel hierzu ist der Aufsatz von Luigi Mazza: „If Strategic ‚Planning Is Everything, Maybe It's Nothing‘".[8]

Ein Beispiel dafür, wie zu allgemeine Begriffe scheitern, wenn es darum geht, sie auf reale (und damit spezifische) Kontexte anzuwenden, liefert ein Buch zum Thema Strategie.[9] In diesem Buch mit dem Titel *Strategic Planning. An International Perspective*[10] werden mehr als ein Dutzend Fälle strategischer Planungen aus aller Welt beschrieben und analysiert. Wenn es aber darum geht, den Begriff *Strategic Planning* zu präzisieren, also den gedanklichen Schirm, unter dem all die verschiedenen Beiträge zusammengeführt werden sollen, findet man dazu (abgesehen von einer sehr knappen, hochabstrakten und deshalb zu allgemeinen Definition) die folgende Textpassage: „Strategic planning [...] has been defined in many different ways and has been called many different things {p 1} [...] the meaning which has been attributed to the term strategic has often been unclear and sometimes even contradictory. As strategic planning will be influenced by the available and effective policy levers and by past patterns of spatial and institutional development it is unlikely that it means the same thing when it has been translated into a different culture setting, political system, policy context and planning tradition."[11]

Mit diesen Sätzen konzedieren die Autoren, dass keine übergreifenden Definitionen des Begriffs *Strategie* zur Verfügung stehen, die sich für die Beschreibung der verschiedenen, in dem Buch zusammengetragenen Planungsfälle eignen. Hier zeigt sich die oben beschriebene methodische Falle: Eine Definition, die übergreifend ist und zugleich den spezifischen Kontexten gerecht wird, bekommt man mit solchen Ein-Wort-Definitionen nicht zustande.

Fazit

Das Nachdenken über und das Arbeiten an unseren Planungsbegriffen ist hilfreich, vor allem, weil sich dadurch die Möglichkeit bietet, unsere Planungen zu analysieren und zu verbessern. Wer – vor diesem Hintergrund – jedoch annimmt, an diesem Thema würde eifrig gearbeitet, wird enttäuscht sein. Man hat sogar den Eindruck, dass dieses Themenfeld von manchen Kolleginnen und Kollegen bewusst ignoriert wird. Es wird Zeit, dies zu ändern. Schließlich kann es sich keine Profession leisten, Möglichkeiten der Selbstreflexion, der Selbstüberprüfung und in der Folge der Verbesserung des eigenen Denkens und Handelns bewusst ungenutzt zu lassen – und dies gilt auch für die Planungsprofession.

Wien *Vienna*, 05.05.2016

Wien *Vienna*, 05.05.2016

Hamburg, 21.11.2013

Hamburg, 20.11.2013

THE ROLE OF THE PLANNER IN THE PLANNING PROCESS

for a preventive adaptation of housing in the context of disaster risk reduction—based on examples from the Asia-Pacific region (Indonesia, India, Sri Lanka, Philippines)

SABRINA BRENNER

Natural hazards can have a devastating impact on human life and the built environment. Some of these hazards are amplified by climate change, which presents a significant problem. It is therefore necessary to develop adaptation strategies for housing, which include the immediate physical environment, both inside and outside, of buildings where people live and which serve as a shelter from external influences.

The vulnerability of a region, dependent on the socio-economic conditions and on the coping and adaptation capacity of the affected community, determines to a large extent whether loss or damage occur and whether a natural hazard, including climatological, meteorological, hydrological, and geophysical hazards, becomes a natural disaster. A lack of money and resources, inadequate planning laws and regulations, and a lack of monitoring are reasons why people in developing countries are particularly vulnerable to the impact of natural hazards. Furthermore, during the design and planning process, the natural influences, some of which are affected by climate change, are often not taken sufficiently into account.

In many cases, there is a lack of information and knowledge about what can be done to adapt housing appropriately.

Ninety per cent of international aid funds is not handed out until *after* a natural disaster, namely for emergency aid and reconstruction. After a disaster there is usually no time for careful planning, which leads to grave problems: the replacement buildings are often even more poorly adapted to local conditions than the houses which were destroyed by the event. A shift in focus from emergency aid to preventive adaptation to local conditions can save lives as well as time, money, and other resources.

A further central aspect of this field of research is the exchange and sharing of knowledge. Every planning context and every project is different, and yet there are still parallels, which is why certain measures and procedural steps can be applied to different areas, presenting a true opportunity to share and exchange knowledge and experience, especially with regard to reconstruction projects.

This thesis involves developing a planning process for the preventive adaptation of housing to natural hazards in the research area. The focus of the research is on the role of the planner within such a process. This role is studied on the basis of reconstruction and housing projects in an Asia-Pacific context.

DIE ROLLE DES PLANERS IM PLANUNGSPROZESS
für eine vorsorgliche Anpassung von Wohnbau im Kontext von Katastrophenrisikominimierung – basierend auf Beispielen aus dem asiatisch-pazifischen Raum (Indonesien, Indien, Sri Lanka, Philippinen)

SABRINA BRENNER

Naturgefahren können einen schwerwiegenden Einfluss auf das menschliche Leben und die gebaute Umwelt haben. Einige dieser Gefahren werden durch den Klimawandel verstärkt, was ein erhebliches Problem darstellt. Daher ist es nötig, Anpassungsstrategien für den Wohnbau (*housing*) zu entwickeln. Wohnbau umfasst das unmittelbare physische Umfeld sowohl innerhalb als auch außerhalb von Gebäuden, in denen Menschen leben und die als Schutz vor äußeren Einflüssen dienen.

Die Anfälligkeit einer Region, abhängig von den sozio-ökonomischen Rahmenbedingungen als auch den Bewältigungs- und Anpassungskapazitäten einer betroffenen Gesellschaft, bestimmt wesentlich, ob Verlust oder Schaden entsteht und eine Naturgefahr, darunter klimatologische, meteorologische, hydrologische und geophysikalische Gefahren, zu einer Naturkatastrophe wird. Geld- und Ressourcenknappheit, unzureichende Planungsregeln und -vorschriften sowie eine fehlende Überwachung sind Ursachen dafür, dass Menschen in Entwicklungsländern besonders anfällig für Naturgefahren sind. Zudem wird im Zuge des Entwurfs- und Planungsprozesses häufig nicht ausreichend Rücksicht auf die natürlichen und durch den Klimawandel bedingten Einflüsse genommen.

Häufig fehlen auch die Information und das Wissen darüber, was getan werden kann, um den Wohnbau entsprechend anzupassen. 90 Prozent der internationalen Hilfsgelder werden erst nach einer Naturkatastrophe ausgegeben, vor allem für Soforthilfe und den Wiederaufbau. Dabei bleibt nach einer Katastrophe meist keine Zeit für eine präzise Planung, was zu schwerwiegenden Problemen führt: Die Ersatzbauten sind oft schlechter an die lokalen Bedingungen angepasst, als die ursprünglichen Häuser, die durch das Ereignis zerstört wurden. Eine Schwerpunktverschiebung von der Soforthilfe hin zur präventiven Anpassung an die lokalen Bedingungen kann Leben retten sowie Geld, Zeit und andere Ressourcen einsparen.

Ein weiterer zentraler Punkt dieses Forschungsfelds ist der Wissensaustausch: Jeder Planungskontext und jedes Projekt ist unterschiedlich und trotzdem gibt es Parallelen, weshalb bestimmte Maßnahmen und Prozessschritte in unterschiedlichen Gebieten eingesetzt werden können – eine wichtige Chance, Wissen und Erfahrungen insbesondere aus Wiederaufbauprojekten auszutauschen.

In der Arbeit wird der Planungsprozess für eine vorsorgliche Anpassung von Wohnbau an Naturgefahren im Untersuchungsgebiet entwickelt. Der Forschungsschwerpunkt liegt dabei auf der Rolle des Planers innerhalb eines solchen Prozesses. Diese Rolle wird auf Basis von Wiederaufbau- und Wohnbauprojekten im asiatisch-pazifischen Kontext untersucht.

PROVISIONAL POLICIES AS A FOUNDATION FOR PLURALITY PARTICIPATION IN URBAN DEVELOPMENT

HANNES ROCKENBAUCH

The controversy surrounding the infrastructure project Stuttgart 21 has shown that the existing formal and informal processes for implementing complex projects in Germany are no longer adequate. The present-day civic protest goes beyond criticism of individual inadequate processes, with increasing criticism of the established policy and planning procedures. This discontent leads to two different reactions among the civic population. Firstly, some of them withdraw into privacy and political apathy, with voting and parties increasingly losing significance. In many areas, voter participation and party membership numbers are decreasing. Alternatively, citizens rebel when they are affected and intervene in infrastructure projects, airport noise, or global issues such as the occupy or anti-nuclear movements.

In planning discourse, "cooperation and participation" have for a long time been a matter of common sense. Even back in the 1970s there was a call to "risk greater democracy." It is acknowledged almost without exception that the results of processes that take the ideas and demands of citizens into account are richer, more suitable, and more widely accepted. However, the dispute about the large-scale project in Stuttgart shows that the so-called *communicative turn* in planning theory has evidently not been able to fulfil its promise of planning on an equal footing with citizens.

An approach according to the motto "bringing everyone together around one table," in order to consider policies, planning, and participation together from the outset, is lacking. In practice, politics administration, and citizens often exist as parallel worlds, each with their own principles and little mutual understanding. This leads to a paradoxical situation: although the number of informal procedures is steadily increasing, the involvement and participation of citizens is often non-binding and a dead end. Based on the notion of "provisional policy," this thesis is designed to provide impulses for a change of culture in the world of communal policy and planning. It turns away from the illusion that everything can be planned rationally, in favour of a shared process of knowledge generation among all those involved. "Collective wisdom" can serve as a pool of experience and feedback for policies and planning in the solving of complex problems. However, as knowledge and the world are constantly changing, it is necessary to view policy and planning decisions as being subject to human error. For each decision, in order to really learn from cooperation, the "provisional policy" takes into account the aim of ensuring the ability and opportunity to act in future. In this sense, "provisional" means proactive, protective, and reversible. Provisional policies and planning should deliver decisions that are not only democratically legitimate, but also tolerant and therefore robust.

PROVISORISCHE POLITIK ALS GRUNDLAGE FÜR DIE MITWIRKUNG DER VIELEN AN DER STADTENTWICKLUNG

HANNES ROCKENBAUCH

Die Auseinandersetzungen um das Infrastrukturprojekt Stuttgart 21 haben gezeigt, dass die existierenden formellen und informellen Verfahren zur Umsetzung komplexer Vorhaben in Deutschland nicht mehr ausreichen. Dabei geht das heutige Aufbegehren der Bürger über die Kritik einzelner unzureichender Verfahren hinaus. Verstärkt wird der etablierte Politik- und Planungsbetrieb kritisiert.

Dieser Unmut führt zu zwei unterschiedlichen Reaktionen bei den Bürgern. Zum einen zieht sich ein Teil von ihnen ins Private und in die politische Gleichgültigkeit zurück: Wahlen und Parteien verlieren für viele immer mehr an Bedeutung. Vielerorts sinken die Wahlbeteiligung und die Mitgliederzahlen der Parteien. Zum anderen begehren die Bürger bei Betroffenheit auf und mischen sich bei Infrastrukturprojekten, Flughafenlärm oder globalen Themen wie der Occupy- oder Anti-AKW-Bewegung ein.

Im Planungsdiskurs gehören „Kooperation und Partizipation" längst zum common sense. Bereits in den 1970er Jahren hieß es „mehr Demokratie wagen". Fast ausnahmslos wird anerkannt, dass die Ergebnisse von Prozessen, die Ideen und Belange der Bürger berücksichtigen, reicher, passgenauer und akzeptierter sind. Doch die Auseinandersetzungen um das Stuttgarter Großprojekt zeigen, dass der sogenannte Communicative Turn in der Planungstheorie offensichtlich seine Versprechungen auf eine Planung auf Augenhöhe mit dem Bürger bis heute nicht einlösen konnte.

Ein Ansatz nach der Devise „alle an einen Tisch" fehlt, um Politik, Planung und Partizipation von Anfang an zusammenzudenken. In der Praxis existieren Politik, Verwaltung und Bürger oft als Parallelwelten mit eigenen Gesetzmäßigkeiten und wenig gegenseitigem Verständnis. Das führt zu einer paradoxen Situation: Obwohl die Zahl informeller Verfahren stetig wächst, bleiben Engagement und Beteiligung der Bürger oft unverbindlich und laufen ins Leere. Unter dem Begriff einer „provisorischen Politik" soll diese Arbeit Impulse für einen Kulturwandel der kommunalen Politik- und Planungswelt liefern. Weg von der Illusion, alles sei rational planbar, hin zu einem gemeinsamen Wissensgenerierungsprozess aller Beteiligten. Die „Weisheit der Vielen" kann bei der Lösung komplexer Probleme als Erfahrungsschatz und Rückkopplungsebene von Politik und Planung dienen. Weil sich aber Wissen und Welt ständig verändern, ist es nötig, politische und planerische Entscheidungen unter Vorbehalt menschlicher Fehlbarkeit zu stellen. Um aus Zusammenarbeit tatsächlich lernen zu können, berücksichtigt die „provisorische Politik" bei jeder Entscheidung das Ziel Handlungsfähigkeit und -möglichkeit für zukünftiges Handeln zu erhalten. Mit „provisorisch" ist in diesem Sinne vorausschauend, schützend und reversibel gemeint. Provisorische Politik und Planung sollen nicht nur demokratisch legitime, sondern auch fehlerfreundliche und damit robuste Entscheidungen liefern.

BOTTOM-UP ENERGY TRANSITION

Energy transition as a social learning process

MARIO SCHNEIDER

The energy transition is one of the most complex transformation processes of the current century. In view of the threat of climate change, the energy supply system developed over a period of over 100 years, with its energy supply chains and energy consumption patterns, is set to be replaced by 2050 to a large extent by a new system that protects the climate and environment. An optimisation of the existing system would not be enough to achieve the necessary climate protection goals.

Owing to the increased opting out of nuclear power due to the reactor accident in Fukushima in 2011, the pressure to act and time pressure are especially great in Germany. This is because switching off nuclear power plants leads to an increased burning of coal for energy production, which has a negative impact on climate change. The major energy suppliers have so far invested very little in developing renewable energy sources and are economically dependent on their fossil fuel plants. The corporations are still refraining from major investment, unsure of which new technologies will establish themselves on the market.

In light of the narrow timeframe, which involved parties can drive energy transition forwards? How can and must these groups be supported to make success more likely? Up until now, citizens and private investors in particular have invested in renewable energy sources. This thesis is designed to show both that a bottom-up approach with many involved parties can accelerate the energy transition and how this process can be made operational. Small social niches, for example, can serve as laboratory spaces for the transformation process of energy transition.

Contrary to major projects with high investment costs and lengthy planning schedules, the cooperation of niche parties and established partners can realise smaller and more cost effective projects more quickly. As it cannot yet be foreseen which technologies and forms of cooperation are the most promising for implementing the energy transition, various alternatives have to be tried out. For planners and policy-makers, this approach to energy transition leads to a bottom-up opportunity to try out various solutions in a process of trial and error, thereby driving the energy transition forwards. This method can be quicker and promise greater success than pushing for the development of large-scale infrastructures. This also spreads the risk of bad investments. Potential setbacks and failures can be compensated for more easily by society as a whole. The energy transition is a learning process and must be understood as such in planning. The sharing of knowledge between project initiators, administrations, politics, companies, and planners must be strengthened in order to accelerate the energy transition.

BOTTOM-UP-ENERGIEWENDE
Energiewende als gesellschaftlicher Lernprozess

MARIO SCHNEIDER

Die Energiewende ist einer der komplexesten Transformationsprozesse dieses Jahrhunderts. Das über die Dauer von über 100 Jahren geschaffene Energieversorgungssystem mit seinen Energiebereitstellungsketten und Energieverbrauchsmustern soll angesichts der Bedrohung durch den Klimawandel bis zum Jahr 2050 größtenteils durch ein neues, klima- und umweltschonendes System ersetzt werden. Eine Optimierung des bestehenden Systems allein wird nicht ausreichen, um die notwendigen Klimaschutzziele zu erreichen. Aufgrund des durch den Reaktorunfall 2011 in Fukushima beschleunigten Atomausstiegs ist der Zeit- und Handlungsdruck in Deutschland besonders groß. Denn das Abschalten der Atomkraftwerke führt zu einer zunehmenden Verbrennung von Kohle zur Energiegewinnung, was negative Auswirkungen auf die Klimaentwicklung nach sich zieht. Die großen Energieversorgungsunternehmen haben bisher sehr wenig in den Ausbau der erneuerbaren Energiegewinnung investiert und sind wirtschaftlich auf ihren fossilen Kraftwerkspark angewiesen. Unsicher, welche neuen Technologien sich an den Märkten durchsetzen werden, halten sich die Unternehmen vorerst mit großen Investitionen zurück.

Doch mit welchen Akteuren und Akteursgruppen kann angesichts des engen Zeitrahmens eine Energiewende vorangetrieben werden? Und wie können und müssen diese Gruppen unterstützt werden, um einen Erfolg wahrscheinlicher zu machen? Bisher haben vor allem Bürger und private Investoren in die erneuerbare Energiegewinnung investiert. Diese Arbeit soll zeigen, dass der Bottom-up-Ansatz mit vielen Akteuren eine Energiewende beschleunigen kann und wie sich dieser Prozess operationalisieren lässt. Denn so können beispielsweise kleine gesellschaftliche Nischen als Laborräume für den Transformationsprozess Energiewende dienen.

Im Gegensatz zu Großprojekten mit hohen Investitionskosten und langen Planungszeiträumen lassen sich durch die Zusammenarbeit von Nischenakteuren und Regimeakteuren Projekte kleiner, günstiger und schneller realisieren. Da noch nicht absehbar ist, welche Technologien und Kooperationsformen die vielversprechendsten sind, um die Energiewende zu realisieren, müssen verschiedene Alternativen erprobt werden. Für Planer und Politiker ergibt sich durch den Ansatz einer Energiewende von unten die Möglichkeit, im Trial-and-Error-Verfahren unterschiedliche Lösungsansätze gleichzeitig zu erproben und so die Energiewende voranzutreiben. Dieser Weg kann schneller und erfolgsversprechender sein, als auf den Ausbau von Großinfrastrukturen zu drängen. Des Weiteren wird so das Risiko von Fehlinvestitionen gestreut und eventuelle Rück-/Fehlschläge können gesamtgesellschaftlich leichter kompensiert werden. Die Energiewende ist ein Lernprozess und muss in der Planung als ein solcher verstanden werden. Der Wissensaustausch zwischen Projektinitiatoren, Verwaltungen, Politik, Unternehmen und Planern muss gestärkt werden, um eine Energiewende zu beschleunigen.

URBAN HEAT:
targeting planning tools towards an ideal urban climate

FLORIAN STADTSCHREIBER

The heat wave in summer 2003, with around 70,000 casualties, was one of the most devastating natural disasters in the last 100 years in Europe. It showed what an impact such extreme weather conditions can have. It also showed, however, that the most severely affected areas are European cities. On the one hand, heat leads to significantly higher mortality rates, on the other hand it also compromises the quality of life, including in public spaces. In view of urbanisation, this means significant problems for European cities. Owing to their dense development, cities' urban heat islands will be intensified considerably in forthcoming decades due to climate change. Apart from increasing average temperatures every year, cities can expect prolonged periods of heat in terms of intensity and frequency, characterised by high maximum daytime temperatures and, at the same time, reduced nocturnal cooling. The city of Vienna, for example, the focus of this work, will have to be prepared for an annual average temperature increase of two to four degrees over the course of this century. This is caused not only by the city's geographical location, but also by its physical characteristics.

The spatial distribution of hot and cool areas is the result of spatially-related planning processes. What options does spatial planning have in terms of formal tools (development plan, land allocation plan, development concept), in order to minimise the consequences of increased thermal stress? Are these tools sufficient, in terms of the required adaptation measures, or is it necessary to complement them with informal tools? What contribution can be made by associations, authorities, or organisations, as well as by changes in attitude? This thesis seeks to examine these questions critically and to take the spatial planning requirements from the point of view of climate research into account.

The need to adapt to changing climatic conditions is not questioned in scientific discourse, but it is still a novel topic in planning practice.

It is certain that adaptation will be an impulse for a gradually unfolding transformation process in forthcoming years, which will change the face of our cities. If one takes into account the durability of around 100 years of urban structures and the foreseeable intensification of the aforementioned effects until the middle of this century, it is high time to integrate adaptation to these thermal changes into planning tools as an integral aspect as quickly as possible.

HITZE IN DER STADT:
Ausrichtung der Planungsinstrumente auf den Umgang mit der thermischen Belastung in Städten

FLORIAN STADTSCHREIBER

Die Hitzewelle im Sommer 2003 zählt mit rund 70.000 Todesopfern zu den schwersten Naturkatastrophen der letzten 100 Jahre in Europa. Sie hat vor Augen geführt, mit welchen Auswirkungen bei derart extremen Wetterereignissen zu rechnen ist. Sie zeigte aber auch, dass die Brennpunkte in den europäischen Städten liegen. Hitze führt einerseits zu signifikant steigenden Morbiditäts- und Mortalitätsraten, beeinträchtigt aber auch die Aufenthaltsqualität öffentlicher Räume und schränkt schließlich die Lebensqualität erheblich ein. Unter Berücksichtigung der Urbanisierung ergeben sich erhebliche Probleme für europäische Städte.

Städte weisen aufgrund ihrer dichten Bebauung ausgeprägte urbane Wärmeinseln auf, die durch den Klimawandel in den kommenden Jahrzehnten zusätzlich verstärkt werden. Sie erwarten neben jährlich steigenden Durchschnittstemperaturen vor allem hinsichtlich Intensität und Häufigkeit zunehmende Hitzeperioden, die sich durch hohe Tagestemperaturmaxima und gleichzeitig reduzierte nächtliche Abkühlung auszeichnen. Im Durchschnitt wird sich beispielsweise die Stadt Wien, auf welche der Fokus der Arbeit gelegt wurde, in diesem Jahrhundert auf eine Zunahme der jährlichen Durchschnittstemperatur von zwei bis vier Grad Celsius einstellen müssen. Die Ursachen finden sich nicht nur in der geografischen Lage, sondern vor allem im physischen Erscheinungsbild der Stadt.

Die räumliche Verteilung von thermischen Be- und Entlastungsgebieten ist das Ergebnis von raumbezogenen Planungsprozessen. Über welche Möglichkeiten verfügt die Raumplanung in ihren formellen Instrumenten (Bebauungsplan, Flächenwidmungsplan, Entwicklungskonzept), um die Folgen der zunehmenden Erwärmung zu minimieren? Sind diese Instrumente in Anbetracht der erforderlichen Anpassungsmaßnahmen ausreichend oder ist eine Ergänzung durch informelle Instrumente notwendig? Welcher Beitrag kann durch die Ausrichtung von Vereinigungen, Behörden oder Betrieben und durch Verhaltensänderungen geleistet werden? Diesen Fragen versucht die Arbeit kritisch auf den Grund zu gehen und dabei vor allem die Anforderungen an die Raumplanung aus Sicht der Klimaforschung im Auge zu behalten.

Die Notwendigkeit der Anpassung an die wandelnden klimatischen Gegebenheiten steht im wissenschaftlichen Diskurs außer Frage, stellt jedoch in der Planungspraxis noch ein junges Thema dar. Sicher ist, dass die Anpassung in den nächsten Jahren ein Anstoß für einen graduell verlaufenden Transformationsprozess sein wird, welcher das Gesicht unserer Städte verändern wird. Berücksichtigt man die Bestandskraft städtebaulicher Strukturen von rund 100 Jahren und die abzusehende Intensivierung der genannten Auswirkungen bis Mitte dieses Jahrhunderts, so wäre es jetzt an der Zeit, die Anpassung an diese thermischen Veränderungen möglichst rasch als festen Bestandteil in den Planungsinstrumenten zu integrieren.

NEW USAGE AND BUILDING TYPOLOGIES
NEUE NUTZUNGS- UND BEBAUUNGSTYPOLOGIEN

THE ROLE OF USAGE AND BUILDING TYPOLOGIES IN URBAN LANDSCAPE TRANSFORMATION

MARKUS NEPPL

Transformation processes unfold on different scales in urban and rural areas. While large-scale changes are only noticeable over a longer period of time, small-scale "restructuring" is immediately visible. The face of the city is changing rapidly and radically. These spatial changes are becoming more extreme and the usage mix is becoming ever more complex. The yearning for a smaller-scale usage mix and for green spaces in the landscape is countered in reality by uniform, large-scale structures and public spaces that are difficult to use. There is growing scepticism among the population towards these far-reaching changes, which can lead to an openly-expressed rejectionist attitude.

This state of mind was expressed cautiously, but unequivocally in the introductory text of the documentation *Auf dem Weg zum Räumlichen Leitbild Karlsruhe*[1] *(The Path to the Spatial Model of Karlsruhe)*: "The city of Karlsruhe is changing. Many Karlsruhe citizens still speak fondly of their 'village of Karlsruhe.' However, those who look around the city today witness extensive construction work that will change the cityscape in the centre and in the districts significantly. Is this 'new Karlsruhe' still just as liveable and endearing as the one the locals have hitherto appreciated, or are the changes too radical and hasty?"

Is transformation necessary?

Politics, administration, and the urban planning discipline should try to prevent these processes and to limit changes to the strictly necessary, in order to provide an adequate response to this general mood. However, it is clear that this suggestion does not correspond to the interests of the urban parties involved and has little to do with reality. In this respect, is transformation more of an artificial process, which is used in a targeted manner by some involved parties in order to enforce singular interests, or does the change occur automatically through a kind of "law of nature," which can only be halted by means of far-reaching interventions?

On the one hand, there are of course some understandable reasons for change. The on-going population growth in metropolitan regions is leading to a shortage of surface space and to competition between residential and commercial uses. The maintenance and development of urban infrastruc-

DIE ROLLE VON NUTZUNGS- UND GEBÄUDETYPOLOGIEN IN URBANEN TRANSFORMATIONEN

MARKUS NEPPL

Transformationsprozesse spielen sich in Stadt- und Landschaftsräumen auf unterschiedlichen Maßstabsebenen ab. Während großräumige Veränderungen nur über einen längeren Zeitraum wahrnehmbar sind, ist das kleinräumige „Umbauen" unmittelbar sichtbar. Das Gesicht der Stadt verändert sich schnell und radikal. Die räumlichen Maßstabssprünge werden extremer und die Mischung der Nutzungen wird komplizierter. Der Sehnsucht nach kleinräumiger Nutzungsmischung und grünen Landschaftsräumen stehen in der Realität uniforme Großstrukturen und schlecht nutzbare öffentliche Räume gegenüber. In der Bevölkerung wächst die Skepsis gegenüber diesen tiefgreifenden Veränderungen, was zu einer offen artikulierten Verweigerungshaltung führen kann.

Im Einleitungstext der Dokumentation *Auf dem Weg zum Räumlichen Leitbild Karlsruhe*[1] wurde diese Stimmung noch vorsichtig, aber unmissverständlich formuliert: „Die Stadt Karlsruhe verändert sich. Viele Karlsruher Bürger sprechen immer noch liebevoll von ihrem ‚Dorf Karlsruhe'. Wer sich heute aber in der Stadt umschaut, erlebt eine enorme Bautätigkeit, die das Stadtbild in der Stadtmitte und in den Stadtteilen deutlich verändern wird. Ist dieses ‚neue Karlsruhe' noch genauso lebens- und liebenswert wie das, was seine Bewohner bislang so schätzen oder sind die Veränderungen zu radikal und überhastet?"

Ist Transformation notwendig?

Um dieser allgemeinen Stimmungslage gerecht zu werden, müsste die Politik, die Verwaltung und die Disziplin Stadtplanung versuchen, diese Prozesse zu verhindern und die Veränderung auf ein absolut notwendiges Maß zu beschränken. Dieser Vorschlag entspricht aber offensichtlich nicht den Interessen der städtischen Akteure und hat mit der Realität wenig zu tun. Ist Transformation in diesem Zusammenhang ein eher künstlicher Prozess, wird er also von einigen Akteuren gezielt eingesetzt, um singuläre Interessen durchzusetzen oder entsteht die Veränderung automatisch durch eine Art „Naturgesetz", das nur durch sehr grundsätzliche Eingriffe aufgehalten werden kann?

Auf der einen Seite stehen sicherlich gut nachvollziehbare Gründe für den Wandel. Das anhaltende Bevölkerungswachstum in den Großstadt-

ture has to be adapted to requirements. The competition between urban regions demands prestige projects in order to be perceived as an attractive location. The ecological urban redevelopment and the energy transition are leaving clear traces on the cityscape and the appearance of the landscape. On the other hand, a healthy scepticism is by all means justified and it should be permissible to ask who is benefitting from these processes and who has to fear disadvantages.

An example of this, which had an impact on me personally, was the "total restructuring" of the Netherlands in the 1990s. Driven by extreme growth scenarios and very optimistic economic prognoses, an unprecedented

1 *Skyline of Rotterdam, 1997*
1 *Skyline von Rotterdam, 1997*

building boom was unleashed. The rather modest peripheral area between Rotterdam and Amsterdam became a very dense metropolitan region and various Vinex programmes[2] promoted suburban growth. The Netherlands were celebrated as an architectural wonderland and the architects propagated their "Superdutch."[3] However, this process had no defined end. The transformation developed its own momentum and could not be halted. The global bank crises in 2007 and 2008 and the collapse of the major property investment banks in 2011 inevitably led to a crash.

It emerged retrospectively that the prognoses had been too optimistic and the cheap credit terms had artificially fuelled the demand for housing. It can therefore definitely be said that this radical form of restructuring encouraged many experiments and also enabled remarkable buildings, but overall this "intoxicating feast" resulted in a respective "hangover." ▶1

How does a successful transformation work?

If the transformation of the urban fabric is indeed inevitable, it raises the question as to which laws it obeys and how it can be influenced. The notion of "urbanity" plays an important role in this context. It serves as a form of objective, but, in reality, it is difficult to define. Many attempts to make urbanity plannable have failed in recent urban planning history. Unplanned urbanity, on the other hand, appears to be rather fleeting if one is trying to exploit it. Instead of seeking new formulas, one should concentrate on how to achieve a wider range of usages and a more individual and intelligent implementation. Many buildings are created very schematically today and make no contribution to their surroundings. "Urban buildings" should follow a simple logic. Due to a horizontal organisation of functions, public

regionen führt zu einer Verknappung der Flächenressourcen und zu einer Konkurrenz zwischen Wohn- und Gewerbenutzungen. Der Erhalt und der Ausbau der städtischen Infrastruktur muss den Bedürfnissen angepasst werden. Die Konkurrenz unter den Stadtregionen verlangt nach Prestige-projekten, um als attraktiver Standort wahrgenommen zu werden. Der ökologische Stadtumbau und die Energiewende hinterlassen deutliche Spuren im Stadt- und Landschaftsbild. Auf der anderen Seite ist aber auch eine gesunde Skepsis angebracht und es sollte erlaubt sein zu fragen, wer von diesen Prozessen profitiert und wer eher Nachteile befürchten muss.

Ein Beispiel in diesem Zusammenhang, das mich persönlich sehr geprägt hat, ist der „Totalumbau" der Niederlande in den 1990er Jahren. Angeheizt durch extreme Wachstumsszenarien und sehr optimistische ökonomische Prognosen, wurde ein beispielloser Bauboom entfacht. Die eher beschau-liche Randstaad zwischen Rotterdam und Amsterdam wurde zu einer hochverdichteten Metropolregion und die unterschiedlichen Vinex-Pro-gramme[2] sorgten für ein suburbanes Wachstum. Die Niederlande wurden als architektonisches Wunderland gefeiert und die Architekten propagier-ten ihr „superdutch"[3]. Es gab aber kein definiertes Ende in diesem Prozess. Die Transformation hatte eine Eigendynamik entfacht und war nicht mehr aufzuhalten. Die globalen Bankenkrisen 2007 und 2008 sowie der Zusam-menbruch der großen Immobilienbanken 2011 führten dann unweigerlich zum Crash.

Im Nachhinein stellte sich heraus, dass die Prognosen viel zu optimistisch waren und die günstigen Kreditbedingungen die Wohnungsnachfrage künstlich angefacht hatten. Man kann sicher behaupten, dass diese radi-kale Form des Umbaus viele Experimente gefördert und auch bemerkens-werte Gebäude ermöglicht hat. Insgesamt aber bleibt ein gehöriger Kater nach diesem „rauschenden Fest". ▶1

Wie funktioniert eine erfolgreiche Transformation?

Wenn also die Transformation der urbanen Gefüge unausweichlich ist, stellt sich die Frage, nach welchen Gesetzmäßigkeiten sie abläuft und wie sie beeinflusst werden kann. In diesem Zusammenhang spielt der Begriff der „Urbanität" eine wichtige Rolle. Er dient als eine Art Zielvorstellung, ist aber in der Realität schwer zu fassen. In der jüngeren Stadtbaugeschichte sind viele Versuche gescheitert, Urbanität planbar zu machen. Ungeplante Urbanität scheint dagegen eher flüchtig zu sein, wenn man sie instrumen-talisieren will.

Anstatt nach neuen Formeln zu suchen, sollte man sich darauf konzen-trieren, wie man eine größere Vielfalt der Nutzungen und eine individu-ellere und intelligentere Ausprägung erreichen kann. Viele Gebäude ent-stehen heute sehr schematisch und leisten keinen Beitrag für das Umfeld. „Urbane Gebäude" sollten einer einfachen Logik folgen. Durch eine hori-zontale Anordnung der Funktionen sortieren sich die öffentlichen Angebo-te eher in die Sockelzonen, während in den oberen Geschossen privatere

amenities tend to be concentrated at ground level, with the upper floors dedicated to more private uses. These houses could also be referred to as "urban packhorses." It does not really matter what they transport, as long as they contribute to the collective idea of what is urban.

How important is the versatility of buildings with regard to their use?

All clients plan their buildings according to their requirements and budgets and make maximum use of the leeway allowed by building regulations. The increasing constructional and energetic requirements are detrimental to versatility. Current trends such as co-working and co-living are approaches that are conceived on a small scale and are therefore easy to integrate. Even if these fail, they do not cause a structural problem. However, they are not formulaic, but serve as an interpretation and enrichment of the respective local conditions. Each district ultimately has its own mentality, history, and potential. In this respect, small-scale transformation always signifies a balancing act with an uncertain outcome.

The aforementioned issues show the scope of factors that play a role on the different scales. The following examples serve as illustrations of these issues and provide an insight into how they can be handled in concrete project work.

Stealthy transformation

The observation that cities change is very generalised and not very precise. The public only notices the change if something specific happens. A building is demolished and rebuilt, or a road is pulled up and reconfigured. This small-scale restructuring is part of everyday life in urban areas. If it does not involve prominent buildings or important public spaces, then the result may be noticed and commented on, but after a while one gets used to it and it is no longer worth mentioning.

Viewed over a longer period of time, the sum of these small changes is by all means visible and meets with a very varied response. This restructuring is driven forwards by energetic renovation, more complex usage requirements, and a maximum economic exploitation of building regulations. Planning does not come into these processes. Design matters play a subordinate role in permission processes and must often be accompanied laboriously by advisory boards or expert committees. The results of these stealthy transformations are, in my experience, very varied. If a city has a clear urban structure and a highly developed planning culture, these changes can by all means bring synergetic effects that generate an overall positive mood in the city. On the other hand, if municipal authorities and local policy have no concept for further development, it is very likely that the cityscape will be damaged and that public spaces will not have a coherent atmosphere.

The two examples in Karlsruhe show the contemporary further development of a stable urban situation. Existing buildings are replaced on the

Nutzungen entstehen können. Man könnte diese Häuser auch als „urbane Packesel" bezeichnen. Dabei ist relativ egal, was sie transportieren, Hauptsache es entsteht ein Beitrag zur kollektiven Idee der Stadt.

Wie wichtig ist dabei eine Wandlungsfähigkeit von Gebäuden hinsichtlich ihrer Nutzung?

Jeder Bauherr plant sein Gebäude nach seinen Bedürfnissen, seinem Budget und nutzt den Spielraum der Bauvorschriften möglichst aus. Durch die größeren bautechnischen und energetischen Anforderungen funktioniert die Wandlungsfähigkeit immer schlechter. Aktuelle Trends wie Co-working und Co-living sind Ansätze, die kleinräumig konzipiert und damit gut integrierbar sind. Dadurch entsteht auch bei einem Misserfolg kein strukturelles Problem. Sie funktionieren aber nicht als Rezept, sondern nur als Interpretation und Anreicherung der jeweiligen lokalen Bedingungen. Jedes Quartier hat letztendlich seine Mentalität, seine Historie und seine Potenziale. In diesem Zusammenhang bedeutet die kleinräumige Transformation immer einen Balanceakt mit unsicherem Ausgang.

Die vorangestellten Fragen zeigen die Bandbreite der Faktoren, die in den unterschiedlichen Maßstabsebenen eine Rolle spielen. Die folgenden Beispiele dienen der Illustration dieser Fragestellungen und geben einen Einblick, wie damit in der konkreten Projektarbeit umgegangen werden kann.

Schleichende Transformation

Die Beobachtung, dass sich Städte verändern, ist sehr allgemein und wenig präzise. In der Öffentlichkeit wird die Veränderung erst wahrgenommen, wenn etwas Konkretes passiert. Ein Gebäude wird abgerissen und neu gebaut oder eine Straße wird aufgerissen und umgestaltet. Dieses kleinräumige Umbauen gehört zum Alltag in der Stadt. Wenn es nicht um prominente Gebäude oder wichtige öffentliche Räume geht, wird das Ergebnis zwar wahrgenommen und auch kommentiert, aber nach einer gewissen Zeit der Gewöhnung ist es nicht mehr der Rede wert.

Über einen längeren Zeitraum betrachtet ist die Summe dieser kleinen Veränderungen aber durchaus wahrnehmbar und wird sehr unterschiedlich empfunden. Dieser Umbau wird durch die energetische Sanierung, durch kompliziertere Nutzungsanforderungen und durch eine maximale ökonomische Ausnutzung der Bauvorschriften vorangetrieben. Von Planung kann man bei diesen Prozessen nicht sprechen. Die Gestaltungsfragen spielen in den Genehmigungsprozeduren eine untergeordnete Rolle und müssen oft durch Beiräte oder Expertenkommissionen mühsam begleitet werden. Die Ergebnisse dieser schleichenden Transformationen sind nach meiner Erfahrung höchst unterschiedlich. Wenn eine Stadt eine klare stadträumliche Struktur und eine hoch entwickelte Planungskultur hat, können durch diese Veränderungen durchaus Synergieeffekte entstehen, die eine insgesamt positive Stimmung in der Stadt erzeugen. Wenn

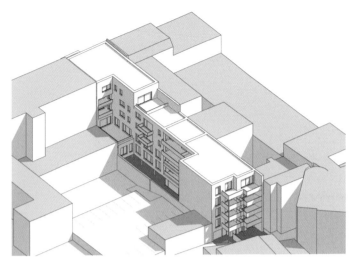

2 *Façade drawing, planned building Karlstrasse 26, Karlsruhe. Architect: ASTOC, Cologne*
2 *Fassadenzeichnung, geplantes Gebäude Karlstraße 26, Karlsruhe. Architekt: ASTOC, Köln*

3 *Isometry, planned building Karlstrasse 26, Karlsruhe. Architect: ASTOC, Cologne*
3 *Isometrie, geplantes Gebäude Karlstraße 26, Karlsruhe. Architekt: ASTOC, Köln*

4 *Building on Herren-strasse 26–28, Karls-ruhe. Architect: LRO, Stuttgart*
4 *Gebäude Herrenstraße 26–28, Karlsruhe. Archi-tekt: LRO, Stuttgart*

aber in der Verwaltung und der Ortspolitik keine Vorstellung über die Wei-terentwicklung besteht, ist die Wahrscheinlichkeit groß, dass das Stadtbild beschädigt wird und die öffentlichen Räume keine zusammenhängende Atmosphäre entfalten können.

Die beiden Beispiele in Karlsruhe zeigen eine zeitgemäße Weiterentwick-lung einer stadträumlich stabilen Situation. In den beiden Straßenzügen werden bestehende Gebäude ersetzt. Es werden hochverdichtete Hofge-bäude eingefügt, die sich in der Nutzungsverteilung und Gebäudestruktur an ihrer Umgebung orientieren. Die Fassadensprache und der Materialge-brauch sind hingegen eigenständig und zeitgemäß. ▶2, 3, 4

Weiche Transformation

Die Stadt Köln beschäftigt sich seit vier Jahren mit der Entwicklung der so-genannten Parkstadt Süd[4]. Zwischen den Stadtteilen Bayenthal, Neustadt-Süd und Radertal befindet sich das Großmarktareal. Mit der Verlagerung der gesamten Marktlogistik entsteht die einmalige Chance, den Kölner Grüngürtel bis zum Rhein fortzusetzen und die angrenzenden Stadttei-le zu arrondieren. Dieses Vorhaben wurde im Masterplan durch das Büro AS&P[5] vorbereitet und soll in den nächsten zehn Jahren umgesetzt wer-den. Das Gelände ist ein hochkomplexer Flickenteppich von Einzelgrund-stücken, bestehenden Gebäudestrukturen und Infrastrukturfragmenten. Die Stadt Köln hat im Jahr 2015 ein kooperatives Werkstattverfahren durchgeführt und versucht durch eine möglichst offene Planungsatmo-

two streets. Very dense courtyard buildings are inserted, whose usage allocation and building structure are orientated towards their surroundings. The language of the façade and the use of materials, on the other hand, are individual and contemporary. ▶2, 3, 4

Soft transformation

The city of Cologne has been involved in the development of the so-called Parkstadt Süd for four years.[4] The large commercial area is between the districts of Bayenthal, Neustadt-Süd, and Radertal. The relocation of the entire market logistics presents the unique opportunity to extend the Cologne green belts as far as the Rhine and to encompass the adjacent districts. This project was prepared by the firm AS&P[5] in a master plan and should be implemented over the next ten years. The terrain is a highly complex patchwork of individual sites, existing building structures, and infrastructure fragments. The city of Cologne carried out a cooperative workshop procedure in 2015 and is seeking to secure public approval in the surrounding districts by means of a planning atmosphere that is as open as possible. Over the course of a year-long participatory marathon, five planning teams were confronted with civil demands, infrastructural necessities, and especially the wish for a major inner-city park. The spe-

5 *Planning workshop
Parkstadt Süd, Cologne*
5 *Planungswerkstatt
Parkstadt Süd, Köln*

sphäre, die Bürger der angrenzenden Stadtteile „mitzunehmen". Fünf Planungsteams wurden ein Jahr lang in einem Beteiligungsmarathon mit Bürgerwünschen, Infrastrukturnotwendigkeiten und vor allem mit dem Wunsch nach einem großen innerstädtischen Park konfrontiert. Das Besondere an diesem Verfahren war der Versuch, „Stadtplanung auf Augenhöhe" zu etablieren. Die Teams, das hochrangige Begleitgremium, die Verwaltung, die Politik und die Stadtgesellschaft wurden durch akribisch geplante Veranstaltungsformate permanent herausgefordert, sich miteinander zu beschäftigen. Das Ziel dieser Bemühungen war es, eine möglichst breite Akzeptanz und Identifikation mit der Vision für diesen neuen Stadtteil zu erzeugen. Die Veranstaltungen waren turbulent, manchmal laut, aber immer erstaunlich zielorientiert. Der Dialog zwischen den externen Planern und der Bürgerschaft diente hierbei als eine Art „geschütztes Territorium". Die Verwaltung hielt sich zunächst zurück. Die direkten Reaktionen beeinflussten die jeweils nächsten Planungsschritte. Nach einigen Workshops wurden zumindest die Missverständnisse ausgeräumt und das Klima verbesserte sich.

Ein weiteres Thema bei solchen großen Projekten ist natürlich die Schaffung von innerstädtischem Wohnraum. Hierbei ging es weniger um die konkreten städtebaulichen Entwürfe, sondern um eine Zielvereinbarung über die Charaktere der zu entwickelnden Quartiere. Die Diskussionen über die Maßstäblichkeit der öffentlichen Räume, die typologische Ausprägung der Wohnbebauung, die Gestaltung der Erdgeschosszonen und über das Mobilitätskonzept standen hierbei im Vordergrund. Letztendlich entschied dann doch das Begleitgremium, welches der fünf Konzepte die Grundlage der weiteren Planung werden sollte.

In den nächsten Jahren wird man sehen, ob dieser aufwendige Prozess eine wirklich tragfähige und vor allen Dingen von einem breiten Konsens getragene Basis für die neue Parkstadt sein kann. ▶5

Radikale Transformation

In der politischen Debatte nimmt die Schaffung von bezahlbarem Wohnraum eine immer stärkere Rolle ein. Durch die teilweise Privatisierung des öffentlichen Wohnraumbestands versuchten viele Kommunen, die öffentliche Wohnraumversorgung auf den privaten Markt zu verlagern. Dadurch wurden die bestehenden Siedlungsbereiche systematisch vernachlässigt. Für die privaten Eigentümer waren sie ökonomisch uninteressant und für die städtischen Gesellschaften eine Belastung.

Jede deutsche Stadt hat mehr als eine von ihnen: leicht angestaubte Siedlungen aus den 1950er Jahren in Zeilenbauweise, die schon zu ihrer Bauzeit nicht viel mehr boten als günstigen Wohnraum und weitläufige, unstrukturierte Freiflächen. Die Siedlung am Buchheimer Weg im Osten von Köln war dafür ein Beispiel. Zwei Generationen nach dem Bau, müssen viele dieser Siedlungen technisch erneuert und oft auch strukturell über-

cial feature of this procedure was the attempt to establish "collaborative urban planning." The teams, the high-level advisory board, administration, politics, and urban society were constantly challenged to face each other through meticulously planned event formats. The aim of these efforts was to engender the widest possible acceptance of and identification with the vision for this new district. The events were turbulent, sometimes loud, but always surprisingly target-orientated. The dialogue between the external planners and the civil population served as a form of "safe territory." The administration initially took a back seat. The immediate reactions influenced the next planning steps. After a few workshops, any misunderstandings were clarified and the atmosphere improved.

Another issue presented by such major projects is of course the creation of inner-city residential space. It was less about concrete urban development

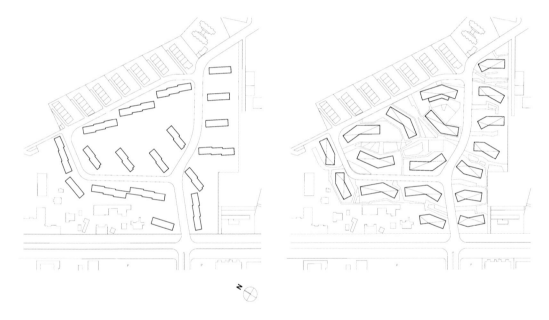

designs and more about agreeing on objectives regarding the characteristics of the districts to be developed, with a focus on discussions about the scale of public spaces, the typological features of the housing, the design of ground-floor zones, and the mobility concept. In the end it was the advisory body that decided which of the five concepts was to become the basis of further planning.

The forthcoming years will show whether this laborious process can be a truly viable basis for a new city park supported by a wide consensus. ▶5

6 *Layering of existing buildings and new planning, drawing: ASTOC, Cologne*

6 *Überlagerung Bestand und Neuplanung, Zeichnung: ASTOC, Köln*

Radical transformation

The creation of affordable housing is playing an increasing role in political debates. Owing to the partial privatisation of public housing, many communities tried to privatise the provision of public housing entirely. This led

dacht werden. Bei dem Kölner Beispiel stellte sich nach umfangreichen Untersuchungen heraus, dass ein Abriss der Siedlung und ihr Wiederaufbau ökonomisch wesentlich günstiger sein würden als eine aufwendige technische Instandsetzung der Häuser. Hinzu kamen die Möglichkeiten, das Freiraumkonzept grundlegend zu überarbeiten, die Grundrisse den heutigen Standards anzupassen sowie weitere Nutzungen wie Kindertagesstätte, Stadtteilbüro und Altenwohngruppen zu integrieren und den ruhenden Verkehr neu zu organisieren.

Der Entwurf für die Siedlung am Buchheimer Weg in Köln versteht sich als kritische Fortschreibung der 1950er-Jahre-Konzepte. Er versucht zu beweisen, dass die Lebensbedingungen in einem sozial schwierigen Stadtteil verbessert und der Nachkriegsstädtebau um neue Qualitäten ergänzt werden kann. ▶ 6, 7

7 Housing layouts, before and after, drawing: ASTOC, Cologne
7 *Wohnungsgrundrisse vorher – nachher, Zeichnung: ASTOC, Köln*

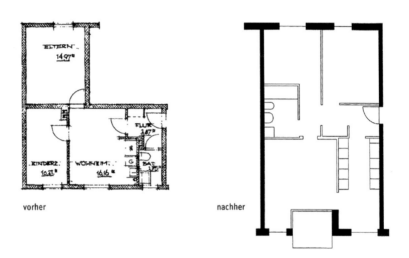

Wie kann die Wechselwirkung zwischen städtebaulicher Vision und architektonischer Wirklichkeit verbessert werden? In den beschriebenen Beispielen geht es immer um den Zusammenhang von Leitbildkonzepten und städtebaulichen Entwürfen mit der konkreten architektonischen Umsetzung. Genau an diesem Punkt ist in den letzten Jahren in meiner Wahrnehmung eine „Zuständigkeitslücke" entstanden. Die Stadtplaner definieren sich eher über den Planungsprozess und die Architekten sehen jede städtebauliche Festlegung eher als Einschränkung.

Carl Fingerhuth beschreibt dieses Phänomen: „Städtebau ist der Missing Link für eine erfolgreiche Betreuung der Transformation der Stadt. Diese Lücke zwischen Raum- respektive Stadtplanung und Architektur zu schließen ist auch deshalb so wichtig geworden, weil in der Einsamkeit der architektonischen Projekte die Entwerfenden sich der holonischen Struktur der Stadt entzogen haben."[6]

to the systematic neglect of the existing settlement areas. They were of no economic interest to private owners and a burden to urban society.

Every German city has more than one of them: rather dusty housing estates from the 1950s built in rows, which did not offer much more than cheap housing even at the time they were built, along with extensive, unstructured open spaces. The estate on Buchheimer Weg in the east of Cologne is one example. Two generations after being built, many of these estates need technical modernisation and in many cases a structural overhaul. In the Cologne example, after comprehensive studies it emerged that demolishing the estate and rebuilding it would be significantly more cost effective than an extensive technical upgrading of the houses. In addition, there was the opportunity to fundamentally rethink the open space concept, to adapt the structures to modern-day standards, to reorganise stationary traffic, and to integrate further usages such as a childcare centre, a district bureau, and homes for the elderly.

The plan for the estate on Buchheimer Weg is understood as a critical continuation of the 1950s concepts. It seeks to prove that the living conditions in a district with social difficulties can be improved and that post-war urban development can be given new qualities. ▶6, 7

How can the interrelationship between an urban development vision and architectural reality be improved? The aforementioned examples are always about the relationship between model concepts and urban development designs on the one hand, and concrete architectural realisation on the other. It is precisely here, in my view, that a "responsibility gap" has emerged in recent years. Urban planners define themselves more through the planning process, while architects tend to see each urban development regulation as a restriction.

Carl Fingerhuth describes this phenomenon: "urban development is the missing link for the successful handling of the transformation of a city. Another reason why closing this gap between spatial and urban planning and architecture has become so important is that designers have turned away from the holonic structure of the city through isolated architectural projects."[6]

Typological considerations play an ambivalent role in current discourse within the architecture discipline. Different "worlds" came face to face with each other in the submitted presentations for the subject of building design at KIT in Karlsruhe in January 2016. Whilst some identified and categorised quite a range of building types, others questioned this approach in principle. For them, a building is a product of conceptual thinking or simply a three-dimensional entity that can be generated by means of various parameters. The unique outcome is the result of a design process only and therefore a product of its creators. The set of laws that emerges through a particular use or local context does not play a significant role, but instead is worked into the conceptual idea more arbitrarily. One of the candidates said: "at our firm we do not design typologically, instead we

Typologische Überlegungen spielen im aktuellen Diskurs der Disziplin Architektur eine zwiespältige Rolle. Bei den Berufungsvorträgen für das Fach Gebäudelehre im Januar 2016 am KIT in Karlsruhe trafen „Welten" aufeinander. Während die einen durchaus unterschiedliche Gebäudetypen identifizierten und kategorisierten, stellten die anderen diese Herangehensweise grundsätzlich infrage. Für sie ist ein Gebäude ein Produkt konzeptioneller Überlegungen oder schlicht ein dreidimensionales Gebilde, das durch verschiedene Parameter generiert werden kann. Dieses Unikat ist einzig und allein durch einen Entwurfsprozess entstanden und somit ein Produkt seiner Schöpfer. Die Gesetzmäßigkeiten, die durch eine bestimmte Nutzung oder den örtlichen Kontext entstehen, spielen keine besondere Rolle, sondern werden eher beiläufig in der konzeptionellen Idee verarbeitet. Eine der Kandidatinnen bei den Berufungsvorträgen sagte: „Wir entwerfen in unserem Büro nicht typologisch, sondern wir entwickeln aus dem Kontext und aus dem Programm eine Haltung, die wiederum stark geprägt wird durch unsere Persönlichkeit und unseren architektonischen Hintergrund." Man könnte diese Debatte durchaus im akademischen Raum belassen und sie als eine weitere Episode in der Auseinandersetzung zwischen traditionell geprägten Architekten und „Konzeptkünstlern" abtun. Dahinter aber steckt ein grundlegend unterschiedliches Verständnis von urbanen Strukturen.

Die Unzufriedenheit mit den erzielten Ergebnissen in städtebaulichen Großprojekten wird dagegen deutlich artikuliert. In dem Artikel „Klötzchenspiel"[7] formuliert die Autorin Laura Weißmüller eine fundamentale Kritik an der Konzeption und Realisierung des Frankfurter Europaviertels. Vielleicht hat das Eine mit dem Anderen nicht viel zu tun, aber irgendwas liegt im Argen an der Schnittstelle zwischen Architektur und Stadtplanung. Die Akteure reden systematisch aneinander vorbei. Während der städtebauliche Entwurf die glanzvolle Vision transportieren soll, um möglichst viel Akzeptanz in der Öffentlichkeit zu erreichen, bleiben die weiteren Akteure erst einmal im Hintergrund. Mit Beginn der Realisierung, treten die ökonomischen Interessen in den Vordergrund und das Ergebnis hat mit der Vision nicht mehr viel zu tun.

Die einzige Möglichkeit, das zu verhindern, ist eine klare Vorstellung der Stadtöffentlichkeit, was sie mit dem Projekt erreichen will. Die Stadt Tübingen hat in den letzten 20 Jahren konsequent Baugruppenprojekte in den Mittelpunkt ihrer Stadtentwicklung gestellt.[8] Aus dieser Frage der Organisationsform wurde eine klare typologische Vorstellung. Die eindeutig formulierten Grundsätze wurden dann an unterschiedlichen Orten in städtebauliche Entwürfe umgesetzt. Die Frage nach der Typologie hat hier eine zentrale Rolle. Sie ist gleichzeitig eine Art Zieldefinition und Erfolgskontrolle.

Alban Janson beschreibt es sehr viel präziser: „Das Charakteristische am Typus ist ein besonderes Verhältnis von Identität und Differenz oder von Schema und Variation."[9]

develop an approach through the context and the usage, which is strongly influenced in turn by our personality and our architectural background." One could by all means leave this discussion to academic spheres and dismiss it as a further episode in the debate between traditional architects and "conceptual artists." However, there is an understanding of urban structures behind it that differs fundamentally.

The dissatisfaction with the achieved results in major urban development projects, however, is expressed very clearly. In the article "Klötzchenspiel"[7] (Game of Blocks), the author Laura Weißmüller formulates a fundamental criticism of the design and realisation of the Europaviertel in Frankfurt. Perhaps one has little to do with the other, but evidently architecture and urban planning are at sixes and sevens. The involved parties regularly talk at cross-purposes. While the urban development plan is supposed to convey a glossy vision, in order to achieve the greatest possible public acceptance, the other involved parties initially remain in the background. When implementation starts, economic interests become a point of focus and the result has little in common with the vision.

The only way to prevent this is for the urban public to have a clear idea of what the project is supposed to achieve. The city of Tübingen has consistently placed building group projects at the centre of its urban development in the last 20 years.[8] This question of organisational form became a clear typological concept. The clearly formulated principles were then implemented at various stages of the urban development plans. The question of typology plays a central role here. It serves both to define the objective and to monitor success.

Alban Janson describes it much more precisely: "what is characteristic of a type is a special relationship between identity and difference, or between a formula and variation."[9]

Conclusion

The concept of transformation is used in many different ways and often in a very generalised manner. The reflection of the visible effects of the various types of transformation plays a secondary role in this. An effective and reliable steering of these processes will remain an illusion, in my view. The dissertations currently being developed attempt to illuminate this topic area from various perspectives and to formulate the terms more precisely, in order to enable a differentiated approach to the processes required in the future. It is about a better understanding and sounding out the scope of planning. Whether this can succeed will be shown by the results.

Fazit

Der Begriff Transformation wird unterschiedlich und oft sehr pauschal benutzt. Die Reflexion der sichtbaren Auswirkungen der unterschiedlichen Transformationsarten spielt dabei eine untergeordnete Rolle. Eine wirksame und zuverlässige Steuerung dieser Prozesse wird nach meiner Überzeugung eine Illusion bleiben.

Die gerade entstehenden Dissertationen versuchen, dieses Themenfeld von unterschiedlichen Positionen zu beleuchten und die Begrifflichkeiten wesentlich präziser zu fassen, um dadurch einen differenzierteren Umgang mit den zukünftig notwendigen Prozessen zu ermöglichen. Es geht dabei um ein besseres Verstehen und ein Ausloten der planerischen Spielräume. Ob dies gelingen kann, werden erst die Ergebnisse zeigen können.

INTERNATIONALES
DOKTORANDENKOLLEG
FORSCHUNGSLABOR RAUM

Curriculum 2013 – 2016
Urbane Transformationslandschaften

INTERNATIONAL
DOCTORAL COLLEGE
SPATIAL RESEARCH LAB

riculum 2013 – 2016
formation of Cities and Landscapes

el Koch, HafenCity Universität Hamburg
pl, KIT Karlsruhe
noll, ETH Zürich
önwandt, Universität Stuttgart
gl, TU Wien
r, TU München

Mailand Milan, 18.03.2015

Wien Vienna, 03.05.2016

Stuttgart, 19.03.2014

Hamburg, 21.11.2013

Wien Vienna, 05.05.2016

SCOPE FOR DENSITY

Problem-orientated procedural approach to densification represented as an aspect of inward city development, based on the example of small- and medium-sized municipalities in the Swiss Plateau region

ANITA GRAMS

The revised Spatial Planning Act that came into effect in Switzerland in 2014 and the minimum strategy of "inward city development before external development" obliges communities to shift their spatial development to the most built-up areas and to coordinate any extension of building zones beyond municipal boundaries. For many small- and medium-sized municipalities in Switzerland, this means a change in their approach to spatial planning practice. In these municipalities in particular, inward city development is confronted with basic problems such as a lack of acceptance of dense building typologies and obstacles to mobilisation which have been secured by building regulations, and restrictive ways of thinking. The research addresses these issues as a starting point and culminates in the hypothesis that inward city development is possible in the main settlement areas in Switzerland, but that the existing formal spatial planning tools alone are inadequate in this respect.

An estimation of the reserves in the main settlement area of Switzerland shows that around two thirds of the settlement area reserves and at least two thirds of the floor space reserves in residential areas are in small and medium-size municipalities, which also account for 93 per cent of all administrative entities in the Swiss Plateau regions. Furthermore, it is estimated that half of floor space reserves are on already built-up but underused plots in residential areas. A systematic "densification refusal" is taking place in small- and medium-sized communities in the main residential areas in Switzerland. In order to assist a breakthrough in the inward city development of this area, a revision of formal tools is required. In addition, more informal procedures are required at an early stage beyond community boundaries, which in turn could lead to a reform of local planning. Informal procedures should not negate the specific organisational form of small- and medium-sized municipalities—i. e. non-professional or "militia" government—but should adapt themselves to this principle. An "internal development compass" brings together the existing knowledge in the "militia" government and presents an informal preamble to the "local planning revision of the third generation." Inward city development in Switzerland requires that politics and spatial planning are orientated towards the starting problems of small- and medium-sized municipalities and adaptation to the operational concepts of public transport in the Swiss Plateau region. If one succeeds in benefitting from the many reserves in small- and medium-sized municipalities through adequate public transport concepts, congestion problems in cities can be avoided, while small- and medium-sized municipalities can be developed further significantly. This would make the concept of "little in many locations, rather than a lot in few locations" have a positive impact on a national level and could initiate the necessary transformation process in the main settlement area of Switzerland.[1]

SPIELRÄUME FÜR DICHTE
Problemorientierter Verfahrensansatz für Verdichtung als Element der Innenentwicklung dargestellt am Beispiel kleiner und mittlerer Gemeinden im Schweizer Mittelland

ANITA GRAMS

Mit dem in der Schweiz 2014 in Kraft getretenen revidierten Raumplanungsgesetz und der Mindeststrategie „Innenentwicklung vor Außenentwicklung" sind die Gemeinden verpflichtet, ihre räumliche Entwicklung auf das weitgehend überbaute Gebiet zu lenken und die Bauzonendimensionierung über Gemeindegrenzen hinaus abzustimmen. Dies bedeutet für viele kleine und mittlere Gemeinden der Schweiz ein Denkmusterwechsel in der raumplanerischen Praxis. Insbesondere in diesen Gemeinden sieht sich eine Innenentwicklung mit Ausgangsproblemen wie mangelnder Akzeptanz dichter Bautypologien, Mobilisierungshindernisse von baurechtlich gesicherten Reserven und fehlenden Denkmustern konfrontiert. Hier setzen die Forschungsfragen an und münden in der Hypothese, Innenentwicklung im Hauptsiedlungsraum der Schweiz sei möglich, die bestehenden formellen Instrumente der Raumplanung allein seien dafür jedoch nicht ausreichend.

Eine Abschätzung der Reserven im Hauptsiedlungsraum der Schweiz zeigt, dass rund zwei Drittel der Siedlungsflächenreserven sowie mindestens zwei Drittel der Geschossflächenreserven in Wohnzonen der kleinen und mittleren Gemeinden liegen, die zudem 93 Prozent aller administrativen Einheiten des Mittellands ausmachen. Außerdem liegen schätzungsweise die Hälfte der Geschossflächenreserven auf bereits bebauten, jedoch unternutzten Parzel-

len. Im Hauptsiedlungsraum der Schweiz findet in kleinen und mittleren Gemeinden ein systematischer „Dichteverzicht" statt. Um der Innenentwicklung im Hauptsiedlungsraum der Schweiz zum Durchbruch zu verhelfen, ist vor allem in diesen Gemeindekategorien eine Revision der formellen Instrumente nötig. Dazu sind vermehrt informelle Verfahren in einer frühen Phase über Gemeindegrenzen hinweg nötig, die in der Konsequenz zu einer Reformation der Ortsplanung führen. Informelle Verfahren sollten dabei die spezifische Organisationsform der kleinen und mittleren Gemeinden – das Milizsystem – nicht negieren, sondern sich in dieses Prinzip einpassen. Ein „Innenentwicklungskompass" vereint das im Milizsystem vorhandene Wissen und bildet den informellen Vorlauf zur „Ortsplanungsrevision der Dritten Generation".

Innenentwicklung in der Schweiz bedingt vor allem eine Hinwendung der Politik und Raumplanung zu den Ausgangsproblemen kleiner und mittlerer Gemeinden und die Anpassung der Betriebskonzepte des öffentlichen Verkehrs im Schweizer Mittelland. Gelingt es, die in kleinen und mittleren Gemeinden zahlreich vorhandenen Reserven durch adaptierte Konzepte des öffentlichen Verkehrs zu erschließen, können einerseits Probleme der Überlastung in Städten vermieden und andererseits die kleinen und mittleren Gemeinden maßvoll weiterentwickelt werden. Damit entfaltet das Konzept „an vielen Orten wenig statt an wenigen Orten viel" auch auf nationaler Ebene seine Wirkung und könnte den nötigen Transformationsprozess im Hauptsiedlungsraum der Schweiz einleiten.[1]

THE DISAPPEARANCE OF THE URBAN BACK AND THEIR VALUE FOR A DIVERSE AND SUSTAINABLE EUROPEAN METROPOLIS

JANNA HOHN

As in other growing European metropolises, one can identify strong densification tendencies in London, Hamburg, and Berlin. Statistics confirm that urban populations are rising and that remaining land areas in cities are diminishing. Drives towards the densification of urban cores and efficient site recycling dominate current planning practice. The last large abandoned sites are currently either in planning or have already been developed with highly profitable projects. Consequently, the economic pressure on the remaining commercial and industrial areas in inner cities is increasing.

These areas are to be found in unused spaces, peripheral areas, and transition zones along railway tracks, around harbour areas, large market areas, and infrastructure corridors. A wide-ranging usage mix has emerged on these "Urban Backs," owing to their compromised location, low land value, and the available industrial infrastructure. Workshops, warehouses, small production plants, and other usages have emerged here which are important for supply and disposal, urban logistics, and the functioning of the overall urban cycle. Urban Backs are commonly found on the periphery of large-scale master plan areas in the inner city. These formerly often inaccessible and closed off areas have formed a fertile ground for many of the aforementioned functions. However, through the current redevelopment process and the associated increase in land value, these peripheral areas have become a focus of interest for authorities and investors.

Many cities have already recognised this issue, but no adequate solutions have yet been found and developed. The thesis intends to show that Urban Backs, with their wide range of usages, their inner-city locations, and their local networks, are necessary for the functioning of the city as a whole from a social, ecological, and economic point of view. They provide a wide range of workplaces, allow a high degree of interconnectivity, and offer niches and potential for future developments.

A significant aim of the thesis is to answer the question of how diversity and heterogeneity can be preserved in the city, despite densification and intensification. Do Urban Backs need to be protected, carefully regenerated, or integrated into new master plans in order to do so? Various scenarios are to be developed to answer this question. Current transformation processes are mapped and spatial solutions are illustrated by analysing selected case studies in London, Hamburg, and Berlin. This thesis will contribute to generating visions and processes for a holistic and socially inclusive inward city development, without compromising diversity and sustainability.

The thesis was funded by the Brigitte-Schlieben-Lange programme of the Ministry of Science, Research, and Art in Baden-Württemberg.

DAS VERSCHWINDEN DER STÄDTISCHEN RÜCKSEITEN UND IHR WERT FÜR EINE DIVERSE UND NACHHALTIGE EUROPÄISCHE METROPOLE

JANNA HOHN

Wie in anderen wachsenden europäischen Metropolen sind in London, Hamburg und Berlin starke Verdichtungstendenzen zu verzeichnen. Die Statistiken belegen, dass die Einwohnerzahlen steigen und die Flächenreserven in den Städten schrumpfen. Innenentwicklung und Flächenrecycling bestimmen die aktuelle Planungspraxis. Die letzten großen brachliegenden Flächen befinden sich nun entweder in Planung oder sind bereits mit hochprofitablen Projekten aufgefüllt. In der Folge nimmt der ökonomische Verdrängungsdruck auf die verbleibenden gewerblich und industriell geprägten Flächen in der Innenstadt zu.

Diese Flächen finden sich in Zwischenräumen, Randgebieten und Übergangszonen entlang von Bahnschienen, Hafengebieten, Großmarktarealen und Infrastrukturkorridoren. Auf diesen „Städtischen Rückseiten" ist aufgrund der beeinträchtigten Lage, dem niedrigen Bodenwert und der vorhandenen industriellen Infrastruktur eine vielfältige Nutzungsmischung entstanden. Werkstätten, Lagerhäuser, kleine Produktionsbetriebe und weitere Nutzungen haben sich angelagert, die für Ver- und Entsorgung, Stadtlogistik und das Funktionieren des gesamten Stadtkreislaufs wichtig sind.

Die Rückseiten sind besonders in den Randbereichen der großen Masterplangebiete in der Inneren Stadt anzutreffen. Diese ehemals oft unzugänglichen und abgeschlossenen Gebiete bildeten einen fruchtbaren Nährboden für eine Vielzahl der oben genannten Funktionen. Durch den aktuellen Aufwertungsprozess und den damit verbundenen Anstieg des Flächenwertes geraten die angrenzenden Rückseiten nun in den Fokus von Verwaltung und Investoren.

Vonseiten der Städte ist dieses Problem oft schon erkannt worden, aber es wurden noch keine ausreichenden Lösungen gefunden und entwickelt. Die Arbeit soll aufzeigen, dass die „Städtischen Rückseiten" mit ihren vielfältigen Nutzungen, ihrer Lage in der Innenstadt und ihren lokalen Netzwerken für das Funktionieren der Stadt in sozialer, ökologischer und wirtschaftlicher Hinsicht notwendig sind. Sie sorgen für ein vielfältiges Arbeitsplatzangebot, ermöglichen eine Stadt der kurzen Wege und bieten Nischen und Potenziale für zukünftige Entwicklungen.

Ein wesentliches Ziel der Arbeit ist die Beantwortung der Frage, wie Diversität und Heterogenität trotz Nachverdichtung und Intensivierung in der Stadt erhalten werden können. Müssen die „Städtischen Rückseiten" dafür geschützt, behutsam saniert oder in neue Masterpläne integriert werden? Zur Beantwortung dieser Frage sollen verschiedene Szenarien entwickelt werden. Durch die Untersuchung ausgewählter Fallbeispiele in London, Hamburg und Berlin werden aktuelle Veränderungsprozesse dargestellt und räumliche Lösungsansätze aufgezeigt. Diese Arbeit leistet einen Beitrag, Bilder und Prozesse für eine ganzheitliche und sozialverträgliche Innenentwicklung zu generieren, ohne Diversität und Nachhaltigkeit in der Stadt zu verlieren.

Die Arbeit wurde durch das Brigitte-Schlieben-Lange-Programm des Ministeriums für Wissenschaft, Forschung und Kunst des Landes Baden-Württemberg gefördert.

PLANNING WITH PLACE ATTACHMENT

FRANZISKA DRASDO

Place attachment is the emotion that people develop towards a place, such as one's own home or the place of birth.[1] These relationships can be formed by various processes, for instance everyday routines, "milestone moments," and memories, but also appropriation and control.

A range of concepts have been generated to describe the emotions people feel towards places. This has been primarily done by human geographers and environmental psychologists. The best-known concepts are *place attachment, sense of place,* and *place identity*. But what have these concepts got to do with planning? Place attachment influences how people respond to a planning process: "planners can benefit from environmental and community psychology perspectives on individual and community place attachments to help understand who gets involved in neighbourhood change and planning efforts, as well as why people resist or support change efforts."[2]

However, there is no monocausal link between the physical environment and the people's behaviour. People's reactions depend on many factors e.g. whether they see their existence, or the character of the place, threatened by the place change, how extensively and quickly the change occurs, and whether they can influence the process of change.[3] For this reason, generalisations such as design guidelines do not work.

Taking place attachment into account in a planning process is enriching, but must be carried out individualised in each planning process. However, for planners, the appropriate theory of place attachment is difficult to use. As the concepts of place attachment have been developed in different fields of research, there is no unified theoretical basis.[4] Furthermore, notions such as *space* and *place* are defined differently than is common in planning.

The aim of the thesis is to improve the incorporation of place attachment into planning processes by making the existing theory applicable and by analysing concepts in terms of their notion of space. Secondly, this work aims to formulate recommendations for a planning process that takes place attachment into account.

FRANZISKA DRASDO

zepte mit Planung zu tun? Ortsbeziehungen beeinflussen, wie Menschen auf Planungen reagieren: „Planners can benefit from environmental and community psychology perspectives on individual and community place attachments to help understand who gets involved in neighborhood change and planning efforts and why, as well as why people resist or support change efforts."[2]

Der Zusammenhang zwischen der physischen Umwelt und dem Verhalten von Menschen ist jedoch nicht monokausal. Wie Menschen auf Veränderungen ihres physischen Umfeldes reagieren, hängt unter anderem davon ab, ob sie sich, ihre Existenz oder den Charakter des Ortes bedroht sehen, wie stark und schnell aus ihrer Sicht die Veränderung ausfällt und ob sie Einfluss auf den Veränderungsprozess haben.[3] Daher funktionieren Verallgemeinerungen wie Design-Richtlinien auch nicht.

Ortsbeziehungen in Planungen miteinzubeziehen ist bereichernd, muss jedoch in jedem Planungsprozess individualisiert erfolgen. Die Theorie zu Ortsbeziehungen ist für Planer jedoch schwer zugänglich: Da die Konzepte zu Ortsbeziehungen in unterschiedlichen Forschungsbereichen entstanden sind, gibt es keine einheitliche Theoriebasis.[4] Zudem werden Begriffe wie *Raum* und *Ort* anders definiert, als es in der Planung üblich ist.

Das Ziel der Arbeit ist es, den Miteinbezug von Ortsbeziehungen in Planungsprozesse zu erleichtern. Zum einen soll dies dadurch geschehen, dass die vorhandene Theorie verständlich und anwendbar gemacht wird. Hierfür werden Konzepte auf ihren Raumbegriff hin analysiert. Zum anderen soll ein Vorschlag formuliert werden, wie ein Planungsprozess, in dem Ortsbeziehungen berücksichtigt werden, aussehen und ablaufen könnte.

Ortsbeziehungen sind Emotionen, die Personen zu einem Ort entwickeln. Beispiele für Orte können das eigene Zuhause oder der Geburtsort sein.[1] Menschen bauen Beziehungen zu Orten durch unterschiedliche Prozesse auf: durch alltägliche Routinen, besondere Erlebnisse, Erinnerungen, aber auch Aneignung und Kontrolle.

Zur Beschreibung dieser Emotionen von Personen zu Orten wurden unterschiedliche Konzepte entwickelt, vorwiegend von Humangeografen und Umweltpsychologen. Die bekanntesten Konzepte sind *place attachment, sense of place,* und *place identity.* Doch was haben diese Kon-

BELGRADE
BELGRAD

RESTRUCTURING OF PLANNING: THE SAVA RIVER WATERFRONT, BELGRADE—A CASE STUDY

MILICA BAJIĆ-BRKOVIĆ

A shift in planning

The radical changes which took place in Serbia at the beginning of the century decoupled spatial development from both the socialist ideology and an ideal which saw planning as solely a method of guiding territorial development. The shift generated significant impact on the sectorial and structural responsibilities for development, and affected planning with regard to its position, the parties involved, its methodology and the instruments planners employ. Decision procedures and planning schemes have become more open to the needs and aspirations of potential investors, which in turn leads to intensive collaboration between investors and local governments. Often, planning follows investors' project proposals, adapting its procedures or redesigning already endorsed plans and strategies.

Belgrade Waterfront project: Redevelopment as an opportunity for development

Belgrade is home to a unique set of challenges in spatial development which can be found nowhere else. One such challenge is a long-standing commitment to redevelop the 100 hectare area at the confluence of the Danube and Sava Rivers. It is a mixed-use zone housing the Belgrade Bus Station, Main Railway Station (both of which have been pending relocation for a long time) and the Belgrade Tourist Port. Residential area and small-scale services complement the main uses. This area is also known for its architectural heritage, which has been

NEUSTRUKTURIERUNG DER PLANUNG: DAS SAVE-UFER, BELGRAD – EINE FALLSTUDIE

MILICA BAJIĆ-BRKOVIĆ

Neue Gewichtungen in der Planung

Durch die radikalen Veränderungen, denen Serbien zu Beginn dieses Jahrhunderts unterworfen war, löste sich die Raumentwicklung von der sozialistischen Ideologie und einem Ideal, das in der Planung lediglich eine Methode zur Durchsetzung territorialer Entwicklung sah. Diese Verschiebung rief einen signifikanten Einfluss auf bereichsspezifische und strukturelle Entwicklungsaufgaben hervor und wirkte sich auf die Planung hinsichtlich ihrer Bedeutung, der beteiligten Parteien, ihrer Methodik und der planerischen Instrumente aus. Entscheidungsprozesse und Flächennutzungspläne sind den Bedürfnissen und Erwartungen potenzieller Investoren gegenüber offener geworden, was wiederum zu einer intensiven Zusammenarbeit von Investoren und Kommunalverwaltungen führte. Oft folgt die Planung den Projektvorschlägen von Investoren, passt ihre Prozesse an diese an oder ändert bereits beschlossene Pläne und Strategien.

Das Belgrader Ufer-Projekt: Sanierung als Entwicklungschance

Was die Herausforderungen der Raumentwicklung angeht, findet sich in Belgrad ein einzigartiges Konglomerat von Besonderheiten, das seinesgleichen sucht. Eine Schlüsselposition nehmen hier wohl die jahrelangen Bemühungen um die Sanierung des 100 Hektar großen Areals am Zusammenfluss von Donau und Save ein: ein Gebiet mit Mischnutzung, in dem sich der Busbahnhof, der Hauptbahnhof (deren Umsiedlung schon seit langem vorgesehen ist)

neglected for a long time, remaining reminiscent of past glory.

The initiative for redevelopment of the area came in response to the newly developed partnership between local and state officials from Serbia and investors from Abu Dhabi. The large-scale development and total reconstruction were decided as strategies for the recovery and rebirth of Belgrade. This philosophy is based on the premise that only large-scale projects can provide an impetus for development and enhance Belgrade's appeal to investors and businesses.

The key elements of the planning scheme include integration of Old and New Belgrade, opening the city towards the river, relocating the two stations, and keeping the area as a mixed-use zone. Densities and area coverage are high, while the urban morphology is to be changed in accordance with the accepted model of freestanding multi-story buildings and towers.

The project raised a rigorous debate and questioned both the scheme and decision procedures. Regarding the spatial aspects, arguments went against the proposed urban morphology, as it appeared to conflict with local values and culture. The magnitude of planned activities was estimated to generate additional traffic challenges, leading to further restructuring of the city, since the existing infrastructure does not have the capacity to support the intensity of the planned development.

Much stronger arguments were raised regarding the decision procedure. The usual regulation was overruled and a special act was adopted for this particular case. The plan developed for the area was adopted after the project scheme had already been accepted through direct negotiation between the Abu Dhabi partner and the Serbian/Belgrade government, a precedent in the Serbian planning practice. Public involvement was reduced to public hearings at final stage only, even though the project is of a crucial importance to the city. This case clearly indicates the change in planning practice and shifting roles within the triangle of key actors: planning—government—investors.

und der Belgrader Touristenhafen befinden. Wohngebiete und Kleinbetriebe vervollständigen die Mischung. Das Areal ist auch für sein architektonisches Erbe bekannt, das, seit langem vernachlässigt, an vergangenen Glanz erinnert.

Die Initiative zur Sanierung des Areals entstand aus einer neu entwickelten Partnerschaft zwischen kommunalen und staatlichen Stellen einerseits und Investoren aus Abu Dhabi andererseits. Die groß angelegte Entwicklung und Totalsanierung sollte der Rettung und Wiedergeburt Belgrads dienen. Diese Philosophie geht von der Prämisse aus, dass nur Großprojekte Entwicklungen anstoßen und Belgrads Attraktivität für Investoren und Unternehmen erhöhen können.

Kernpunkte des Flächennutzungsplans sind die Integrierung der Belgrader Altstadt und Neu-Belgrads, was die Stadt zum Fluss hin öffnen soll, die Verlegung der beiden Bahnhöfe und der Erhalt des Areals als ein Gebiet mit Mischnutzung. Die bauliche Verdichtung ist hoch, die urbane Morphologie muss also verändert werden, um das beschlossene Planungsmodell mit seinen freistehenden mehrgeschossigen Gebäuden und Türmen umzusetzen.

Das Projekt rief eine erregte Debatte hervor, die sowohl die Planung als auch die Entscheidungsprozesse infrage stellte. Was den Aspekt des Stadtraums anging, richtete sich die Argumentation gegen die vorgeschlagene urbane Morphologie, weil sie den lokalen Werten und der Lebenskultur entgegenstehe. Das Ausmaß der geplanten Maßnahmen führe zu weiteren verkehrstechnischen Herausforderungen, während die umfangreiche Entwicklungsplanung durch die vorhandene Infrastruktur nicht bewältigt werden könne.

Noch heftiger argumentierte man jedoch gegen den Entscheidungsprozess: Das übliche Prozedere wurde in diesem speziellen Fall verworfen und ein Sondergesetz angewandt. Der für das Areal entwickelte Plan wurde angenommen, nachdem das Projekt in direkten Verhandlungen zwischen den Partnern aus Abu Dhabi und der serbischen bzw. Belgrader Verwaltung bereits akzeptiert worden war. Dieses Vorgehen sollte zum Präzedenzfall für die serbische Planungspraxis werden. Die öffentliche Beteiligung wurde auf öffentliche Anhörungen zu einem sehr späten Zeitpunkt reduziert, obwohl das Projekt für die Stadt von enormer Bedeutung ist. Dieser Fall verdeutlicht die Veränderungen in der Planungspraxis Serbiens und die Rollenverschiebung unter den drei Hauptakteuren: Planer – Verwaltung – Investoren.

Belgrad Belgrade, 12.06.2014

Belgrad Belgrade, 09.06.2014

Belgrad Belgrade, 14.06.2014

Belgrad Belgrade, 08.06.2014

Belgrad Belgrade, 11.06.2014

Belgrad Belgrade, 12.06.2014

PUBLIC SPACE AND EXPERIMENTAL SPACES

ÖFFENTLICHER RAUM UND MÖGLICHKEITSRÄUME

PUBLIC SPACE AND EXPERIMENTAL SPACES

ANDREAS VOIGT

The framework theme of "Urban Landscape Transformation" and the associated notion of an active "transformation of cities and landscapes" lead to an "inward development"[1] of the landscape and settlement system, understood as the transformation and regeneration of spatial structures and the corresponding spatial usage processes by means of a coordinated and strategic approach. This requires an intense struggle for spatial qualities and densification possibilities. First of all, this requires a study of the "scope for density,"[2] sounded out in a series of steps. Qualities of the whole supporting landscape, infrastructure, and settlement system, including open and recreational spaces, and in particular public spaces, are of equal significance for inward development. It requires the improvement of the functionality and "vitality" of spatial structure elements, of the quality of their spatial relationships and their spatial "fit,"[3] of the integration of spatial infrastructures. It especially requires people to have a conscious attitude that is compatible with the space and the city, which must evidently form the actual core of a *smart city*.

> "I could tell you how many steps make up the streets rising like stairways, and the degree of the arcade's curves, and what kind of zinc scales cover the roofs; but I already know this would be the same as telling you nothing. The city does not consist of this, but of the relationships between the measurements of its space and the events of its past (…)"[4]

Initially the analysis of the term "public space" evokes the whole colourful spectrum of notions of space, which is differentiated by disciplinary and transdisciplinary background knowledge. Each discipline necessarily has "its" concept or concepts of space. This often leads to arguments, also due to claims that one's own concept of space is "correct." In view of this multiplicity, it is presumably merely a question of finding and using the concept of space that is suitable, usable, and helpful for the concrete problem or situation (and for the appropriate planning approach in this context[5]).

The range of aspects and notions of space to be taken into consideration includes:[6] an everyday understanding of space, objective space, scientific spatial concepts, absolute space, container space, relational space, space

ÖFFENTLICHER RAUM UND MÖGLICHKEITSRÄUME

ANDREAS VOIGT

Das Rahmenthema „Urbane Transformationslandschaften" und der damit zu verknüpfende Gedanke einer aktiven „Transformation urbaner Landschaften"[1] führen in weiterer Folge zur „Innenentwicklung"[2] des Landschafts- und Siedlungssystems, verstanden als Transformation und Erneuerung räumlicher Strukturen und korrespondierender Prozesse der Raumnutzung mittels einer koordinierten, strategischen Vorgehensweise. Dies erfordert ein intensives Ringen um räumliche Qualitäten und Möglichkeiten ihrer Nachverdichtung. Dazu müssen zunächst die „Spielräume für Dichte"[3] erkundet und in mehreren Näherungsschritten ausgelotet werden. Gleichrangig sind Qualitäten des gesamten tragenden Landschafts-, Infrastruktur- und Siedlungssystems, einschließlich der Frei- und Erholungsräume, insbesondere der öffentlichen Räume für die Innenentwicklung bedeutsam. Es bedarf der Verbesserung der Funktionsfähigkeit und „Vitalität" raumstruktureller Elemente, der Qualität ihrer räumlichen Beziehungen und ihrer räumlichen „Passung"[4], der Integration räumlicher Infrastrukturen. Vor allem bedarf es eines bewussten raum- und stadtverträglichen Verhaltens der Menschen, das vermutlich den eigentlichen Kern einer *Smart City* bilden muss.

> „Ich könnte dir sagen, wie viele Stufen die treppenartig angelegten Straßen aufweisen, welches Maß die Bögen der Laubengänge haben, mit was für Zinkplatten die Dächer gedeckt sind; doch ich weiß schon, daß dies wäre, als sagte ich dir nichts. Nicht daraus besteht die Stadt, sondern aus Beziehungen zwischen ihren räumlichen Abständen und den Geschehnissen ihrer Vergangenheit [...]."[5]

Zunächst führt die Befassung mit dem Begriff „Öffentlicher Raum" die gesamte, schillernde Vielfalt des Raumbegriffs vor Augen, der durch disziplinäres und transdisziplinäres Hintergrundwissen differenziert wird. Notwendigerweise verfügt jede Disziplin über „ihren" Raumbegriff beziehungsweise „ihre" Raumbegriffe. Häufig entsteht bereits darüber Streit, weil mitunter der Anspruch erhoben wird, über den „richtigen" Raumbegriff zu verfügen. Vermutlich geht es lediglich darum, angesichts dieser Vielfalt, den für die konkrete Problemsituation (und für den in diesem Zu-

as a form of intuition, space as a formal organising structure, subject-related spatial concepts, experienced space, space for action, social space—socio-psychological and phenomenological spatial concepts, symbolic spaces, organisational and political space ("territory"), relational economic space, space as an economic force field, space as an economic milieu, 'matrix space' as a socio-economic space, space in spatial structuring, and regional planning.

The notion of space is characterised by a high "variability of meaning."[7] In this regard, Blotevogel recommends: "the semantic plurality and multidimensionality of the term 'space' and its associated concepts such as 'place' prompts a reformulation of the object in an extended, multidimensional sense, from which the demand for an extended dynamic approach is to be derived. The multiplicity of perspectives with regard to space has to be acknowledged and taken seriously, without losing oneself in an unfounded relativism. One must always take account of the fact that planning practice is at the interface of different perspectives (physical-material, economic, political, aesthetic, regarding the living environment etc.)."[8]

The semantic plurality of concepts, including the concept of space, widens again if the linguistic context—even within a common language area—varies in different areas or if one leaves one's own language area. As part of the 2013–2016 curriculum, we had the opportunity to get to know other linguistic and cultural areas, namely Belgrade (Serbia) and Milan (Italy). Dealing with other languages and cultures helps to specify terms. It mostly helps to clarify their "core" and, at the same time, fascinating new attributes or aspects can emerge at the "periphery" of the terms. The word for space in in Greek language (chóros) also draws attention—with a different emphasis—to dancing (chorós), to movement in space, *spaces for movement*. From this perspective, space constitutes movement in space, concrete actions.[9] This may approximate the points of view in the disciplines of transport science, environmental psychology, urban culture research, urban sociology, etc.

If these semantic-etymological aspects are combined with the thought that planning involves language, culture, and ways of thinking and that planning cultures are based on this,[10] it leads first of all to the insight that planning approaches (even in neighbouring European spaces) require great circumspection, caution, and an understanding of a potentially differing planning culture. This challenge presents itself to an even greater extent if one wishes to work in totally different cultures and spaces worldwide. Different living environments and urban structures, which became visible, audible, and tangible exemplarily when visiting the Spatial Research Labs, are also bound up with different planning cultures. Differing urban climates—which can be experienced in the diurnal and annual cycle—make the concrete spatial experiences distinctive, as do the respective cultural landscapes, the "attitude to life" of the people, etc.

sammenhang zu wählenden Planungsansatz[6]) geeigneten, brauchbaren, gleichsam hilfreichen Raumbegriff zu finden und zu verwenden.

Die Vielfalt zu betrachtender Aspekte und Raumverständnisse umfasst unter anderem[7]: das „alltagsweltliche Raumverständnis": „Gegenständlicher Raum"; „Wissenschaftliche Raumkonzepte": „Absoluter Raum", „Behälter-Raum": „Relationaler Raum, Raum als Anschauungsform, Raum als formale Ordnungsstruktur; subjektbezogene Raumkonzepte: Anschauungsraum, gelebter Raum, Handlungsraum, Gesellschaftlicher Raum – sozialpsychologische und phänomenologische Raumkonzepte, symbolische Räume, organisatorischer und politischer Raum (‚Territorium'), relationaler Wirtschaftsraum, Raum als ökonomisches Kräftefeld, Raum als ökonomisches Milieu, ‚Matrix-Raum' als sozio-ökonomischer Raum"; „Raum in der Raumordnung und Landesplanung".

Der Raumbegriff ist durch eine hohe „Bedeutungsvariabilität"[8] geprägt. Blotevogel empfiehlt in diesem Zusammenhang: „Die semantische Vielfalt und Mehrdimensionalität des Terminus ‚Raum' (*space*) und seiner verwandten Begriffe wie zum Beispiel Ort (*place*) wird zum Anlass, den Gegenstand in einem erweiterten mehrdimensionalen Sinn zu reformulieren und daraus die Forderung nach einem erweiterten dynamischen Planungsansatz abzuleiten. Die Vielfalt der raumbezogenen Perspektiven sei anzuerkennen und ernst zu nehmen, ohne sich dadurch in einem standpunktlosen Relativismus zu verlieren. Stets sei zu beachten, dass sich die planerische Praxis im Schnittpunkt unterschiedlicher Perspektiven (physisch-materiell, ökonomisch, politisch, ästhetisch, lebensweltlich usw.) bewege."[9]

Die semantische Vielfalt der Begriffe, so auch des Raumbegriffs, vergrößert sich nochmals, wenn der sprachliche Kontext – selbst innerhalb eines gemeinsamen Sprachraumes – räumlich variiert wird oder darüber hinaus der eigene Sprachraum verlassen wird. Wir hatten im Rahmen des Curriculums 2013 bis 2016 mit Belgrad (Serbien) und Mailand (Italien) Gelegenheit, weitere Sprach- und Kulturräume kennenzulernen. Die Auseinandersetzung mit anderen Sprachen und Kulturen hilft bei der Schärfung der Begriffe – es verdeutlicht sich zumeist ihr „Kern", gleichzeitig tauchen an den „Rändern" der Begriffe mitunter faszinierend neue Attribute bzw. Aspekte auf. So lenkt das Wort für Raum im Griechischen (*chóros*) – mit anderer Akzentuierung – das Augenmerk auch auf Tanz (*chorós*), gleichsam Bewegung im Raum, auf *Bewegungsräume*. Raum wird in dieser Denkweise durch Bewegung im Raum, durch konkrete Handlungen konstituiert.[10] Dies kommt vermutlich disziplinären Sichtweisen der Verkehrswissenschaften, Umweltpsychologie, Stadtkulturforschung, Siedlungssoziologie etc. durchaus nahe.

Überlagert man diese semantisch-etymologischen Erkundungen mit dem Gedanken, dass Planung mit Sprache, Kultur und Denkweisen zu tun hat und auf dieser Basis Planungskulturen begründet werden[11], so entsteht zunächst die Einsicht, dass planerische Vorgehensweisen (selbst in

The attribute "public" is often used in key spatial planning concepts, such as *public space*, as well as *public asset, public domain, public interest,* and *public transport*, and shows that the *public* has a special value in planning matters. Communal interests should come before individual interests.

Among those involved in spatial planning, associated disciplines, and specialist areas, the observation of the public dimension, for example with regard to the term "public space," leads to a wide range of interpretations and associations, for example: public spaces overlap fundamentally with public assets mostly dedicated to communal usage; they are therefore freely accessible to all; they are the object of private and communal appropriation and of wide-ranging spatial usages, such as festivals, markets, democratic gatherings and rallies; they are a stage for social exchange and integration; public spaces correspond at their core to the ancient Greek concept of *agora*, a central aspect of the Greek *polis*; a privatisation of public space would endanger and restrict its core functions; the owners of public assets are the regional authorities (for Europe: European Union, states, nations, federal regions or cantons, municipalities); property is understood—on the basis of ancient Roman legal concepts—as a full entitlement to the object, but which principally enables private use that serves the common good (for example temporary *pavement cafés*[11], which do however require official permission); cooperative structures enable a communal use of the space, for example the concept of "commons"[12] (or "common land"), which is enjoying increasing popularity again—also in relation to the "common acquisition and use of knowledge."[13]

Public spaces emerge from the interplay between built-up and open spaces. They display a fascinating range of typological and topological design qualities and design elements (in relation to location and spatial links, function, configuration, form, dimension and proportion, façades and textures, choice of colours and materials, lighting, planting, public fountains, furnishing, shade and shelter from rain, artistic features, access to infrastructural elements such as telephone, wireless Internet access, electricity supply, etc.) which can be differentiated from a cultural, regional, and historical point of view. Different forms and types of squares, streets, and alleys have evolved over centuries and millennia of human settlement activity. Public spaces contain bridges and passageways, they also include "waterways." From a multiscalar perspective, what becomes evident beyond the various scales are the varying details of public spaces, which are the subject of focus of different disciplines.

Public spaces usually carry—both above and below the ground—important spatial infrastructure (energy, supply and disposal, water, sewers, public transport, telecommunications, etc.). They are the spaces where individual transport participants move in various modes (on foot, by bicycle, on a skateboard, by car, in a multimodal form, etc.). They border semi-public and private spaces that have various uses and, in combination, they form different street areas and street types (for example commercial and

benachbarten europäischen Räumen) große Umsicht und Behutsamkeit und Verständnis für eine möglicherweise etwas andere Planungskultur erfordern. Diese Herausforderung stellt sich umso mehr, wenn man in teils gänzlich anderen Kulturen und Räumen weltweit tätig werden möchte. Mit unterschiedlichen Planungskulturen eng verbunden sind ebenso unterschiedliche Lebens- und Stadtkulturen, die im Rahmen der Auseinandersetzung mit den bereisten Forschungslaborräumen beispielhaft sichtbar, hörbar und spürbar wurden. Unterschiedliche Stadtklimata – erlebbar im Tages- und Jahresgang – differenzieren die konkreten Raumerlebnisse in besonderer Weise, ebenso die jeweiligen Kulturlandschaften, die „Lebensgefühle" der Menschen etc.

Das Attribut „öffentlich" findet bei Schlüsselbegriffen räumlicher Planung häufig Verwendung, namentlich zunächst *öffentlicher Raum*, weiters *öffentliches Gut*, *öffentliche Hand*, *öffentliches Interesse*, *öffentlicher Verkehr* und verdeutlicht, dass das *Öffentliche* einen besonderen Stellenwert in Planungsfragen hat: Die Interessen des Gemeinwesens sollen vor Einzelinteressen stehen.

Die Betrachtung des Öffentlichen führt bei den an räumlicher Planung beteiligten und zu beteiligenden Disziplinen und Fachgebieten am Beispiel des Begriffs „öffentlicher Raum" zu durchaus vielfältigen und unterschiedlichen Interpretationen und Assoziationen, beispielhaft:

Öffentliche Räume überlagern sich im Kern mit dem zumeist dem Gemeingebrauch gewidmeten öffentlichen Gut; sie sind daher für alle frei zugänglich; sie sind Gegenstand privater und gemeinschaftlicher Aneignung und vielfältiger Raumnutzungen, wie Feste, Märkte, demokratische Versammlungen und Kundgebungen, gegebenenfalls Gerichtsbarkeit; sie sind Bühne für den gesellschaftlichen Austausch und Integration; öffentliche Räume entsprechen im Kern dem altgriechischen Konzept der *agora*, zentraler Bestandteil der griechischen *polis*; eine Privatisierung des öffentlichen Raumes würde dessen Kernfunktionen gefährden und verunmöglichen; Eigentümer des öffentliche Gutes sind die Gebietskörperschaften (für Europa: Europäische Union, Staaten, Länder (Bundesländer bzw. Kantone) und Gemeinden); Eigentum wird – auf der Grundlage antiker römisch-rechtlicher Vorstellungen – als Vollrecht an der Sache verstanden, das jedoch eine dem Gemeinwohl dienende private Nutzung grundsätzlich ermöglicht (zum Beispiel zeitlich befristete *Schanigärten*[12], die jedoch einer Genehmigung durch die Behörde bedürfen); genossenschaftliche Konstruktionen ermöglichen eine gemeinschaftliche Nutzung des Raumes: beispielhaft benannt sei das Konzept „Allmende"[13] (bzw. „Allmeinde"), das sich – auch bezogen auf die „gemeinsame Schaffung und Nutzung von Wissen"[14] – wieder zunehmender Beliebtheit erfreut.

Öffentliche Räume entstehen aus dem Wechselspiel von gebauten Räumen und Freiräumen; sie weisen eine faszinierende Vielfalt an typologisch und topologisch differenzierbaren Gestaltqualitäten und Gestaltelementen auf (bezogen auf Lage und räumliche Verknüpfung, Funktion,

shopping streets). Public spaces are the object of *spatial production* and of an "attention economy."[14] They have an important significance for the urban climate and ecology.

These associations and interpretations could be continued and extended. Public spaces are, as it were, the central nerve pathways, arteries, and veins of the settlement and urban body: they link public buildings, lead to major train stations, link public transport stops, lead to sports and recreational facilities, connect to parks and leisure amenities, and, ultimately, support the primary spatial infrastructure. A suitable design is a precondition for a thriving social life and for economic development.

> "Images are perceived moments, gained from the world of awareness, through the selection and specification of what has been seen. The bringing together of external impressions (experiences) and inner notions is a complex and lengthy process. Spatial content becomes a pictorial event."[15]

Public spaces are the object of intense, pictorial spatial perception from a static and dynamic viewpoint (spatial sequences). Spatial Research Labs allow—in the case of thorough study and spatial exploration—fascinating insights into the multiplicity of public spaces, in relation, for example, to the appearance of the locality and cityscape, the settlement and urban structure, and the wide-ranging processes of spatial usage. This opportunity was presented during joint explorations over the course of the doctoral college: these Spatial Research Labs are real proof of past and present-day notions of space, which have become reality through countless and repeated actions. Stable usage processes over time tend to lead to stable spatial structures.[16]

The academic study of public space is encouragingly vibrant and wide-ranging. For example, in 2008/2009 the research group "Urban culture and public space" was founded at the Department Department of Spatial Planning Spatial Planning at TU Wien (Vienna University of Technology), with a sponsored guest professor and with the generous support of the municipal authorities. A selection of publications[17] shows the breadth of research interest in public space (in chronological order):

Madanipour, Ali: *Public and Private Spaces of the City*. London 2003
Mitchell, Don: *The Right to the City: Social Justice and the Fight for Public Space*. New York 2003
Tonkiss, Fran: *Space, the City and Social Theory*. Cambridge 2005
Low, Setha/Smith, Neil: *The Politics of Public Space*. London/New York 2005
Frank, Karin A./Stevens, Quentin: *Loose Space: Possibility and Diversity in Urban Life*. London/New York 2006
Watson, Sophie: *City Publics. The (Dis)enchantments of Public Encounters*. London/New York 2006

Konfiguration, Form, Dimension und Proportion, Fassaden und Texturen, Farb- und Materialwahl, Beleuchtung, Bepflanzung, öffentliche Brunnen, Möblierung, Beschattung und Regenschutz, künstlerische Ausgestaltung, Zugang zu infrastrukturellen Gelegenheiten wie Telefon, W-LAN, elektrischer Strom usw.), die beispielhaft in kultureller, regionaler und historischer Betrachtung differenziert werden können; über Jahrtausende und Jahrhunderte menschlicher Siedlungstätigkeit sind unterschiedliche Formen und Typen von Plätzen, Straßen und Gassen entstanden; öffentliche Räume beinhalten Brücken und Durchgänge, sie umschließen auch „Wasserstraßen"; in einer multiskalaren Betrachtung öffentlicher Räume treten über die verschiedenen Maßstabsebenen unterschiedliche Details zu Tage, die Erkenntnisgegenstand verschiedener Disziplinen sind.

Öffentliche Räume tragen zumeist – sowohl ober- als auch unterirdisch – die wesentliche räumliche Infrastruktur (Energie, Ver- und Entsorgung – Wasser, Kanal, öffentlicher Verkehr, Telekommunikation usw.); sie sind Bewegungsraum für individuelle Verkehrsteilnehmerinnen und -teilnehmer in verschiedenen Modalitätsformen (zu Fuß, mit dem Rad, mit dem Skateboard, mit dem Automobil, in multimodaler Form usw.); sie grenzen an halböffentliche und private Räume mit verschiedenen Nutzungen und bilden im Verbund unterschiedliche Straßenräume und Straßenraumtypen (zum Beispiel Geschäfts- und Einkaufsstraßen).

Öffentliche Räume sind Gegenstand der *Raumproduktion* und einer „Ökonomie der Aufmerksamkeit"[15]; sie haben eine wichtige stadtklimatische und stadtökologische Bedeutung.

Diese Assoziationen und Interpretationen ließen sich fortsetzen und erweitern. Öffentliche Räume sind gleichsam die zentralen Nervenbahnen, Arterien und Venen des Siedlungs- und Stadtkörpers: Sie verbinden die öffentlichen Gebäude, führen zu den großen Bahnhöfen und umschließen die Haltestellen öffentlicher Verkehre, sie führen zu den Sport- und Erholungseinrichtungen, zu Park- und Freizeitanlagen, sie tragen die wesentliche räumliche Infrastruktur. Ihre ansprechende Gestaltung ist Voraussetzung für ein gedeihliches gesellschaftliches Leben und für wirtschaftliche Entwicklung.

> „Bilder sind wahrgenommene Augenblicke, gewonnen aus der Erkenntniswelt, durch Selektion und Verdichtung des Gesehenen. Die Zusammenführung von äußeren Eindrücken (Erlebnissen) und inneren Vorstellungen ist ein komplexer, in der Zeit fortschreitender Prozeß. Räumliche Inhalte werden zu bildhaften Ereignissen."[16]

Öffentliche Räume sind Gegenstand intensiver, bildhafter Raumwahrnehmung in statischer und dynamischer Betrachtung (Raumsequenzen). Forschungslaborräume ermöglichen – bei intensiver Befassung und räumlicher Erkundung – faszinierende Einblicke in die Vielfalt öffentlicher Räu-

Stevens, Quentin: *The Ludic City: Exploring the Potential of Public Spaces*. London/New York 2007

Staeheli, Lynn/Mitchell, Don: *The People's Property? Power, Politics and the Public*. New York 2008

Hou, Jeff: *Insurgent Public Space. Guerilla Urbanism and the Remaking of Contemporary Cities*. London/New York 2010

Knierbein, Sabine: *Die Produktion zentraler öffentlicher Räume in der Aufmerksamkeitsökonomie. Ästhetische, ökonomische und mediale Restrukturierungen durch gestaltwirksame Koalitionen in Berlin seit 1980*. Wiesbaden 2010

Madanipour, Ali: *Whose Public Space?* London/New York 2010

Bridge, Gary/Watson, Sophie: *The New Blackwell Companion to the City*. Chichester 2011

Hou, Jeff: *Transcultural Cities. Border Crossing and Placemaking*. New York 2013

Tonkiss, Fran: *Cities by Design: The Social Life of Urban Form*. Cambridge 2013

Madanipour, Ali/Knierbein, Sabine/Degros, Aglaée: *Public Space and the Challenges of Urban Transformation in Europe*. London/New York 2014

Tornaghi, Chiara/Knierbein, Sabine: *Public Space and Relational Perspectives. New Challenges for Architecture and Planning*. London/New York 2015

The city of Vienna is home to numerous activities in public spaces. The relevant sub-department at the municipal department responsible for Urban Development and Urban Planning (MA (i.e. "Magistratsabteilung") 18) was named "Landscape and Public Space." Many publications are available, divided according to the following themes: analyses before planning, quality of life, principles of social space planning, spatial typologies, safety in the public domain, social processes in public space, urban sociology, city district structures, and strategies and concepts for public spaces.[18]

The portraits of the dissertations within the 2013–2016 curriculum of the International Doctoral College "Spatial Research Lab" show a pleasing range of points of contact with the terms "public space" and "experimental space," for example: "From urban interventions to urban practice. Effects of artistic district development—impulses for urban planning?" (Renée Tribble); "OPEN DESIGN—Integrating dynamic change into landscape architecture projects" (Katarina Bajc); "Renaissance of photographic wallpaper in the city. Visual landscape surrogates—a solution for densely populated areas" (Jonas Bellingrodt).

So that the transformation of urban landscapes and an inward development of settlement systems can succeed, "experimental space" must be opened up, in which ideas can be explored in an uncomplicated manner and initially without consequences, and in which problem-based clear hypotheses for spatial development can be set out, strictly monitored, and, if necessary, even rejected again, in order to explore potential solutions and approaches through a step-by-step process of justified "design" and "rejection" of ideas. The International Doctoral College "Spatial Research Lab" was and is to a certain extent such an "experimental space."

me, beispielhaft bezogen auf Orts- und Stadtbild, Orts- und Stadtgestalt, Siedlungs- und Stadtstruktur und vielfältige Prozesse der Raumnutzung. Diese Möglichkeit bot sich im Rahmen gemeinsamer Erkundungen im Verlauf des Doktorandenkollegs: Diese Laborräume sind reale Belege vergangener und gegenwärtiger Raumvorstellungen, welche durch zahllose und wiederkehrende Handlungen Realität geworden sind. Stabile Nutzungsprozesse über die Zeit führen tendenziell zu stabilen räumlichen Strukturen.[17]

Die wissenschaftliche Auseinandersetzung mit dem öffentlichen Raum ist erfreulich intensiv und vielfältig. So wurde etwa 2008/2009 an der Technischen Universität Wien im Department für Raumplanung mit großzügiger Unterstützung durch die Stadt Wien eine Forschungsgruppe „Stadtkultur und öffentlicher Raum" samt Stiftungsgastprofessur eingerichtet. Eine Auswahl an Publikationen[18] zeigt beispielhaft die Vielfalt des Forschungsinteresses am öffentlichen Raum (in chronologischer Reihenfolge):

Madanipour, Ali: *Public and Private Spaces of the City*. London 2003

Mitchell, Don: *The Right to the City: Social Justice and the Fight for Public Space*. New York 2003

Tonkiss, Fran: *Space, the City and Social Theory*. Cambridge 2005

Low, Setha/Smith, Neil: *The Politics of Public Space*. London/New York 2005

Frank, Karin A./Stevens, Quentin: *Loose Space: Possibility and Diversity in Urban Life*. London/New York 2006

Watson, Sophie: *City Publics. The (Dis)enchantments of Public Encounters*. London/New York 2006 2006

Stevens, Quentin: *The Ludic City: Exploring the Potential of Public Spaces*. London/New York 2007

Staeheli, Lynn/Mitchell, Don: *The People's Property? Power, Politics and the Public*. New York 2008

Hou, Jeff: *Insurgent Public Space. Guerilla Urbanism and the Remaking of Contemporary Cities*. London/New York 2010

Knierbein, Sabine: *Die Produktion zentraler öffentlicher Räume in der Aufmerksamkeitsökonomie. Ästhetische, ökonomische und mediale Restrukturierungen durch gestaltwirksame Koalitionen in Berlin seit 1980*. Wiesbaden 2010

Madanipour, Ali: *Whose Public Space?*. London/New York 2010

Bridge, Gary/Watson, Sophie: *The New Blackwell Companion to the City*. Chichester 2011

Hou, Jeff: *Transcultural Cities. Border Crossing and Placemaking*. New York 2013

Tonkiss, Fran: *Cities by Design: The Social Life of Urban Form*. Cambridge 2013

Madanipour, Ali/Knierbein, Sabine/Degros, Aglaée: *Public Space and the Challenges of Urban Transformation in Europe*. London/New York 2014

Tornaghi, Chiara/Knierbein, Sabine: *Public Space and Relational Perspectives. New Challenges for Architecture and Planning*. London/New York 2015

2 Usage traces in public
space, skaters
2 Nutzungsspuren
im öffentlichen Raum,
Skater

Die Stadt Wien entfaltet hinsichtlich öffentlicher Räume zahlreiche Aktivitäten, das zuständige Referat in der für Stadtentwicklung und Stadtplanung zuständigen Magistratsabteilung (MA 18) wurde in „Landschaft und öffentlicher Raum" unbenannt. Zahlreiche Publikationen, gegliedert nach folgenden Themenbereichen, stehen zur Verfügung (in alphabetischer Reihenfolge): Analysen vor der Planung, Aufenthaltsqualitäten, Grundlagen sozialraumorientierter Planung, Raumtypologien, Sicherheit im öffentlichen Raum, Soziale Prozesse im öffentlichen Raum, Stadtsoziologie, Stadtteilstrukturen, Strategien und Konzepte für öffentliche Räume.[19]

Die Porträts der Dissertationen des Internationalen Doktorandenkollegs „Forschungslabor Raum", Curriculum 2013 bis 2016 lassen erfreulich vielfältige Berührungspunkte mit den Begriffen „Öffentlicher Raum" und „Möglichkeitsräume" erkennen, beispielhaft: „Von Urbanen Interventionen zu Urbaner Praxis. Effekte künstlerischer Quartiersentwicklung – Impulse für die Stadtplanung?" (Renée Tribble); „OPEN DESIGN – Integration von dynamischem Wandel in landschaftsarchitektonischen Werken" (Katarina Bajc); „Renaissance der Fototapete in der Stadt. Visuelle Landschaftssurrogate – eine Lösung für dicht besiedelte Areale" (Jonas Bellingrodt).

Damit die Transformation urbaner Landschaften und eine Innenentwicklung der Siedlungssysteme gelingen können, müssen „Möglichkeitsräume" eröffnet werden, in denen unkompliziert und zunächst ohne Konsequenzen Ideen erkundet werden können, in denen problembasiert klare Hypothesen zur räumlichen Entwicklung aufgestellt, streng geprüft und mitunter auch wieder verworfen werden können, um in einem schrittweisen Vorgang des begründeten „Entwerfens" und ebenso zu begründenden „Verwerfens" der Ideen mögliche Lösungsrichtungen und -ansätze zu erkunden. Ein Stück weit ist und war das Internationale Doktorandenkolleg „Forschungslabor Raum" ein solcher „Möglichkeitsraum".

In der realen Welt braucht es ebenfalls Räume, in denen experimentiert werden kann und in denen Möglichkeiten zukünftiger Raumnutzung – zunächst als Ausnahme zu bestehenden Regimes der Raumnutzung – erprobt werden können. Der öffentliche Raum – im Übergang zu halböffentlichen und privaten Räumen – ist die ideale „Bühne" für solche Experimente. Diese können – ergänzend zu Experimenten in der realen Welt – in Teilaspekten auch im virtuellen Raum simuliert werden oder durch Überlagerung realer und virtueller Welten Anschaulichkeit erhalten. Mittels verschiedener Methoden raumbezogener Simulation kann die Raumverträglichkeit konzipierter Eingriffe in die reale Welt vor deren Realisierung erkundet und nach Möglichkeit verbessert werden. In diesem Zusammenhang sind „bildgebende Verfahren", die zunächst strategischen Überblick zu den jeweiligen Problemstellungen, vertiefenden Einblick in Probleme und Schlüsselräume und sodann Ausblick in Lösungsrichtungen bieten, unerlässlich. ▶1, 2, 3, 4

In the real world, spaces are also required where one can experiment and where possibilities of future spatial usage can be explored, initially as an exception to existing spatial usage schemes. Public space—at the transition to semi-public and private spaces—is the ideal "stage" for such experiments. These can also be partially simulated in virtual space, to complement experiments in the real world, or be illuminated by layering real and virtual worlds. By means of various methods of spatial simulation, the spatial compatibility of conceived interventions into the real world can be explored and, if necessary, improved before realisation. In this regard, "imaging processes," which provide a strategic overview of the respective issues, more in-depth insights into problems and key areas, and then indicate potential solutions, are essential. ▶ **1, 2, 3, 4**

Language and the concept of space, two examples

The word "space," *chóros* (χῶρος) in Greek, equivalent to *chóra* (χώρα), was already used in the epic Ilias by Homer (850 BC). Its meaning was originally "area, region, territory." Later, it gained the meaning of "a special locality in the region" or a "particular place", where certain events took place, without being mistaken for the term "place." Even later still, the two words *chóros* and *chóra* were endowed with different meanings: the word *chóra* is mentioned in texts by Thucydides as *choríon* (diminutive form of *chóra*), but is also used with the meaning of "area." In time, this meaning was restricted and the word *chorion* or *chóra* referred concretely to the town and the village. This meaning exists up until today in the modern Greek language. The word *chóros* (χῶρος) s also used to refer to the space in an ancient Greek theatre where the choir dances and sings (dance = *chorós* (χορός)). However, this derivation cannot be verified. One explanation states that the word *chorós* (χορός) = dance originates from the root *cher* = hand, as the dancers held hands. The word *chóros* (χῶρος) is used in modern Greek with the meaning of "space, place," and by extension: *chorotaxia* (χωροταξία)= choros + taxis = arrangement of space = spatial planning. (Konstantinos Fisoglou)[19]

In Croatian and in Serbian, *prostor* means space: this lexeme is known to all Slavic language families and reaches back to the ancient Slavonic and Old Church Slavonic languages. It is derived from **sterti, (today: prostirati)*, which in turn goes back to the Latin *sternere* (to extend, stretch out). The Slavic concept of space therefore refers to extension, which does not have to be limited. *Prostor* can refer either to an unlimited spatial expanse or a clearly defined, more restricted space, i. e. a delimited surface. The philosophical meaning of the lexeme also represents the basic form or category of human existence (space and time). The term "public space" is expressed by means of attribution: *javni prostor* (javno = public). Another term for space in the sense of a region, a territory, or a definable geographical unit, is the lexeme *područje*. From an etymological point of view, this term is derived from the combination of pod + ruka = under the hand. The thought

3 *Gaining an overview,*
Karlsruhe and Vienna
3 *Überblick gewinnen,*
Karlsruhe und Wien

Sprache und Raumbegriff, zwei Beispiele

Das Wort „Raum" auf Griechisch *chóros* (χῶρος), gleichwertig mit *chóra* (χῶρα), wird bereits im Epos *Ilias* von Homer (850 v. Chr.) verwendet. Seine Bedeutung war ursprünglich „Gegend, Gebiet, Region". Später bekommt es die Bedeutung von „besonderer Ort des Landes" oder „bestimmter Ort", wo manche Ereignisse stattfinden, ohne aber mit dem Begriff „Ort" verwechselt zu werden. Noch später wurden die beiden Worte *chóros* und *chóra* mit unterschiedlichen Bedeutungen versehen: Das Wort *chóra* wird

concept behind this lexeme therefore does not so much express extension and expanse, but rather an attribution and possible delimitation. What fits "under the hand" can, on the one hand, have a particular owner (whose hand?), and, on the other hand, vary in size (how big is the hand?). The semantic meaning of the term područje is therefore often used also for administrative units, which is not the case for prostor. (Katharina Tyran)[20]

bereits in den Texten von Thukydides als *choríon* (Verkleinerung von *chóra*) erwähnt, aber auch mit der Bedeutung „Gegend" verwendet. Mit der Zeit wurde diese Bedeutung eingegrenzt und das Wort *chorion* oder *chóra* bezeichnete konkret die Stadt und das Dorf. Diese Bedeutung existiert bis heute in der neugriechischen Sprache. Das Wort *chóros* (χώρος) wird auch für die Bezeichnung des Platzes im altgriechischen Theater, wo der Chor tanzt und singt, verwendet (Tanz = *chorós* (χορός)). Dies ist aber nicht nachweisbar. Eine Erklärung besagt, dass das Wort *chorós* (χορός) = Tanz aus der Wurzel *cher* = Hand stammt, da sich die Tänzer an den Händen gehalten haben. Das Wort *chóros* (χώρος) wird im Neugriechischen mit der Bedeutung „Raum, Platz" verwendet; weiterführend: *chorotaxia* (χωροταξία) = *choros* + *taxis* = Ordnung des Raumes = Raumordnung.
(Konstantinos Fisoglou)[20]

Im Kroatischen und Serbischen bezeichnet *prostor* den Raum: Dieses Lexem ist allen slawischen Sprachfamilien bekannt und reicht bis in die urslawische und altkirchenslawische Sprache zurück. Abgeleitet ist es von **sterti, (heute: prostirati)*, das wiederum auf das lateinische *sternere* (verbreiten, ausdehnen) zurückgeht. Der Raumbegriff im Slawischen bezieht sich damit also auf die Ausdehnung, die noch nicht begrenzt sein muss. *prostor* kann dabei sowohl eine unbegrenzte Raumausdehnung als auch einen klar definierten, engeren Raum, eine abgegrenzte Oberfläche bezeichnen. Des Weiteren steht das Lexem in seiner philosophischen Bedeutung auch für die Grundform oder Kategorie der menschlichen Existenz (Raum und Zeit). Der Begriff „öffentlicher Raum" wird ebenso wie im Deutschen durch Attribuierung ausgedrückt: *javni prostor* (*javno* = öffentlich). Ein weiterer Begriff für Raum im Sinne einer Region, eines Territoriums, einer bestimmbaren geografischen Einheit ist das Lexem *podru je*. Etymologisch betrachtet stammt dieser Begriff aus der Verbindung *pod* + *ruka* = unter die Hand. Das Gedankenkonzept hinter diesem Lexem drückt also weniger die Ausdehnung und Weite aus, sondern eher die Zugehörigkeitsbestimmung und mögliche Abgrenzung: Was „unter die Hand" passt, kann einerseits einen bestimmten Besitzer haben (wessen Hand?), andererseits in der Größe variieren (wie groß ist die Hand?). Der Begriff *podru je* wird daher in seiner semantischen Bedeutung oft auch auf Verwaltungseinheiten angewandt, was bei *prostor* nicht der Fall ist.
(Katharina Tyran)[21]

Stuttgart, 20.03.2014

Hamburg, 21.11.2013

Belgrad Belgrade, 13.06.2014

Karlsruhe, 23.06.2015

179

OPEN DESIGN
Integrating dynamic change into landscape architecture projects

KATARINA BAJC

The awareness that natural systems, as well as society and its requirements, are constantly changing has a significant influence on environmental design. Contemporary landscape architects have been influenced in particular by *non-equilibrium* theories—theories of ecological imbalance—which state that ecosystems develop unpredictably to a certain extent. The development path that they follow is often not determined, but probabilistic and multidirectional. Adaptability is therefore important for such self-regulating and open systems, in order to enable biological diversity and promote the health of our environment.

Adaptability and dynamic natural processes are therefore increasingly becoming an integral aspect of landscape designs and part of the sustainability agenda. Spontaneous ecological change has become an active design tool, instead of being an undesirable side effect when working with organic material. Consequently, contemporary concepts in landscape architecture take account of biological succession, the spontaneous processes of growth and decay, and slow or rapid spontaneous adaptation to new circumstances.

These landscapes often display a transitory, disturbed, and unfinished appearance and, in many cases, do not appeal to the aesthetic preferences of the user, which may include scenic aesthetics or the aesthetics of care. Traditional landscape design tools that abstracted the organic material, for example by reshaping plants or suppressing natural processes, are losing their validity due to the influence of ecological theories. Traditional design elements are therefore no longer compatible with contemporary aims of supporting dynamic change in designed landscapes. For this reason, new design strategies must be found that support ecological goals and are, at the same time, capable of stimulating strong aesthetic experiences in the landscape that trigger compassion and a sense of attachment to the environment.

This thesis analyses various design approaches by several landscape architects based in the US and Europe with regard to their flexibility and adaptability to natural dynamic change. What kind of aesthetic effect do these works have, compared to classical designs that often follow a set scheme? Based on formal and contextual analyses, spatial structures are identified that ensure anchor points, identity, orientation, and a lasting image in a designed landscape that is constantly changing. Qualitative interviews are designed to establish which visual, bodily, and multisensory perceptions, prompted by ecological dynamics, have a particular effect on the users of these landscapes to make it a pleasant, stimulating, or memorable experience. A typological catalogue of design methods and implemented examples will serve future designers as a reference work when combining ecological and aesthetic aims in design.

OPEN DESIGN
Integration von dynamischem Wandel in landschaftsarchitektonischen Werken

KATARINA BAJC

Das Bewusstsein, dass sich natürliche Systeme sowie die Gesellschaft und ihre Bedürfnisse ständig verändern, hat einen großen Einfluss auf die Gestaltung der Umwelt. Zeitgenössische Landschaftsarchitekten wurden insbesondere durch die *non-equilibrium*-Theorien – die Ungleichgewichtstheorien der Ökologie – beeinflusst. Danach entstehen Ökosysteme gewissermaßen unvorhersehbar, da sie oft keinem bestimmten, vorgegebenen Entwicklungspfad folgen, sondern sich probabilistisch und multidirektional entwickeln. Wandlungsfähigkeit ist somit für solche selbstregulierenden und offenen Systeme wesentlich. Sie ermöglicht die biologische Vielfalt und unterstützt die Gesundheit unserer Umwelt.

Anpassungsfähigkeit und Prozesse, die für natürliche Systeme typisch sind, werden deshalb immer stärker zu einem integralen Bestandteil von Landschaftsentwürfen. Anstelle eines ungewünschten Nebeneffekts bei der Arbeit mit organischem Material wird das *Prozesshafte* zu einem Instrument. Zeitgenössische Konzepte in der Landschaftsarchitektur beziehen infolgedessen die biologische Sukzession, die spontanen Prozesse von Wachstum und Verfall, von Mutationen sowie die langsame oder plötzliche Anpassung an neue Umstände mit ein.

Das Erscheinungsbild dieser Landschaften wirkt oft transitorisch, gestört und unvollendet und kann sich nur schwer an die ästhetischen Präferenzen des Nutzers wie zum Beispiel szenische Ästhetik oder Ästhetik der Pflege anpassen. Traditionelle gestalterische Werkzeuge, welche die Landschaft oder organisches Material abstrahierten, beispielsweise durch Umformung von Pflanzen und Unterdrückung natürlicher Prozesse, haben dennoch ihre Geltung durch den Einfluss ökologischer Theorien verloren. Die traditionellen Gestaltungselemente sind mit zeitgenössischen Zielen und dynamischem Wandel nicht mehr kompatibel. Deshalb müssen neue Entwurfsstrategien gefunden werden, die die ökologischen Ziele unterstützen und gleichzeitig die Fähigkeit besitzen, starke ästhetische Erlebnisse in der Landschaft mit neuen Mitteln anzuregen.

Verschiedene Ansätze unterschiedlicher Landschaftsarchitekten werden in der Arbeit hinsichtlich ihrer Flexibilität und Anpassungsfähigkeit an den dynamischen Wandel analysiert. Welche Art von Auswirkung in Bezug auf ihre Ästhetik erzeugen diese Werke im Vergleich zu klassischen und damit oftmals festgelegten Entwürfen? Anhand formaler Analysen werden räumliche Strukturen identifiziert, die für visuelle Ankerpunkte, Identität, Orientierung und dauerhaftes Image sorgen, in einem Entwurfsplan, der sich ständig verändert. Mithilfe qualitativer Interviews soll festgestellt werden, welche optischen, körperlichen und multisensorischen Wahrnehmungen, die von ökologischen Dynamiken ausgelöst werden, auf die Nutzer dieser Landschaften besonders einwirken und Vergnügen erregen. Ein typologischer Katalog von Entwurfsmethoden soll künftig Entwerfern als Nachschlagewerk bei der gestalterischen Verbindung ökologischer und ästhetischer Ziele dienen.

RENAISSANCE OF PHOTOGRAPHIC WALLPAPER IN THE CITY
Visual landscape surrogates—a solution for densely populated areas

JONAS BELLINGRODT

We love authenticity, like driving through the prairie or through a surging stream in an off-road vehicle. Advertising messages of this kind with a wealth of such images are presented to us daily in the city on façades and large-format screens. These images of the landscape evoke a yearning that can scarcely be fulfilled in reality. Aesthetic access to nature is a significant factor determining the quality of life in the city. The most important source of perception are visual stimuli. How we see our living environment is the result of social change that has been occurring for centuries, over the course of which there has been an increasing loss of nature. The mastery of natural forces was followed by a period in which more attention was paid to the beauty and sublimity of nature. The English landscape garden, for example, emerged in the eighteenth century as a walk-through, built-up landscape scene, an image of beautiful nature. How do we interact today with images of nature in the city and what design potential does this harbour for the future?

For people today, the image of nature is more important than nature itself. Digital media produce pictorial worlds whose effect can scarcely be avoided. The possibility to integrate nature as a motif on photographic wallpaper or as a built artefact into the cityscape is put to significant commercial use. It also represents a strategy for city planning, in order to provide at least visual access to nature in densely built-up areas. This replacement for living nature satisfies a basic need for city dwellers, visual contact with nature, so as to counteract the controlled environment of the built-up city dominated by technology.

To ensure that pictorial applications on buildings do not erode perceptive faculties, they must be specifically selected and designed for the particular location and not be applied randomly according to advertisements.

Depicting nature on façades is not a present-day invention. This way of representing nature has existed since antiquity. However, in contemporary landscape architecture, this kind of design has hitherto been rejected, as nature is merely simulated, instead of having the function of integrating nature into the city, which should be its aim. In view of limited resources, in future we will not have the luxury of turning down this form of surface design.

Landscape architects, planners, and urban developers are already designing images and spatial scenarios, in order to have a positive influence on the future development of particular spaces. If images within spaces change the perception of the user on a one-to-one basis, then they can also stimulate a transformation process in the mind. Sparking discussions with photographic wallpaper and simulating nature in the city as a public experience represent a previously unused method. Although it is a manipulation of the senses, it is also an extension of the repertoire of the planning discipline when actively designing aesthetic transformation processes.

RENAISSANCE DER FOTOTAPETE IN DER STADT
Visuelle Landschaftssurrogate – eine Lösung für dicht besiedelte Areale

JONAS BELLINGRODT

Wir lieben das Authentische. Mit dem Geländewagen durch die Prärie oder durch den rauschenden Bachlauf fahren. Bildgewaltig begegnen uns alltäglich solche Werbebotschaften in der Stadt, an Fassaden, auf großformatigen Bildschirmen. Diese Landschaftsbilder wecken Sehnsüchte die sich in Realität kaum noch einlösen lassen. Der ästhetische Zugang zur Natur ist ein wesentlicher Faktor, der die Lebensqualität in der Stadt bestimmt. Die wichtigste Wahrnehmungsquelle ist dabei der visuelle Reiz. Wie wir unsere Lebensumwelt sehen, ist das Resultat eines bereits Jahrhunderte andauernden gesellschaftlichen Wandels, in dessen Verlauf wir einen zunehmenden Naturverlust verzeichnen. Nach der Beherrschung der Naturgewalten folgte eine Hinwendung zu dem Schönen und Erhabenen der Natur. Der englische Landschaftsgarten beispielsweise entstand im 18. Jahrhundert als ein begehbares gebautes Landschaftsbild, ein Abbild der schönen Natur. Wie interagieren wir heute mit Abbildungen von Natur in der Stadt und welche Gestaltungsmöglichkeiten liegen darin für die Zukunft verborgen?

Für den Menschen ist das Bild der Natur heute wichtiger als die Natur selbst. Digitale Medien produzieren Bildwelten, deren Wirkung man sich kaum entziehen kann. Die Möglichkeiten, Natur als Motiv einer Fototapete oder als gebautes Artefakt in das Stadtbild zu integrieren, werden von der Werbung massenhaft genutzt.

Sie stellen aber auch für die Stadtplanung eine Strategie dar, in baulich verdichten Gebieten zumindest einen visuellen Zugang zur Natur herzustellen. Dieser Ersatz für die lebendige Natur befriedigt ein Grundbedürfnis des Stadtbewohners: den visuellen Kontakt zur Natur als Ausgleich zur technisch beherrschten, kontrollierten Umwelt der gebauten Stadt. Wenn Bildapplikationen an Bauwerken nicht zur Erosion der Wahrnehmungsfähigkeit beitragen sollen, dann müssen sie für den jeweiligen Ort spezifisch ausgesucht und gestaltet werden, anstatt wie in der Werbung beliebig.

Natur auf Fassaden abzubilden ist keine Erfindung unserer Zeit, diese Art der Naturdarstellung existiert schon seit der Antike. In der aktuellen Landschaftsarchitektur wird diese Art der Gestaltung aber bisher abgelehnt, da Natur nur vorgetäuscht wird, anstatt die Funktion lebendiger Natur in die Stadt zu integrieren, was das Ziel sein sollte. Angesichts mangelnder Ressourcen können wir uns den Luxus in Zukunft nicht erlauben, auf diese Art der Oberflächengestaltung zu verzichten.

Landschaftsarchitekten, Planer und Stadtgestalter entwerfen bereits Bilder und räumliche Szenarien, um zukünftige Entwicklungen eines bestimmten Raumes positiv zu beeinflussen. Wenn Bilder im Raum die Wahrnehmung der Nutzer eins zu eins verändern, wird damit ein Transformationsprozess in den Köpfen angeregt. Mit Fototapete Diskussionen anzustoßen, Natur in der Stadt öffentlich erfahrbar zu simulieren, stellt eine bisher nicht genutzte Methode dar. Es handelt sich zwar um eine Manipulation der Sinne, aber gleichzeitig auch um eine Erweiterung des Repertoires der planenden Zunft, Transformationsprozesse ästhetisch aktiv zu gestalten.

FROM URBAN INTER-VENTIONS TO URBAN PRACTICE
An alternative way of neighbourhood development?

RENÉE TRIBBLE

Urban interventions are now widely used as a description for stepping in and changing urban spaces with artistic and, in some cases, participative methods for a temporary period of time. Having their origin in art, urban interventions have long since gone beyond a brief moment of temporary interaction in favour of an urban practice that criticizes the failure to incorporate everyday knowledge into urban development processes. Urban practice claims to practice an alternative urban planning that enables specific local characteristics to be taken into account and local residents to participate in the planning. However, this practice is often still associated solely with the fields of art and culture in the context of art festivals or temporary, exceptional circumstances. The achieved results, on the other hand, indicate a long-term potential that would appear to be worthwhile for the development of neighbourhoods.

Laws, regulations, and political targets, along with defined areas of responsibility and limited decision-making powers, ensure that creative involvement with the authorities is deemed to fail. Urban practice, on the other hand, creates an opportunity to act, despite normative restrictions in everyday urban planning. Does this also change planning practice? What does this mean for the future planning of urban development processes? Which fields of practice, involved parties, and disciplines must be taken into account when developing districts?

Six european case studies show the characteristics and potentials of urban practice relevant for neighbourhood development. Based on the case study *PlanBude* in Hamburg, the decision-making processes and areas of responsibility within urban practice cooperating with municipal planning are analysed and the various involved parties and their roles in urban practice and communal planning are identified. The effects of urban practice on communal planning activity, defined according to the *PlanBude* process, are categorised and serve later on as a critical examination model in order to differentiate and verify the conclusions reached on the basis of the exemplary cases studied. A conscious differentiation of the various starting situations could show a range of possibilities for neighbourhood development that takes local everyday knowledge into account. This could provide a valuable contribution to the understanding of planning disciplines, as well as to the practice of neighbourhood development, which can apply urban practice impulses to planning and the local community. The underlying principle here could be summarised as: Urban interventions created through art and understood through planning.

VON URBANEN INTERVENTIONEN ZU URBANER PRAXIS
Eine alternative Quartiersentwicklung parallel zur Stadtplanung?

RENÉE TRIBBLE

Urbane Interventionen haben sich als Beschreibung für das Einschreiten in und Verändern von städtischen Räumen mit künstlerischen und zum Teil partizipativen Mitteln für einen temporären Zeitraum etabliert. Ursprünglich aus der Kunst kommend gibt es mittlerweile eine große Bandbreite an Urbanen Interventionen, die längst aus dem kurzeitigen Moment der temporären Interaktion herausgetreten sind. Vielmehr hat sich eine Urbane Praxis gebildet, die sich aus einem künstlerischen Selbstverständnis heraus kritisch mit dem fehlenden Einbezug von Alltagswissen in Stadtentwicklungsprozesse auseinandersetzt. Urbane Praxis reklamiert für sich, eine alternative Stadtplanung zu praktizieren, die eine auf ortsspezifische Charakteristika eingehende und mit der lokalen Bewohnerschaft geplante Stadtentwicklung ermöglicht. Diese Urbane Praxis findet jedoch nach wie vor zumeist im Rahmen von Kunstfestivals oder temporären Ausnahmezuständen statt. Die Ergebnisse, die erzielt werden, zeugen aber von einem langfristigen Potenzial, das für die Entwicklung von Quartieren lohnenswert erscheint.

Gesetze, Vorschriften und politische Zielsetzungen sorgen neben abgesteckten Zuständigkeitsbereichen und beschränkten Handlungsfreiräumen dafür, dass kreatives Engagement in Behördengängen scheitert. Urbane Praxis hingegen schafft Handlungsspielräume trotz normativer Zwänge im Stadtplanungsalltag. Verändert sich dadurch auch die Planungspraxis? Was bedeutet dies für die zukünftige Gestaltung von Stadtentwicklungsprozessen? Welche Handlungsfelder, Akteure und Disziplinen müssten bei der Entwicklung von Quartieren berücksichtigt werden?

Anhand von sechs europäischen Fallbeispielen werden die für die Entwicklung von Quartieren relevanten Eigenschaften und Potenziale Urbaner Praxis untersucht. Am Fallbeispiel *PlanBude* in Hamburg werden die Entscheidungsabläufe und Verantwortungsbereiche innerhalb einer in Kooperation mit Planung praktizierenden Urbanen Praxis analysiert und die unterschiedlichen Akteure und ihre Rollen in Urbaner Praxis und kommunaler Planung herausgearbeitet. Die anhand des PlanBuden-Prozesses definierten Effekte und Wirkungsebenen Urbaner Praxis auf kommunales Planungshandeln werden kategorisiert und dienen anschließend als kritisches Untersuchungsraster, um die getroffenen Schlussfolgerungen anhand der untersuchten Fallbeispiele zu differenzieren und verifizieren. Eine bewusste Differenzierung der unterschiedlichen Ausgangslagen könnte vielfältige Möglichkeiten für eine Quartiersentwicklung mit Einbezug des lokalen Alltagswissens aufzeigen. Damit könnte ein wertvoller Beitrag für das Selbstverständnis der Planungsdisziplinen wie für die Praxis der Quartiersentwicklung gewonnen werden, der die Impulse Urbaner Praxis auf die Planung und die Bewohnerschaft zu übertragen vermag. Grundsätzlich scheint hierfür zu gelten: Was Kunst macht und Planung versteht.

URBAN (SPACE) PRODUCERS
STADT(RAUM)-PRODUZENTEN

URBAN TRANSFORMERS

MICHAEL KOCH

Urban/Rural

The debate about urban landscape transformation includes not only the question of target images, but also the question of influential factors and mutual effects. Disciplinary conventions regarding the ideal city of the future have become more difficult, at the latest since the onset of the postmodern era. Since then, doubt has been cast on the omnipotent claims of urban design's supposed certainty about what constitutes the right viable city.[1,2]

In addition, there are increasing insights into which parties and which constellations actually influence urban development. The "real existing city" reflects the possibilities and conditions with regard to building the "ideal city." The title of the doctoral college "Urban *Landscape* Transformation" consciously includes the category of *landscape*. The modern notion of *Stadtlandschaft (urban landscape)* represents an attempt, especially in the 1940s and 1950s, to identify the observed transformation, assimilation, and pervasion processes of the city and the landscape as a whole and to make them the basis for a new guiding model. Looking back, this revealed further "rurban"[3] parties and influential factors that make the "merging of city and landscape"[4] easier to explain in terms of a new urbanity. In this context, the term "rurbanity" seeks to capture the growing phenomenon of the convergence of rural and urban lifestyles.

The magazine *Stadtaspekte – die dritte Seite der Stadt*[5] *(Aspects of the city – the third side of the city)*, which has been published at irregular intervals since 2012, can be taken as representative published evidence of how interdisciplinary groups are vying for a contemporary and appropriate understanding of the city and for participation in the processes of change. Landscape elements and landscape territories are of course also part of this. The facts and arguments in the new building culture reports from the Bundesstiftung Baukultur (Federal Foundation for Building Culture) contribute to identifying the developmental forces and the potential of the city and landscape. A special edition of *Stadtaspekte*, with key messages from the building culture report 1, became a magazine for building culture: "Neue Räume"[6] (New Spaces).

The building culture report 2, "City and Landscape," showed the rurban living environments beyond the core cities. Awareness of the interpenetration and dependence of rural and urban everyday life will add a necessary new dimension to urbanist discourses fixated on the core city. The major-

URBANE TRANS-FORMATOREN

MICHAEL KOCH

StadtLand

Die Auseinandersetzung mit urbanen Transformationslandschaften schließt die Frage nach Zielbildern ebenso ein wie die Frage nach Wirkungskräften und Wirkungszusammenhängen. Disziplinäre Konventionen über das anzustrebende Ideal einer Stadt der Zukunft sind spätestens mit der Postmoderne schwieriger geworden. Infrage steht seither der omnipotente Gestaltungsanspruch der Stadt auf Grundlage vermeintlicher Gewissheit darüber, was denn die richtige zukunftsfähige Stadt sei.[1,2]

Hinzu kommen zunehmende Erkenntnisse darüber, welche Akteure und welche Konstellationen die Stadtentwicklung tatsächlich beeinflussen. Die „real existierende Stadt" spiegelt die Möglichkeiten und Bedingungen, die „ideale Stadt" zu bauen. Der Titel des Doktorandenkollegs „Urbane Transformations*landschaften*" schließt bewusst die Kategorie *Landschaft* mit ein: Mit dem modernen Begriff der *Stadtlandschaft* wurde besonders in den 1940er und 1950er Jahren versucht, die beobachteten Transformations-, Angleichungs- und Durchdringungsprozesse von Stadt und Landschaft gesamthaft zu fassen und einem neuen Leitbild zugrunde zu legen. Mit zeitlichem Abstand betrachtet, sind damit weitere „rurbane"[3] Akteure und Wirkungskräfte sichtbar geworden, die das „Verschmelzen von Stadt und Landschaft"[4] in Richtung auf eine neue Urbanität erklärbarer machen. In diesem Kontext versucht der Begriff der „Rurbanität", das zunehmend zu beobachtende Phänomen der Konvergenz ruraler und urbaner Lebensstile einzufangen.

Das seit 2012 in loser Folge erscheinende Magazin *Stadtaspekte – die dritte Seite der Stadt*[5] kann stellvertretend als publizistischer Beleg genommen werden, wie interdisziplinäre Gruppen um ein zeitgemäßes und angemessenes Verständnis von Stadt und um die Teilhabe an Veränderungsprozessen ringen. Landschaftselemente und Landschaftsterritorien tauchen dabei selbstverständlich ebenso auf. Die neuen Baukulturberichte der Bundesstiftung Baukultur tragen mit Fakten und Argumenten zur Verständigung über die Entwicklungskräfte und die Entwicklungspotenziale von Stadt und Land bei. Mit einer Sonderausgabe von *Stadtaspekte* wurde mit zentralen Botschaften des Baukulturberichtes 1 daraus ein Magazin für Baukultur: „Neue Räume".[6]

Der Baukulturbericht 2 „Stadt und Land" wird die rurbanen Lebenswelten jenseits der Kernstädte sichtbar machen. Die Vergegenwärtigung der Durchdringung und Abhängigkeit ruraler und urbaner Lebensalltage wird die notwendige Ergänzung der kernstadtfixierten urbanistischen Diskur-

ity of city dwellers live outside of the core city, in any case. In fact, those living in the "suburban agglomerate" are the modern-day city dwellers and urban territories are *urban landscapes*. Those who would like to influence urban transformations intentionally must know what the "urban transformers" are. The following text seeks to illuminate the significance of this interplay between disciplinary responsibility for the transformation of a city and the influencing factors that (re)produce the city every day, and to relate it to individual aspects of the thesis research by the college participants.

Disciplinary responsibility

Urban development and urban planning, in their present-day form, are the result of the industrial and civil revolution. Hitherto unprecedented urban growth and a newly negotiated balance between economic, social, and political aspects have determined the framework conditions and concrete structural developments of cities since the end of the nineteenth century. The problems cities are faced with have been illuminated and commented on by many experts (hygienists, biologists, sociologists, etc.), as well as by authors and artists.[7] Currently, the engineering and architectural disciplines seemed to be called on the most to propose conceptual solutions as to how the newly emerging cities could function and become liveable environments. Reinhard Baumeister, for example, explained the tradition of city planning in the German-speaking area on the basis of infrastructure projects,[8] while Camillo Sitte based the tradition of urban design on spatial and architectural rules.[9]

Democracy as an urban building contractor

Apart from the question of how the "New City" should look, the matter of the "building contractor" had to be clarified. Who could be in charge of the implementation and realisation of the "New City," backed by which power structure? And who was legitimised by whom to play this role? Which tools were required to achieve the desired urban restructuring?

With the emerging democracies, state and municipal authorities were politically legitimised to assume this restructuring power. This sovereign responsibility and power to direct developed step by step. Building law focused on averting danger gradually evolved into modern planning law that sought to shape the city even in the widest sense. The protection of private property and the requirements of the community became the object of special procedural regulations. The interplay of private and public interests had to be balanced and appropriate, democratically legitimised evaluation processes had to be "invented." The aim was to achieve a balanced, appropriate, and viable development of the city.

se möglich machen. Ohnehin lebt die Mehrheit der Städter jenseits der Kernstädte. Eigentlich ist der „Agglomerit" der Städter der Gegenwart und urbane Territorien sind *StadtLand*. Wer urbane Transformationen absichtsvoll beeinflussen möchte, muss die „urbanen Trans-Formatoren" kennen. Der folgende Text möchte die Bedeutung dieses Spannungsfeldes zwischen disziplinärer Zuständigkeit für die Transformation der Stadt und den Wirkungskräften, die die Stadt alltäglich (re-)produzieren, ausleuchten und einzelne Aspekte der Promotionsforschungen der Kollegteilnehmer in diesen Zusammenhang stellen.

Disziplinäre Zuständigkeit

Städtebau und Stadtplanung sind als Tätigkeiten in der heutigen Form ein Kind der industriellen und bürgerlichen Revolution: Ein bis anhin nicht gekanntes Stadtwachstum und ein neu zu verhandelndes Zusammenspiel wirtschaftlicher, gesellschaftlicher und politischer Akteure bestimmten ab Ende des 19. Jahrhunderts Rahmensetzungen und konkrete bauliche Entwicklungen der Städte. Die in den Städten zu lösenden Probleme wurden von vielen Fachleuten (Hygieniker, Biologen, Soziologen etc.), aber auch von Schriftstellern und Künstlern beleuchtet und kommentiert.[7] Die Disziplinen der Ingenieure und der Architekten schienen damals am ehesten berufen, konzeptionelle Lösungen dafür, wie die sich neu herausbildenden Städte funktionieren und zu lebenswerten Umwelten werden könnten, vorschlagen zu können. Reinhard Baumeister beispielsweise begründete im deutschsprachigen Raum die Tradition der Planung der Stadt via Projekte der Infrastruktur[8], Camillo Sitte diejenige der Gestaltung der Stadt durch räumliche und architektonische Regeln[9].

Demokratie als Stadt_Bauherrin

Neben der Frage, wie die „Neue Stadt" auszusehen habe, war die Frage der „Bauherrschaft" zu klären. Mit welchem Machtgefüge ausgestattet, kann wer für eine Umsetzung und Realisierung der „Neuen Stadt" sorgen? Und: Wer ist wodurch legitimiert, diese Rolle zu spielen? Außerdem war zu klären, mit welchen Instrumenten die angestrebte städtische Neuordnung erreicht werden könnte.

Mit den entstehenden Demokratien wurden staatliche Instanzen und Kommunen zur Ausübung dieser Gestaltungsmacht politisch legitimiert. Diese hoheitliche Zuständigkeit und Weisungsbefugnis wurde schrittweise entwickelt. Aus dem auf Gefahrenabwehr fokussierten Bauordnungsrecht ging nach und nach das moderne, auch im weitesten Sinne gestalten wollende Planungsrecht hervor. Der Schutz des Privateigentums und die Belange der Gemeinschaft wurden Gegenstand besonderer prozeduraler Vorschriften. Das Zusammenspiel privater und öffentlicher Interessen war auszutarieren, entsprechende demokratisch legitimierte Abwägungsprozesse waren zu „erfinden". So sollte eine ausgewogene gerechte und zukunftsfähige Entwicklung der Stadt erreicht werden.

Invention of urban planning

The building and urban development boom of the 1960s and 1970s led to criticism of the resulting urban realities in many countries. The introduction of a new discipline through interdisciplinary urban and spatial planning study courses appeared to be a fitting and overdue curricular reaction to the evident complexity of the city. It was an attempt to widen the monodisciplinary, one-sided answers of the architecture profession to address the social, economic, and political challenges in cities.

This also questioned the modern, omnipotent design aspirations of architecture, namely that architecture could contribute causally to a good society or, in other words, that good architecture could build a good society. These design aspirations were supplemented with social science in planning courses: integrated socio-economic, technical, political, and urban development strategies were set out to ensure socially-responsible urban development. Democratically-legitimised and official planning was to supply the parameters for this: good (urban) society through good urban planning under official responsibility.

The introduction of this new discipline went hand in hand with a regrettable mutual alienation of architecture and urban and spatial planning, based on misunderstandings about which conceptual aspects causally influence the development of the city and how they do so, i. e. through which forces, in the social context of the city.[10]

Experiences on the disciplinary borderline

For a number of years, many graduates of architecture and planning studies, as well as of other disciplines involved in urban development processes, have been sounding out new fields of work in explorative and experimental practice. The relevant understanding of the "co-production" of a city in this context reflects the vying for new cooperative design possibilities in the widest sense and for new urban responsibility cooperatives.[11] It follows that the culture initiative *"Urbane Künste Ruhr"* (Urban Arts Ruhr) places its programme for 2016 under the title "We are building a new city."

The collective Assemble in London, awarded the Turner Prize in 2015, seeks to restructure urban space and living environments co-productively "on the border between design, architecture, and social work." "Assemble succeeds where urban planners and architects fail."[12,13] Furthermore, the group Teleinternetcafe in Munich, together with the landscape architects from Treibhaus, proposed a new urbanist strategy at varying rates of development for the "Kreativquartier" (creative district) in Munich. In a type of laboratory situation, there is an attempt to enable innovative development processes within existing procedural and instrumental requirements and administrative responsibilities.[14] Numerous more recent publications offer collectively-gathered experience and knowledge about self-initiated projects relating to the communal appropriation and pro-

Erfindung der Stadtplanung

Im Bau- und Stadtentwicklungsboom der 1960er und 1970er Jahre entwickelte sich in vielen Ländern eine Kritik an den Ergebnissen der entstandenen städtischen Realitäten. Die Einführung einer neuen Disziplin durch die interdisziplinär alimentierten Stadt- und Raumplanungsstudiengänge schien die angemessene und überfällige curriculare Reaktion auf die offensichtliche Komplexität der Stadt. Es war der Versuch, die disziplinär gebundenen einseitigen Antworten der Architektenschaft auf die sozialen, ökonomischen und politischen Herausforderungen in den Städten angemessen zu ergänzen.

Damit wurde auch der moderne omnipotente Gestaltungsanspruch der Architektur infrage gestellt: nämlich durch gute Architektur auch ursächlich zu einer guten Gesellschaft beitragen, also die gute Gesellschaft bauen zu können. Zumindest wurde dieser Gestaltungsanspruch auf die Planungsstudiengänge sozialwissenschaftlich ausgeweitet: integrierte sozioökonomische, technische, politische und städtebauliche Strategien sollten für eine gesellschaftlich verantwortbare Stadtentwicklung sorgen. Die Maßstäbe dafür sollte die demokratisch legitimierte hoheitliche Planung liefern: gute (Stadt-)Gesellschaft durch gute Stadtplanung in hoheitlicher Verantwortung.

Die Einführung dieser neuen Disziplin ging einher mit einer bedauerlichen gegenseitigen Entfremdung von Architektur, Stadt- und Raumplanung, die auf Missverständnissen darüber basiert, welche konzeptionellen Artefakte wie im sozialen Kontext der Stadt durch welche Kräfte die Entwicklung der Stadt ursächlich und maßgeblich beeinflussen.[10]

Disziplinäre Grenzerfahrungen

Seit etlichen Jahren loten zahlreiche Absolventinnen und Absolventen der Architektur- und Planungsstudiengänge, aber auch anderer sich in Stadtentwicklungsprozessen engagierenden Disziplinen in explorativer und experimenteller Praxis neue Arbeitsfelder aus. Das in diesem Kontext gelebte Verständnis von der „Co-Produktion" von Stadt spiegelt das Ringen um neue kooperative Gestaltungsmöglichkeiten im weitesten Sinne und um neue städtische Verantwortungsgemeinschaften.[11] Sinnfällig, dass die Kulturinitiative Urbane Künste Ruhr ihr Programm für 2016 unter den Titel stellt „Wir bauen eine neue Stadt".

In London sucht das 2015 mit dem Turner-Preis dotierte Kollektiv Assemble, „an der Grenze zwischen Design, Architektur und Sozialarbeit" Stadt- und Lebensräume co-produktiv neu zu gestalten: „Assemble gelingt, woran Stadtplaner und Architekten scheitern."[12,13] Und die Gruppe Teleinternetcafe hat in München zusammen mit den Landschaftsarchitekten von Treibhaus eine neue urbanistische Strategie unterschiedlicher Entwicklungsgeschwindigkeiten für das „Kreativquartier" in München vorgeschlagen. In einer Art Laborsituation wird versucht, innovative Entwicklungsprozesse im Rahmen bestehender prozeduraler und instrumenteller

duction of space. Examples of this are *Self Made City*[15] or *Handmade Urbanism*.[16] Furthermore, under the catchphrase "guerrilla urbanism," there are countless reports about urban practices beyond disciplinary or institutional authorities.

The term "co-production" of the city raises the question not only of who is co-producing districts with whom, but also of associated and adequate new professional fields. This is linked to the question of new possibilities of democratic legitimisation for the changes to the city agreed in this manner.[17] Terms originating from different planning theory or political contexts, such as "community of solidarity" or "community of responsibility" refer to discussions that could be applied to the topics addressed here. How can communal participation in development processes be made compatible with a responsibility for resources and for coordinating interests and budgets? George Franck brings in the idea of the "urban commons" in this respect.[18] Commons are a publicly accessible area in small communities that can be used according to communally decided rules. Under the concept of "urban commons," Franck discusses possible procedures for reaching cooperatively decided rules for urban development.

Situational practice

Despite their quite different thematic focuses, a recurring theme in the individual dissertation research projects for this college was the relationship between disciplinary specialist knowledge, "on-site" knowledge, "everyday knowledge," and relevant knowledge from other, "new" disciplines involved with urban development and which are also concerned with the intentional and target-oriented influence of changes.

Anita Grams sees possibilities for mobilising inward city development potential in smaller and medium-sized communities and postulates that informal processes, including the "militia" government system that is effective in communities of this size, have to supplement formal procedures in order to be able to achieve an inward city development on a suitable scale.[19]

The project by Karin Hollenstein also investigates the potential of inward city development and asks whether inward city development per se can lead to energy savings? Perhaps it can in terms of the concentrated use of materials, but how about beyond that? The answer is also yes if people change their behaviour and no longer constantly demand more living space per person, or arrange their everyday lives so that they can get around on foot.[20]

Mario Schneider formulates the theory in his work that the "energy transition" can be implemented quicker through bottom-up processes if the necessary learning processes among architects, planners, politicians, and citizens unfold "on site," including with regard to consumer behaviour, thereby stimulating behavioural changes successfully. In other words, if

Erfordernisse und administrativer Zuständigkeiten möglich zu machen.[14] Zahlreiche jüngere Publikationen bieten gesammeltes Erfahrungswissen über selbst initiierte und verantwortete Projekte gemeinschaftlicher Raumaneignung und Raumproduktion. Beispielhaft sind hierbei *Self Made City*[15] oder *Handmade Urbanism*[16] zu nennen. Und unter dem Schlagwort „Guerilla Urbanism" finden sich unzählige Berichte urbaner Praktiken jenseits disziplinärer oder institutioneller Zuständigkeiten.

Der Begriff „Co-Produktion" von Stadt wirft außer der Frage, wer hier mit wem Stadtteile co-produziert, unmittelbar auch die Frage nach damit verbundenen neuen auskömmlichen beruflichen Tätigkeitsfeldern auf. Verbunden damit ist wiederum die Frage nach neuen Möglichkeiten demokratischer Legitimierung der so vereinbarten Veränderungen von Stadt.[17] Aus anderen planungstheoretischen oder politischen Kontexten stammende Begriffe wie „Solidargemeinschaften" oder „Verantwortungsgemeinschaften" zeugen von Diskussionen, die man auf die hier behandelten Themen übertragen könnte: Wie kann gemeinschaftliche Teilhabe an Entwicklungsprozessen auch mit der Verantwortung über Ressourcen sowie mit der Verantwortung für Interessensausgleiche und Unterhalt verknüpft werden? Georg Franck bringt hierfür die Idee der „urbanen Allmende" ein.[18] Die Allmende ist eine in kleinen Kommunen nach gemeinschaftlich festgelegten Regeln allgemein nutzbare Fläche. Unter dem Begriff „urbane Allmende" diskutiert Franck mögliche Verfahren, um zu kooperativ festgelegten Spielregeln für städtebauliche Entwicklungen zu kommen.

Situative Praxis

Ein wiederkehrendes Moment in den einzelnen Dissertationsforschungen dieses Kollegs war trotz der thematisch sehr unterschiedlich fokussierten Dissertationsprojekte das Verhältnis von disziplinärem Fachwissen zu Wissen „vor Ort", zu „Alltagswissen", zu relevantem Wissen anderer und auch „neuer" Disziplinen, die sich mit urbanen Entwicklungen und eventuell auch der Möglichkeit der absichtsvollen und zielorientierten Beeinflussung von Veränderungen befassen.

Anita Grams sieht Möglichkeiten der Mobilisierung der Potenziale der Innenentwicklung in kleineren und mittleren Gemeinden und postuliert, dass informelle Verfahren unter Einschluss des „Milizsystems", das in Gemeinden dieser Größenordnung wirksam ist, die formellen Verfahren zwingend ergänzen müssen, um eine Innenentwicklung in relevantem Ausmaß erreichen zu können.[19]

Die Arbeit von Karin Hollenstein geht ebenfalls den Potenzialen der Innenentwicklung nach und fragt, ob Innenentwicklung per se zu Energieeinsparungen führen kann? Was den konzentrierten Materialeinsatz angeht vermutlich ja, aber darüber hinaus? Auch ja, wenn Menschen ihr Verhalten ändern, nämlich nicht ständig mehr Wohnfläche pro Person beanspruchen, oder ihren Lebensalltag so organisieren, dass sie mehr Wege zu Fuß erledigen können.[20]

daily routines are changed and everyday knowledge can be made (re)productive for this purpose.[21]

In the quite different planning context of "emergency aid," Sabrina Brenner's research indicates the situational conditionality of success: the necessarily rapid reconstruction aid after disasters ignores cultural contexts and local knowledge all too often, so that the resulting aid does not provide protection from any future disasters. The challenge appears to lie in how follow-up measures can bring together external expertise and local everyday cultures and learning processes, in order to implement truly long-term protection.[22]

Bettina Wyss probes these aspects of local knowledge and local culture further in her work, using "subjective cartographies" to examine the reasons why people develop place attachment, in order to illuminate the psychological and therefore subjective dimension of identification with spaces and places.[23]

New parties, new accomplices

Aesthetics, meaning "perceptibility in general" and "beauty in particular," is a demand placed on public space architecture that seeks to shape urban development concretely. The longstanding question is how to prove that the outcome can be causally attributed to architecture. There are regular claims that architecture engenders emotional effects and doubts are refuted by accusations of folksy prejudice. Now art and cultural initiatives are increasingly involving themselves in urbanistic matters and processes of change with their work and are reopening the question about the causal effect of architecture. In her work "Spatial Stimuli," Anna Kirstgen[24] investigates the effects of targeted spatial productions and seeks viable evaluation criteria.

In the meantime, individual urban interventions by artists, as artistic urban practice, are part of everyday experience in cities. This has an effect on civil society and spatial function for the development of the districts they take place in. Renée Tribble researches to what extent these effects challenge those responsible disciplinarily and administratively for urban development and planning.[25] How and under what conditions can one achieve synergy effects between local knowledge and the claim to official responsibility?

Steffen Braun approaches the new parties involved in urban development from a material point of view: based on the observation that technical progress has a significant influence on the development of cities, he investigates to what extent the knowledge of technical futures gained through innovation research could be used for a more harmonious and controlled implementation of technical progress.[26]

Mario Schneider formuliert in seiner Arbeit unter anderem die These, dass die „Energiewende" schneller durch Bottom-up-Prozesse umzusetzen sei, dann nämlich, wenn die notwendigen Lernprozesse bei Architekten, Planern, Politikern und Bürgern unter anderem gerade auch im Hinblick auf das Verbrauchsverhalten quasi „vor Ort" ankommen und so Verhaltensänderungen erfolgreich stimulieren können. Mit anderen Worten, wenn Alltagsroutinen verändert werden und Alltagswissen hierfür (re-)produktiv gemacht werden kann.[21]

Im ganz anderen Planungskontext der „Katastrophenhilfe" stößt Sabrina Brenner in ihren Recherchen auf die situative Bedingtheit von Erfolg: Die in der Regel notwendigerweise schnelle Aufbauhilfe nach Katastrophen ignoriert zu häufig kulturelle Kontexte und lokales Wissen, sodass die daraus resultierende Vorsorge vor Katastrophen nicht wirklich vorzubeugen vermag. Die Herausforderung scheint hier darin zu liegen, wie schon in der Nachsorge externe Expertise mit lokalen Alltagskulturen und Lernprozessen verknüpft werden kann, um wirklich nachhaltigen Schutz zu implementieren.[22]

Bettina Wyss stößt noch spezifischer in diese Dimensionen von lokalem Wissen und lokaler Kultur vor, wenn sie mit ihrer Arbeit über Ursachen und Bedingungen der Ortsverbundenheit von Menschen quasi „subjektiven Kartografien" nachgeht, um mitunter die psychische und damit subjektive Dimension der Identifikation mit Räumen und Orten auszuleuchten.[23]

Neue Akteure, neue Komplizen

Ästhetik, also „Wahrnehmbarkeit im Allgemeinen" und „Schönheit im Besonderen" sind Ansprüche an die Architektur im öffentlichen Raum, die konkret gestaltender Städtebau erreichen möchte. Diese Wirkungsweise kausal als architektonischen Effekt nachzuweisen, ist eine schon lange währende Fragestellung. Gerne werden ursächlich durch Architektur bedingte emotionale Wirkungen behauptet und gegen Zweifel mit dem Vorwurf volkstümelnder Befangenheit verteidigt. Nun bringen sich Kunst und Kulturschaffende vermehrt mit ihren Arbeiten in urbanistische Auseinandersetzungen und Veränderungsprozesse ein und werfen die Frage nach deren ursächlicher Wirkung neu auf. Anna Kirstgen geht in ihrer Arbeit *Raumreiz*[24] den Wirkungsweisen von engagierten Raumproduktionen nach und sucht nach belastbaren Bewertungskriterien.

Inzwischen gehören einzelne urbane Interventionen von Künstlern als eigentliche künstlerische Urbane Praxis zum Erfahrungsalltag in Städten. Dadurch werden relevante zivilgesellschaftliche und auch raumfunktionale Effekte für die Entwicklung derjenigen Quartiere ausgelöst, in denen sie stattfinden. Renée Tribble recherchiert, inwieweit diese Effekte die für die Stadtentwicklung und -planung disziplinär und administrativ Zuständigen herausfordern.[25] Wie und unter welchen Voraussetzungen können hier Synergieeffekte von lokalem Wissen und reklamiertem hoheitlichem Zuständigkeitsanspruch erreicht werden?

Shared learning processes

The desire to be able to incorporate "collective wisdom" more productively into the development of our cities, beyond existing participatory and collaborative formats, flows into the research being conducted by Hannes Rockenbauch into the postulation of "provisional politics and planning."[27] The associated preliminary and temporary aspect of planning policy and decisions necessarily brings a requirement for shared learning processes. These joint learning processes are meeting places for expert and everyday knowledge and are a challenge for all those involved. New models of civil co-responsibility for development projects could be negotiated within these shared learning processes. Shared responsibilities structured in this new manner would be able to give civil participation a greater significance.

Disciplinary reinvention

Even if the individual doctoral research theses documented in this book address quite different topics and aspects of urban landscape transformations, in almost all of the projects "urban transformers" are central factors in urban transformation processes.

The resulting findings underline the fact that the relationship between conceptual models for transformation processes and the influential parties and factors needs to be explored in greater depth and re-evaluated.

For the subsequent disciplinary self-examination and readjustment, it could be helpful to discuss the self-understanding of urbanist disciplines in the context of the "transformative science" postulated by Uwe Schneidewind and Mandy Singer-Brodowski.[28] Transformative science proposes an understanding of science as a catalyst for processes of social change. This postulation is a response to the theory that after the Neolithic and industrial revolution, humanity is standing once again on the threshold of epochal change, which the Nobel prize winner Paul Crutzen refers to as "Anthropocene" and which requires a fundamental new definition of the relationship between science and society. The central challenges include overcoming disciplinary and institutional divisions, as well as countering the "justice and participation challenge" by means of a new relationship between basic and applied knowledge and situational, contextual, and everyday knowledge.[29]

Applied to urbanist disciplines, it is about reflecting on the specialist conceptual design impetus in the light of insights about the concrete influential forces in urban development and bringing them into the negotiating processes for urban change co-productively.

Uwe Schneidewind and Mandy Singer-Brodowski also stipulate that institutional experiments are necessary in order to accomplish this necessary convergence of university knowledge and everyday practice. In relation to urban development, this could culminate in the call for a new urbanist education experiment, a "Bauhaus 2.0"—a "city Bauhaus" that combines university learning and research with urban everyday practices and general

Steffen Braun nähert sich den neuen Akteuren der Stadtentwicklung von der dinglichen Seite: Ausgehend von der Feststellung, dass der technische Fortschritt die Entwicklung der Städte maßgeblich beeinflusst, untersucht er, inwieweit nicht das via Innovationsforschung erworbene Wissen über technische Zukünfte für eine stärker harmonisierte und kontrollierte Implementierung des technischen Fortschritts genutzt werden könnte.[26]

Gemeinsame Lernprozesse

Der Wunsch, die „Weisheit der Vielen" über bestehende Beteiligungs- und Mitwirkungsformate hinaus noch produktiver in die Entwicklung unserer Städte einbinden zu können, mündet in der Forschung von Hannes Rockenbauch in das Postulat einer „provisorischen Politik und Planung".[27] Die damit zwangsläufig verbundene Vorläufigkeit von planungspolitischen und planerischen Entscheidungen bedeutet notwendigerweise die Forderung nach gemeinsamen Lernprozessen. Diese gemeinsamen Lernprozesse wären Begegnungsräume von Fach- und Alltagswissen und eine Herausforderung für alle Beteiligten. Innerhalb dieser gemeinsamen Lernprozesse könnten auch neue Modelle bürgerschaftlicher Mitverantwortung für Entwicklungsprojekte verhandelt werden. Derartig strukturell verabredete neue Verantwortungsgemeinschaften würden bürgerschaftlicher Mitwirkung ein höheres Gewicht geben können.

Disziplinäre Wieder_Er_Findung

Auch wenn die einzelnen Promotionsforschungen, wie in diesem Buch dokumentiert, sich sehr unterschiedlichen Themen und Aspekten urbaner Transformationslandschaften zuordnen lassen, finden sich in fast allen Arbeiten „urbane Trans-Formatoren" als zentrale Akteure in urbanen Transformationsprozessen.

Die damit verbundenen Befunde bekräftigen, dass das Verhältnis zwischen konzeptionellen Leitbildern für Transformationsprozesse und den wirksamen Akteuren und Kräften vertieft zu erkunden und neu auszutarieren ist.

Für die darauf reagierende disziplinäre Selbstvergewisserung und Neujustierung könnte es hilfreich sein, das Selbstverständnis urbanistischer Disziplinen im Kontext der von Uwe Schneidewind und Mandy Singer-Brodowski postulierten „transformativen Wissenschaft"[28] zu diskutieren. Mit transformativer Wissenschaft wird ein Wissenschaftsverständnis angeregt, dass Wissenschaft als Katalysator für gesellschaftliche Veränderungsprozesse versteht.

Dieses Postulat reagiert auf die These, dass die Menschheit nach der neolithischen und der industriellen Revolution nunmehr wiederum an der Schwelle epochaler Umwälzungen steht, die der Nobelpreisträger Paul Crutzen als „Anthropozän" bezeichnet, und die eine grundlegende Neudefinition des Verhältnisses von Wissenschaft und Gesellschaft erfordern. Dabei gehört zu den zentralen Herausforderungen, die disziplinären und

education requirements, for example in community colleges. For example, the HafenCity University (HCU) in Hamburg, newly founded in 2006 and focusing on "architecture and metropolitan development," would have the potential to do so, if it was allowed to experiment a little more and was provided with suitable personnel and funds.[30]

institutionellen Trennungen ebenso zu überwinden wie der „Gerechtig-keits- und Beteiligungsherausforderung" durch ein neues Verhältnis von Grundlagen- und Anwendungswissen sowie situativem Kontext- und All-tagswissen zu begegnen.[29]

Übertragen auf urbanistische Disziplinen ginge es darum, den fachlichen konzeptionellen Gestaltungsimpetus im Lichte der Erkenntnisse über die konkret wirkenden Kräfte der Stadtentwicklung zu reflektieren und co-produktiv in die Aushandlungsprozesse der Stadtveränderung einzubrin-gen.

Uwe Schneidewind und Mandy Singer-Brodowski postulieren auch, dass institutionelle Experimente erforderlich seien, um diese notwendige Kon-vergenz von universitärem Wissen und Alltagspraktiken zu bewerkstelli-gen. Bezüglich Stadtentwicklung könnte das in die Forderung nach einem neuen urbanistischen Ausbildungsexperiment, einem „Bauhaus 2.0", mün-den – einem „Stadt-Bauhaus", das universitäre Ausbildung und Forschung mit urbanen Alltagspraktiken und dem allgemeinen Bildungsanspruch, zum Beispiel der Volkshochschule, verbindet. Die 2006 als auf „Baukunst und Metropolenentwicklung" fokussierte neu gegründete HafenCity Uni-versität (HCU) in Hamburg zum Beispiel hätte das Potenzial dazu, wenn man sie etwas mehr experimentieren ließe und ihr auch entsprechende Personal- und Sachmittel zur Verfügung stellen würde.[30]

Mailand Milan, 18.03.2015

Hamburg, 21.11.2013

Wien Vienna, 05.05.2016

Hamburg, 21.11.2013

Hamburg, 21.11.2013

"INNOVATE OR DIE ...?"
About the relevance of urban innovations for the city of tomorrow

STEFFEN BRAUN

How is the city changing in light of technological and social evolution in the twenty-first century? What opportunities do existing innovation processes present for the city of tomorrow and how can these be made use of in practice? This dissertation focuses on the systematisation of innovation processes in the context of urban transformation and future-orientated urban development. Characteristics and the usage potential of a prototypical innovation process for future-orientated urban development are identified by analysing previous and current evolution and diffusion processes of urban systems. The aim is to construct a multi-layered model by combining existing approaches such as *transition management* and *living lab typologies*. It will conclude by studying and describing opportunities for targeted innovation processes within a case-study district.

Sustainable urban development is currently increasingly faced with the task of reflecting objectively on modern, in some cases technically-driven, approaches such as *smart cities* and with setting out convergent strategies and methods. The call for self-sufficiency and sustainable consumption alone is no longer enough. It is surmised increasingly in science and practice that the innovation capacity of cities and their subsystems, meaning the basic ability to bring forth something new, can represent a valuable quality for overcoming urban challenges. There must be a rethinking process, both when planning and when implementing viable urban concepts, in which components such as energy, buildings, infrastructure, mobility, logistics, supply, security, health, or administration are closely interlinked. One can expect an increased merging of basic technologies and social requirements, and therefore a changing use of resources. Urban development, technical progress, and innovation research currently represent largely separate domains of science and practice which need to be bridged.

This dissertation addresses this research gap in the context of urban transformation tasks and will show critical influential factors and guidelines for an innovation-orientated transformation of urban structures and processes, by means of an integrative research structure. In view of the increasing speed of innovation in economics and society, the formulation of the central research question would appear to be easy: how does what is new establish itself in the city? The thesis is very application-orientated and pursues the development of theory as a central aim, as well as the construction of a multi-layered conceptual model for preparing and structuring innovation processes for innovative urban development.

„INNOVATE OR DIE …?"
Zur Relevanz urbaner Innovationen für die Stadt von morgen

STEFFEN BRAUN

Wie verändert sich Stadt entlang der technischen und gesellschaftlichen Evolution im 21. Jahrhundert? Welche Chancen ergeben sich aus bestehenden Innovationsprozessen für die Stadt von morgen und wie lassen sich diese in der Praxis nutzen? Das Dissertationsvorhaben befasst sich mit der Systematisierung von Innovationsprozessen im Kontext urbaner Transformation und zukunftsorientierter Stadtentwicklung. Durch Analyse bisheriger und aktueller Evolutions- und Diffusionsprozesse städtischer Systeme werden Charakteristiken und Nutzenpotenziale für einen prototypischen Innovationsprozess für zukunftsorientierte Stadtentwicklung identifiziert. Ziel ist der Aufbau eines Mehr-Ebenen-Modells durch Kombination bestehender Ansätze wie *Transition Management* und *Reallabortypologien*. Abschließend sollen Chancen für gerichtete Innovationsprozesse an einem Referenzquartier überprüft und beschrieben werden.

Nachhaltige Stadtentwicklung hat aktuell immer mehr die Aufgabe, moderne, teils auch technisch getriebene Ansätze wie *Smart Cities* sachlich zu reflektieren und konvergente Strategien und Maßnahmen aufzuzeigen. Der Ruf nach Suffizienz und nachhaltigem Konsum al-

lein reicht nicht mehr aus. In der Wissenschaft und Praxis reift vermehrt die Vermutung, dass dabei die Innovationsfähigkeit von Städten und ihren Subsystemen, also die grundsätzliche Fähigkeit Neues hervorzubringen, eine wertvolle Eigenschaft zur Bewältigung der urbanen Herausforderungen darstellen kann. Ein Umdenken muss sowohl bei der Planung als auch bei der Umsetzung zukunftsfähiger Stadtkonzepte stattfinden, in denen sich Teilsysteme wie Energie, Gebäude, Infrastruktur, Mobilität, Logistik, Versorgung, Sicherheit, Gesundheit oder Verwaltung eng miteinander verzahnen. Dabei ist von einer zunehmenden Verschmelzung zugrunde liegender Technologien, gesellschaftlicher Bedarfe und damit veränderter Ressourceninanspruchnahme auszugehen. Stadtentwicklung, technischer Fortschritt und Innovationsforschung stellen heute weitgehend getrennte Domänen von Wissenschaft und Praxis dar, die es zu überbrücken gilt.

Das Dissertationsvorhaben adressiert diese Forschungslücke im Kontext urbaner Transformationsaufgaben und wird durch ein integratives Forschungsdesign leistungskritische Einflussfaktoren und Leitlinien für eine innovationsorientierte Transformation von städtischen Strukturen und Prozessen aufzeigen. Angesichts der zunehmenden Innovationsgeschwindigkeit in Wirtschaft und Gesellschaft scheint die zentrale Forschungsfrage zumindest in der Formulierung einfach: Wie kommt das Neue in die Stadt? Die Arbeit ist stark anwendungsorientiert und verfolgt neben der Theoriebildung als zentrales Ergebnis den Aufbau eines konzeptionellen Mehr-Ebenen-Modells zur Vorbereitung und Strukturierung von Innovationsprozessen für eine innovationsfähige Stadtentwicklung.

SPATIAL STIMULI

ANNA KIRSTGEN

Producing space is a central task for architects. However, the question of how this space affects later users is often neglected. Although there are regular debates reflecting on the impact of architecture, these are rarely applied in practice. Instead, each architect develops their own concept of space based on practice and an individual theory. Many architects succeed in creating atmospheric spaces. They have an understanding of how to use volumes, materials, light, etc. in such a way that their interplay generates special atmospheres. The handling of physical and non-physical methods is mastered quite expertly by some architects, whilst others create the impression that using design techniques to bring forth atmospheric situations is a game of chance.

The theory is that a better understanding of how space is perceived and what influence it has on the behaviour of the users facilitates spatial communication and contributes to a more conscious approach to the space by planners. Furthermore, broader knowledge enables a more precise application of design methods in the design process and also provides reference points in order to make space more attractive for the later users.

It has been observed in recent years that, alongside urban planning and architecture, other disciplines are getting more involved in the appearance of urban space. The traditional approach of architects is increasingly being confronted with artistic practices in public spaces. Boundaries have been dissolving in art since the 1960s, blurring the divisions between different art genres, between the museum and the city, and between art and non-art.

Producers who act in accordance with this succeed in reviving unaesthetic urban spaces by incorporating new spatial stimuli. Their handling of public space sparks a discussion about its effects and prompts a renewed search for explanatory approaches and guidelines. Creating sensibilities consciously requires a new understanding of how spatial stimuli are engendered. As a precondition for this, it is first of all necessary to set out the spatial concepts relevant for architecture, in order to shed light on spatial stimuli and their contribution to creating atmospheres. In addition, one should establish an epistemological base and provide an aesthetic and psychological illumination of the field of perception for the purpose of discussion in architecture and architectural practice.

The aim of the thesis is to set out practice-orientated spatial concepts for architects and planners. Spatial effects and how they are created are presented on the basis of these concepts, in order to make architects and designers aware of spatial stimuli.

RAUMREIZ

ANNA KIRSTGEN

Eine zentrale Aufgabe der Architekten ist es, Raum zu produzieren. Die Frage, in welcher Weise dieser Raum auf die spätere Nutzerschaft wirkt, wird jedoch häufig außer Acht gelassen. Die Debatte zur Reflexion der Wirkung von Architektur wird zwar immer wieder geführt, ist in der Praxis allerdings nur selten rezipiert worden. Vielmehr entwickelt jeder Architekt seine Raumauffassung praxisbezogen und als individuelle Theorie.

Vielen Architekten gelingt es, stimmungsvolle Räume zu schaffen. Sie verstehen es, Volumetrien, Materialien, Licht etc. so einzusetzen, dass in ihrem Zusammenspiel besondere Atmosphären entstehen. Den Umgang mit körperlichen und nicht-körperlichen Mitteln beherrschen manche Architekten geradezu virtuos, bei anderen hingegen entsteht der Eindruck, das Setzen entwerferischer Mittel zur Hervorbringung atmosphärischer Situationen komme einem Glücksspiel gleich.

Ein besseres Verständnis, wie Raum wahrgenommen wird und welchen Einfluss er auf das Verhalten der Nutzer hat, erleichtert die Verständigung über den Raum und trägt zu einem bewussteren Umgang der Planer mit Raum bei – so die These. Darüber hinaus ermöglicht ein breiteres Wissen einen präziseren Umgang mit gestalterischen Mitteln im Entwurfsprozess und bietet zudem Orientierungspunkte, um Raum für die spätere Nutzerschaft attraktiver zu gestalten.

In den letzten Jahren ist zu beobachten, dass sich neben der Stadtplanung und der Architektur immer häufiger auch andere Disziplinen mit dem Erscheinungsbild von urbanem Raum auseinandersetzen. Im öffentlichen Raum werden der traditionellen Arbeitsweise der Architekten zunehmend künstlerische Praktiken gegenübergestellt. Seit den 1960er Jahren ist in der Kunst ein Entgrenzungsprozess zu beobachten, der Trennlinien zwischen den unterschiedlichen Kunstgattungen, zwischen Museum und Stadt und zwischen Kunst und Nicht-Kunst zunehmend aufhebt.

Den vor diesem Hintergrund agierenden Produzenten gelingt es, anästhetische Stadträume durch das Setzen von neuen Raumreizen wiederzubeleben. Ihr Umgang mit dem öffentlichen Raum fordert eine Diskussion über seine Wirkungsweise heraus und gibt Anlass dazu, neuerlich nach Erklärungsansätzen und Grundlagen zu suchen. Denn um bewusst Befindlichkeiten schaffen zu können, bedarf es eines neuen Verständnisses, wie Raumreize entstehen. Dafür ist zunächst eine Aufbereitung der für die Architektur relevanten Raumkonzepte zur Beleuchtung von Raumreizen und deren Beitrag zur Atmosphärenbildung Voraussetzung. Zudem sollen erkenntnistheoretische Grundlagen sowie eine ästhetische und psychologische Beleuchtung des Feldes der Wahrnehmung für die Diskussion in Architektur und architektonischer Praxis aufbereitet werden.

Ziel der Arbeit ist es, praxisorientierte Raumbegriffe für Architekten und Planer herauszuarbeiten. Auf Basis dieser Begriffe werden räumliche Wirkungsweisen und ihre Entstehungsprozesse beleuchtet, um Architekten und Gestalter für Raumreize zu sensibilisieren.

AT HOME IN THE DISTRICT?
Place attachment and its spatial localisation: a study based on the example of the Wipkingen district (city of Zurich)

BETTINA WYSS

Switzerland is facing major spatial planning challenges: urban sprawl is proceeding unchecked, the population is increasing, and the available space per person is decreasing. Densification appears to be urgently required and is currently being pursued by the basic strategy of "inward city development before external development." However, this densification is meeting with resistance, as there are fears it may be detrimental to the quality of life and living space.

The dissertation therefore addresses, from an interdisciplinary point of view, the question of how the quality of life can be raised in city districts. The concept of place attachment is a focal point among the factors that influence the quality of life in cities. An understanding of place attachment is central for planning, if it is to meet requirements. Various research projects show that experiencing place attachment is a basic human need, which increases one's quality of life if fulfilled. The hypothesis is that place attachment is, on the one hand, a psychological process and, on the other hand, also has clearly spatial, constructed, and geographical components. Place attachment, or a first step towards it, can be supported by city district planning. Enabling or reinforcing place attachment through the built environment requires an understanding of what constitutes place attachment and to what extent elements of it are related to spatial features.

The research project pursues the question of how place attachment is to be understood in the present-day urban environment. What does place attachment mean for people today? Which places have a special meaning for city dwellers, in other words to what places do they develop this attachment, and why to these in particular? What role does the local living environment play for city residents today? What contribution does place attachment make to the subjective quality of life and residence? In order to answer these questions, a study was carried out in the Wipkingen district in Zurich. The data gained from this study is compared to data from the project carried out by the photographer Stefan Dinter in Karlsruhe: "Karlsruhe. Experiencing a City."[1]

ZU HAUSE IM QUARTIER?
Ortsverbundenheit und deren räumliche Verortung: eine Studie am Beispiel des Quartiers Wipkingen (Stadt Zürich)

BETTINA WYSS

dabei das Konzept der Ortsverbundenheit fokussiert. Die Kenntnis von Ortsbeziehungen ist zentral für ein bedürfnisgerechtes Planen. Diverse Forschungsarbeiten zeigen, dass das Erleben von Ortsverbundenheit ein Grundbedürfnis des Menschen ist, das – wenn es erfüllt wird – die Lebensqualität steigert. Die Hypothese ist, dass Ortsverbundenheit einerseits ein psychologischer Prozess ist und andererseits auch klar räumliche, gebaute und geografische Komponenten hat. Ortsverbundenheit kann durch Stadtquartiersplanung gefördert beziehungsweise in einem ersten Schritt ermöglicht werden. Um Ortsverbundenheit durch die gebaute Umwelt konkret zu fördern oder zu ermöglichen, bedarf es des Wissens darüber, was Ortsverbundenheit ausmacht und inwiefern Elemente der Ortsverbundenheit räumlich zu verorten sind.

Das Forschungsprojekt geht der Frage nach, wie Ortsverbundenheit im heutigen städtischen Umfeld verstanden werden kann: Was macht für Menschen heute Ortsverbundenheit aus? Welche Orte haben für Stadtbewohner eine besondere Bedeutung, das heißt, zu welchen Orten bauen sie diese Verbundenheit auf und wieso gerade zu diesen Orten? Welche Rolle spielt das lokale Lebensumfeld für Stadtbewohner heute? Welchen Beitrag leistet Ortsverbundenheit zur subjektiven Lebens- und Wohnqualität? Zur Beantwortung der Fragestellung wurde eine Studie im Quartier Wipkingen in Zürich durchgeführt. Die Daten dieser Studie werden mit Daten des vom Fotografen Stefan Dinter in Karlsruhe durchgeführten Projekts „Karlsruhe. Eine Stadt erleben. Fotografien" verglichen.[1]

Die Schweiz steht vor großen raumplanerischen Herausforderungen: Die Zersiedelung des Landes verläuft nach wie vor ungebremst, die Bevölkerungszahl steigt, der pro Person verfügbare Raum nimmt ab. Verdichtung scheint dringend nötig und kommt aktuell als Mindeststrategie „Innenentwicklung vor Außenentwicklung" zur Anwendung. Diese Verdichtung stößt aber auf Widerstände, eine Verminderung der Lebens- und Wohnqualität wird befürchtet.

Die Dissertation befasst sich deshalb aus interdisziplinärer Sicht mit der Frage, wie die Lebensqualität in Stadtquartieren gefördert werden kann. Unter den Faktoren, welche die Lebensqualität in Städten beeinflussen, wird

MILAN
MAILAND

THE MILAN EXPERIENCE

GIOVANNA FOSSA

Currently, Milan is one of the European cities which is clearly interpreting the theme of the Spatial Research Lab "Urban Landscape Transformation." In the last few years, the Milan skyline has been dramatically changing with the new *Porta Nuova towers*, similar to a US downtown attached to the historic centre, and the *CityLife skyscapers*, landmarking the main highway access to Milan. These two great urban projects dialogue with the background perspective of the Alps and with the European infrastructure corridors crossing the Milan metropolitan region, thus creating several new centres which complement the historic one. The image of Milan has been changing. Indeed, the 2015 Milan Expo launched the discussion about its contemporary identity in relation to the strategic issue of the post-use of the exhibition site.

Among the city plan transformation areas, the most strategic ones are those of the *Bovisa gas tanks* and the attached *Farini railway yard*, starting at the crossing of the two main development axes of Milan (Simplon and Gotthard, still today part of the Genova-Rotterdam corridor). The future of Milan relies on the transformation process of these areas and the Expo site's potential which is close by and is also aligned in the direction of the Malpensa airport.

Bovisa is the heart of this system: a "drop" of 850,000 square metres closed inside a railway junction but served by two train stations. The handicap is the heavy subsoil pollution of its gasometer site, which occupies half of the drop; the attached historic industrial neighbourhood started to be reused for the *Politecnico Bovisa Campus* in 1990 as a kick-off action of the whole Bovisa transformation process.

One shot transformation of such a huge area is no longer possible nowadays: temporary reuses would prevent deterioration, promote the

1 In dark green: The Bovisa and Farini transformation areas, aligned on the Simplon infrastructure axis, in the strategic vision of the Milan City Plan
1 In Dunkelgrün: Die Transformationsareale von Bovisa und Farini, angegliedert an die Simplon-Infrastrukturachse, in der strategischen Vision der Mailänder Stadtplanung

re-appropriation by citizens, and accompany a step-by-step participatory design process. Politecnico and the City just launched (January 2016) a "Call for Ideas" oriented to elaborate guidelines for the reuse of the Bovisa gasometer area.

So far in the process there has been marked by political tension between a transit-oriented development approach (considering the excellent accessibility by rail to the areas involved) and an extreme green vision (the preservation of the polluted forest in the gasometer area and the full park option for the reuse of the yard). The on-going negotiation between the city and the railway company concerns not only Farini but the whole set of underutilized yards, allowing that densification and urban design criteria could vary in a site-specific way.

From a planning point of view, synergies are evident between the use of Bovisa by the University/HT, a various mix of related uses in the Farini redevelopment, and the hypothesis of a

DIE MAILÄNDER PRAXIS

GIOVANNA FOSSA

Zu den strategisch wichtigsten stadtplanerischen Transformationsgebieten gehören die Bovisa-Gasometer und der benachbarte Farini-Bahnbetriebshof, die am Schnittpunkt zwischen den beiden Hauptentwicklungsachsen Mailands liegen (Simplon und Gotthard, bis heute Teil des Bezugssystems des Korridors Rotterdam – Genua). Die Zukunft Mailands hängt vom Transformationsprozess dieser Areale sowie dem Potenzial des Expo-Geländes ab, das in der Nähe liegt und auch auf den Flughafen Malpensa ausgerichtet ist.

Bovisa bildet das Herz dieses Systems: ein 850.000 Quadratmeter umfassendes Areal in Form eines „Tropfens" inmitten eines Eisenbahnknotenpunkts, das an zwei Bahnhöfe angebunden ist. Problematisch ist die starke Belastung des Untergrunds auf dem Gasometer-Gelände, das die Hälfte des Areals einnimmt. Das angrenzende historische Industriegebiet wird seit 1990 durch den Politecnico-Bovisa-Campus genutzt, was den Anstoß für den gesamten Transformationsprozess in Bovisa geben sollte.

Ein solch riesiges Areal kann heutzutage nicht mehr im Handumdrehen transformiert werden: temporäre Neunutzungen würden den Verfall verhindern, die Wiederaneignung durch die Bewohner fördern und einen schrittweisen, partizipativen Planungsprozess begünstigen. Im Januar 2016 haben das Politecnico und die Stadt einen „Ideenaufruf" gestartet, durch den Richtlinien zur Neunutzung des Bovisa-Gasometer-Geländes entwickelt werden sollen.

Bis jetzt gab es in diesem Prozess politische Spannungen zwischen den Vertretern eines auf den Schienenverkehr bezogenen Entwicklungskonzepts (welche die exzellente Anbindung der betroffenen Areale an die Bahn hervorheben) und jenen einer extrem „grünen Vision"

Gegenwärtig ist Mailand ganz eindeutig eine der europäischen Städte, die den vom „Forschungslabor Raum" thematisierten „Urbanen Transformationslandschaften" ein Gesicht gibt. In den letzten Jahren hat sich die Skyline Mailands dramatisch verändert: durch die neuen Türme von Porta Nuova, die an US-amerikanische, sich an historische Stadtzentren angliedernde Innenstädte erinnern, und die CityLife-Hochhäuser, welche die wichtigste Autobahnzufahrt nach Mailand markieren. Diese zwei großangelegten urbanen Projekte stehen im Dialog mit der Silhouette der sie umgebenden Alpen sowie den europäischen Infrastrukturkorridoren, welche die Mailänder Metropolenregion durchkreuzen und so der historischen Stadtmitte neue Zentren hinzufügen. Das Bild Mailands hat sich gewandelt. Die Mailänder Expo 2015 und die Strategien zur Folgenutzung des Ausstellungsgeländes haben eine Diskussion über die Identität der Stadt angestoßen.

2 *The Farini railway yard transformation area, Milan*
2 *Das Transformations-areal des Farini-Bahn-betriebshofs, Mailand*

Human Technopolis in the former Expo site: this system could therefore give birth to a Milan innovation district which could rediscover its historic manufacturing identity and competiveness.

From an urban design point of view, it is clear that there is great potential in the vision of opening up the long barrier of the sequence of these areas, cross-connecting neighbourhoods on both sides top spur on the effects of diffused renewal and increased attraction which are already tangible. The planned greenway ("green ray") would extend the already existing walkable path between the historic core (Duomo/Castle) and the Porta Nuova CBD to the gardens of the Expo site; it is a wide linear strip which could open a landscape perspective stretching itself from the "vertical wood" to outer regional river parks and beyond towards the Monte Rosa, following the "grand axis" which has been shaping the form of Milan and its region since the Napoleon era.

3 *The Bovisa gas tank transformation area, Milan, with the Monte Rosa on the background*
3 *Das Transformationsareal der Bovisa-Gasometer, Mailand, mit dem Monte Rosa im Hintergrund*

(die den Erhalt des belasteten Waldes auf dem Gasometer-Gelände und die Umwandlung des gesamten Bahnbetriebsgeländes in einen Park befürworten). Die noch anhaltenden Verhandlungen zwischen der Stadt und der Bahngesellschaft drehen sich nicht nur um Farini, sondern auch um eine ganze Reihe anderer, wenig genutzter Betriebshöfe. Ziel ist eine Anpassung der Verdichtung und stadtplanerischen Kriterien an die örtlichen Besonderheiten.

Von einem planerischen Gesichtspunkt aus ergeben sich Synergien zwischen der Anbindung Bovisas an die Universität/HT, einem darauf bezogenen Nutzungsmix bei der Neugestaltung des Farini-Geländes und der Idee einer „Human Technopole" auf dem ehemaligen Expo-Gelände: Durch dieses System könnte ein innovativer Mailänder Stadtbezirk entstehen, der sich auf seine historische industrielle Identität und Wettbewerbsfähigkeit besinnt.

Aus Sicht der Stadtentwicklung wird das große Potenzial deutlich, das die Öffnung der langen, durch die ineinander übergehenden Areale geschaffenen Barriere birgt: Dabei werden Gelände beiderseits der Trennlinie verbunden, wodurch eine individuelle Neustrukturierung und Aufwertung des gesamten Areals möglich wird – was schon heute evident ist. Der auf ganzer Länge geplante Grünbereich („grüne Strahl") würde den schon existierenden Fußweg zwischen dem historischen Zentrum (Dom/Schloss) und dem Wirtschaftsviertel Porta Nuova bis zu den durch Wasserflächen strukturierten Gärten des Expo-Geländes verlängern. Es ist ein breiter, geschwungener Streifen, der eine landschaftliche Perspektive eröffnen könnte, die sich vom „vertikalen Wald" („Bosco Verticale") zu den am Fluss gelegenen Parks der Außenregionen und weiter auf den Monte Rosa erstrecken und dabei der „großen Achse" folgen würde, die Mailand und seiner Umgebung seit der Ära Napoleons Form gegeben hat.

Mailand Milan, 13.05.2015

Mailand Milan, 18.05.2015

Mailand Milan, 18.05.2015

Mailand Milan, 18.05.2015

Mailand Milan, 18.05.2015

INFRASTRUCTURE AS SPATIAL DESIGNER

INFRASTRUKTUREN ALS RAUMGESTALTER

INFRASTRUCTURE AS SPATIAL DESIGNER

BERND SCHOLL

This contribution outlines experiences of dealing with infrastructures that design space from the point of view of a spatial planner who has been convinced for a long time of the contribution of infrastructures to shaping environments in the interests of long-term spatial development. An economic approach to dwindling land resources has forced the avoidance of urban sprawl and the transformation of existing structures, which of course also includes infrastructures. We refer to the associated minimalist strategy as inward development. However, many difficult tasks of significant importance still have to be resolved. A doctoral college opens up opportunities for this, which is why dissertation projects related to "infrastructure as spatial designer" were included in the programme.

All long-term basic amenities of a personal, material, and institutional nature are referred to as infrastructures; infrastructures are significant for the functioning of an economy with a division of labour and a highly differentiated society.

Physical infrastructures and their built structures change the physical appearance of living environments. Transport infrastructures can influence spatiotemporal relationships drastically. Social infrastructures such as kindergartens, schools, and universities contribute to social education. High-level medical facilities ensure the best possible state of health among the population.

Physical infrastructures include transport routes, ports, and airports, as well as other technical infrastructures, such as for the generation and distribution of energy, the disposal of waste water, water supply, and defence against natural hazards. Underground infrastructures are often underestimated in terms of their importance as spatial structures. As they are among the particularly expensive infrastructures, also with regard to on-going maintenance, they are set up as very long-term structures. They determine the layout and use of the space above ground. Cities destroyed by wars and earthquakes have often been rebuilt on the old road pattern, because they contained the pipe systems and underground transport routes that influenced property situations. Pathways and street systems, once laid out, can last for centuries or even millennia. Old trade routes have become motorways and railway tracks. Small fishing harbours have turned into major ports, sometimes right by the sea, sometimes by a major river with maritime access, such as in Rotterdam or Hamburg. Once they reached the limits of their capacity, some of them were relocated towards

INFRASTRUKTUREN ALS RAUMGESTALTER

BERND SCHOLL

Dieser Beitrag skizziert Erfahrungen im Umgang mit Infrastrukturen als Raumgestalter aus Sicht eines Raumplaners, der vom gestaltenden Beitrag von Infrastrukturen zum Nutzen einer nachhaltigen Raumentwicklung schon seit längerem überzeugt ist. Der haushälterische Umgang mit der knappen Ressource Boden zwingt zur Vermeidung von Zersiedelung und damit zur Transformation des Bestandes, wozu selbstverständlich auch die Infrastrukturen gehören. Wir bezeichnen die damit verbundene Mindeststrategie als Innenentwicklung. Doch viele schwierige Aufgaben von grundsätzlicher Bedeutung sind noch zu lösen. Ein Doktorandenkolleg eröffnet dafür besondere Möglichkeiten, weshalb Dissertationsvorhaben, die mit „Infrastrukturen als Raumgestalter" in Verbindung stehen, in die Skizze einbezogen wurden.

Als Infrastrukturen werden alle langlebigen Grundeinrichtungen personeller, materieller und institutioneller Art bezeichnet, die für das Funktionieren einer arbeitsteiligen Volkswirtschaft und hoch differenzierten Gesellschaft von Bedeutung sind.

Materielle Infrastrukturen und ihre baulichen Anlagen verändern das physische Erscheinungsbild von Lebensräumen. Transportinfrastrukturen können Raum-Zeit-Verhältnisse drastisch beeinflussen. Soziale Infrastrukturen wie Kindergärten, Schulen und Universitäten tragen zur gesellschaftlichen Bildung und Ausbildung bei. Hochstehende medizinische Einrichtungen sorgen für eine möglichst gesunde Bevölkerung.

Zu den materiellen Infrastrukturen gehören Verkehrswege ebenso wie Häfen und Flughäfen und andere technische Infrastrukturen, beispielsweise zur Erzeugung und Verteilung von Energie, zur Beseitigung von Abwässern, zur Wasserversorgung und zur Abwehr von Naturgefahren. Sehr oft werden unterirdische Infrastrukturen in ihrer Bedeutung als Raumgestalter unterschätzt. Weil sie zu den besonders teuren Infrastrukturen gehören, auch was den dauernden Unterhalt betrifft, sind sie auf eine sehr lange Lebensdauer ausgelegt. Sie disponieren die Gestaltung und Nutzung des oberirdischen Raums. So wurden von Kriegen und Erdbeben zerstörte Städte oft wieder auf dem alten Straßensystem errichtet, weil dies Leitungssysteme sowie Verkehrswege im Untergrund und damit einhergehende Eigentumsverhältnisse nahelegten. Einmal angelegte Wege und Straßensysteme können Jahrhunderte und Jahrtausende überdauern. Aus alten Handelswegen wurden Autobahn- und Eisenbahntrassen. Aus kleinen Fischerhäfen wurden große Häfen, manchmal direkt am Meer,

the sea, which in turn opened up new urban development possibilities for the port facilities that were no longer needed, as shown by recent examples in Rotterdam, Oslo, and Copenhagen.

The title of this contribution stipulates that infrastructures act as spatial designers. However, this is of course an inadmissible simplification as such. There are actors and stakeholders that—led by their interests—have an influence on and shape space with their infrastructural projects and plans; these actions can unfortunately also blemish it. The concept of space includes the physical environment, the possibilities of change, and the resulting opportunities for being, behaviour, and experience.

It must be taken into consideration that years and decades can pass between the planning and the realisation of infrastructures. Furthermore, owing to the great significance of infrastructures, the pros and cons are the subject of public debate. Budget and time overruns during the realisation play an important role. However, the central task is especially the clarification of the intended—and unintended—effects and consequences of the infrastructures. Sectoral commissioning authorities were initially concerned with this. However, what if many parties with different aims and interests want to claim usage of the space? The view evolved in the 1960s that large-scale planning is necessary in light of the dynamic developments in many living environments. The task of spatial planning is therefore also the overall and forward-looking coordination of activities that influence space in the interests of sustainable development and the designing of our living spaces.

Owing to the mostly high investments, their spatial effects, and their contribution to the shaping of living environments, achieving added value when setting up infrastructures presents an additional task, especially for spatial planning. Such added value can only be noticed effectively if there are on-going and envisaged measures important for the future. The laws in many countries therefore rightly task spatial planning with associated aspects, such as the incorporation and communication of added value for public purposes. In order to be able to fulfil these tasks, however, spatial planning and its representatives are required to take a proactive stance. Waiting until involved parties declare their intentions rarely leads to success. Spatial planners must explore involved parties' intentions themselves, offer concepts and ideas for an integrated spatial and infrastructure development for discussion, and put these into motion early on through suitable processes, formal procedures, and, if possible, in cooperation with all the important parties involved. The spatial design discipline is involved in such processes. Markus Nollert, a participant in the first doctoral college in 2007–2011, who addressed this subject area, showed important interconnections and put forward proposals for the use of design in spatial planning practice.[1]

Consequently, initiative is required of those involved in spatial planning, which represents an additional challenge in light of its limited resources,

manchmal an einem großen Fluss mit maritimem Zugang, wie beispielsweise in Rotterdam oder Hamburg. Einmal an die Grenzen ihrer Leistungsfähigkeit gekommen, verlagerte man manche von ihnen Richtung Meer, was wiederum neue städtebauliche Möglichkeiten für die nicht mehr benötigten Hafenanlagen eröffnete, wie jüngere Beispiele aus Rotterdam, Oslo und Kopenhagen zeigen.

Der Titel dieses Beitrags legt nahe, dass Infrastrukturen den Raum gestalten. Aber dies ist natürlich eine an sich unzulässige Vereinfachung. Es sind Akteure, die – interessengeleitet – mit ihren infrastrukturellen Absichten und Vorhaben auf den Raum einwirken, ihn gestalten und leider auch verunstalten können. Der Begriff des Raums umfasst dabei die physische Umwelt, die Möglichkeiten seiner Veränderung und die dadurch entstehenden bzw. begrenzten Möglichkeiten des Daseins, Verhaltens und Erlebens.

Zu bedenken ist, dass von der Planung bis zur Realisierung von Infrastrukturen Jahre und Jahrzehnte vergehen können. Und wegen der großen Bedeutung von Infrastrukturen ist das Für und Wider Gegenstand öffentlicher Diskurse. Kosten- und Zeitüberschreitungen bei der Realisierung spielen dabei eine wichtige Rolle. Vor allem aber ist das Klären der beabsichtigten – und unbeabsichtigten – Wirkungen und Konsequenzen der Infrastrukturen die zentrale Aufgabe. Sektorale Aufgabenträger waren zunächst damit befasst. Was aber, wenn zahlreiche Akteure mit unterschiedlichen Anliegen und Interessen Nutzungen des Raums beanspruchen wollen? In den 1960er Jahren reifte deshalb die Erkenntnis, dass eine großräumige Planung vor dem Hintergrund dynamischer Entwicklungen in vielen Lebensräumen notwendig sei. Aufgabe der Raumplanung ist deshalb auch die ganzheitliche und vorausschauende Koordination raumwirksamer Tätigkeiten in Richtung einer nachhaltigen Entwicklung und Gestaltung unserer Lebensräume.

Aufgrund der meist hohen Investitionen, ihrer Raumwirksamkeiten und ihres Beitrags beim Gestalten von Lebensräumen ist die Erzielung von Mehrwerten bei der Erstellung von Infrastrukturen eine zusätzliche und besonders der Raumplanung zuwachsende Aufgabe. Denn solche Mehrwerte können erst im Überblick laufender, in Aussicht genommener und allenfalls in Zukunft bedeutsamer Vorhaben effektiv wahrgenommen werden. Zu Recht weisen die Gesetzgebungen vieler Länder der Raumplanung deshalb damit verbundene Aufgaben wie etwa die Abschöpfung und Zuführung entstandener Mehrwerte für öffentliche Zwecke zu. Um diese Aufgaben erfüllen zu können, ist allerdings eine proaktive Haltung der Raumplanung und ihrer Akteure erforderlich. Ein Abwarten, bis Akteure ihre Absichten deklarieren, führt selten zum Erfolg. Raumplanerinnen und Raumplaner müssen diese vielmehr selbst erkunden, Vorstellungen und Ideen für eine integrierte Raum- und Infrastrukturentwicklung zur Diskussion stellen und diese durch geeignete Prozesse, als Ergänzung zu den formellen Verfahren, frühzeitig – und möglichst in Zusammenarbeit mit allen wichtigen Akteuren – in Gang bringen. Bei solchen Prozessen

as opposed to the funds which are mostly abundantly available to infra-structure sponsors. It is about acquiring the required means for planning and enabling the necessary discourses at the highest level through suit-able alliances. Examples like the following show that this is achievable.

As a spatial planner, one can undoubtedly best appreciate the significance of infrastructures on the basis of examples. However, the quote that goes back to Goethe also applies with regard to this: "One only sees what one knows." In other words, one only perceives what one is aware of and al-ready understands. The difficult tasks that were solved are important for understanding the examples. Such tasks can also be referred to as prob-lems and in order to understand these problems and their solutions, the relevant background or, as we also say, the respective problem situation, is important. The problem situation includes, for example, the constellations of involved parties and schedules, the technical knowledge available at the time of seeking solutions, etc.

The examples should convey an impression of the multitude of challeng-es, tasks, and solutions in the field of spatial and infrastructural develop-ment.

Flood protection systems—Vienna and the New Danube

An impressive example of infrastructure as spatial designer is the New Danube in Vienna. It goes back to a procedural innovation from the 1970s. The original plan envisaged the creation of space for excess Danube water masses by means of a standard discharge channel, in order to protect the city of Vienna from disastrous floods. After the first kilometre had been built, there was a realisation that steep embankments secured with large stone blocks represented the squandering of the opportunity of the cen-tury for the urban development of this important European city: the use of the Danube area as a recreational area for the Viennese population. ▶ 1, 2

Today, a variously designed space comprising the New Danube and Dan-ube Island provides many hundred thousand people with peace and re-laxation, as well as a wide range of aquatic and recreational amenities, on beautiful summer days. Efficient public transport provides access to the area and a motorway was relocated from its planned location on the crest behind the trans-Danube flood dam and covered with extensive green bridges to shield bordering residential areas and the emerging recreational areas from noise pollution. The infrastructure has also passed its test as a flood protection project. The metamorphosis to a multifunctional infra-structure has generated and shaped a central living environment with ex-tensive additional usages for the local population. The procedural innova-tion of the Viennese model developed for the task was a significant factor in its success.[2] Overcoming time-consuming and often fruitless consec-utive procedures in favour of a dialogue-orientated, cooperative process, serving the purposes of learning through solving problems, contributed significantly to the pool of modern informal processes.[3,4]

kommt die Disziplin des raumplanerischen Entwerfens zum Zug. Markus Nollert, Teilnehmer des ersten Doktorandenkollegs 2007–2011, hat sich mit diesem Themenfeld beschäftigt, wichtige Zusammenhänge aufgezeigt und Vorschläge für den Einsatz des Entwerfens in der Raumplanungspraxis unterbreitet.[1]

Infolgedessen ist bei den Akteuren der Raumplanung Initiative gefragt, was vor dem Hintergrund ihrer knappen Ressourcen, aber meist reichlich vorhandener Mittel von Infrastrukturträgern eine zusätzliche Herausforderung darstellt. Die Kunst besteht darin, durch geeignete Bündnisse die erforderlichen Mittel für Planungen und die dazu notwendigen Diskurse auf höchstem Niveau zu ermöglichen. Beispiele wie die folgenden zeigen, dass dies erreichbar ist.

Man kann die Bedeutung der Infrastrukturen als Raumgestalter wohl am besten anhand von Beispielen erfahren. Allerdings gilt auch in diesem Zusammenhang das auf Goethe zurückgehende Zitat: „Man sieht nur, was mein weiß", eigentlich: Man erblickt nur, was man weiß und schon versteht. Für das Verstehen der Beispiele sind die schwierigen Aufgaben, die gelöst wurden, von Bedeutung. Solche Aufgaben können auch als Probleme bezeichnet werden. Und für das Verständnis dieser Probleme und ihrer Lösungen ist der jeweilige Hintergrund oder, wie wir auch sagen, die jeweilige Problemsituation wichtig. Zur Problemsituation gehören beispielsweise die Konstellationen von Akteuren und Zeiten, das zur Zeit der Lösungsversuche vorhandene technische Wissen etc.

Die Beispiele sollen einen Eindruck der vielfältigen Herausforderungen, Aufgaben und Lösungen im Spannungsfeld von Raum- und Infrastrukturentwicklung vermitteln.

Hochwasserschutzanlagen – Wien und die Neue Donau

Ein beeindruckendes Beispiel für Infrastrukturen als Raumgestalter ist die Neue Donau in Wien. Sie geht zurück auf eine Verfahrensinnovation aus den 1970er Jahren. Der ursprüngliche Plan sah vor, mit einem regelkonformen Entlastungskanal Raum für zusätzliche Wassermassen der Donau zu schaffen, um so die Stadt Wien vor verheerenden Hochwassern zu schützen. Nachdem der erste Kilometer gebaut war, erkannte man, dass mit steilen und durch große Steinblöcke gesicherten Uferböschungen eine Jahrhundertchance für die Stadtentwicklung dieser wichtigen europäischen Stadt vertan würde: Die Nutzung des Donaubereichs als Naherholungsgebiet für die Wiener Bevölkerung. ▶ 1, 2

Heute bietet ein vielfältig gestalteter Raum mit Neuer Donau und Donauinsel an schönen Sommertagen vielen hunderttausend Menschen Ruhe und Erholung, aber auch Bade- und Freizeitvergnügen vielfältiger Art. Leistungsfähige öffentliche Verkehrsmittel erschließen das Gebiet und eine Autobahn konnte von der geplanten Lage auf der Krone hinter den trans-danubischen Hochwasserdamm verlegt und mittels weiträumigen Grünbrücken überdeckt werden, um angrenzende Wohngebiete und die

1, 2 Old (right) and
New Danube with the
developing recreation-
al area in the city of
Vienna
1, 2 Alte (rechts) und
Neue Donau mit entste-
hendem Naherholungs-
gebiet in der Stadt Wien

Bridges—the Holbeinsteg in Frankfurt am Main

Bridge construction is often also referred to as the crowning discipline of
civil engineering. Whether a bridge is perceived as beautiful or not also
depends on whether an optimal technical solution was found for the respective situation. In many cases, problems become the starting point for
the use of novel materials, building techniques, and budget options. Furthermore, as is so often the case, it was pioneers such as the Swiss engi-
neers Maillart and Menn who used complex starting situations smartly to
reach surprisingly simple and elegant solutions.[5,6] One has the impression
that their bridges have become an integral part of the respective (rural and
urban) spaces.

Bridges are conspicuous structures. It is therefore highly important to design them carefully and to integrate them into the respective spatial context. An accomplished example, the planning of which I was able to be
involved with at the beginning of the 1980s as part of the Frankfurt museum embankment planning by the planning consultant office AS&P, is the
so-called Holbeinsteg. Conceived as a pedestrian bridge, it created a new
link to both sides of the Main embankment and to the already existing and
newly-planned museum buildings. ▶3

Building the bridge also symbolised that the fluvial and urban area of the

gerade entstehenden Erholungsflächen vor Lärm zu schützen. Seine Bewährungsprobe als Hochwasserschutzprojekt hat die Infrastruktur ebenfalls bestanden. Die Metamorphose zur multifunktionalen Infrastruktur hat einen zentralen Lebensraum mit weitreichendem Zusatznutzen für die Bevölkerung entstehen lassen und gestaltet. Die mit der Aufgabe entwickelte Verfahrensinnovation des Wiener Modells war maßgeblich für den Erfolg verantwortlich.[2] Das Überwinden zeitraubender und oft ins Leere laufender konsekutiver Verfahren durch einen dialogorientierten, kooperativen und dem Lernen beim Problemlösen verpflichteten Prozess trug maßgeblich zum Fundament moderner informeller Verfahren bei.[3,4]

Brücken – der Holbeinsteg in Frankfurt am Main

Brückenbau wird oft auch als Königsdisziplin der Bauingenieurwissenschaft bezeichnet. Ob eine Brücke als schön empfunden wird oder nicht, hängt auch davon ab, ob in der jeweiligen Situation die optimale technische Lösung gefunden wurde. Nicht selten wurden Probleme zum Ausgangspunkt für die Verwendung neuartiger Materialien, Bautechniken und Berechnungsmöglichkeiten. Und wie so oft waren es Pioniere wie beispielsweise die Schweizer Ingenieure Maillart und Menn, die komplexe Ausgangslagen geschickt nutzten, um zu überraschend einfachen und eleganten Lösungen zu kommen.[5,6] Bei ihren Brücken hat man den Eindruck als seien sie zum unverzichtbaren Teil der jeweiligen (Landschafts- und Stadt-)Räume geworden.

Brücken sind auffällige Bauwerke. Ihre sorgsame Gestaltung und Integration in die jeweiligen räumlichen Kontexte ist deshalb außerordentlich

Main was to become a new and liveable centre in Frankfurt. The pedestrian bridge, which was later christened Holbeinsteg, was conceived as a modern counterpart to the Eiserner Steg (Iron Bridge) from the nineteenth century and links the northern embankment to the nearby Städel Museum. Its high pylons, new and clearly visible landmarks on the silhouette of the Main embankment, were intended to mark the hitherto neglected river area and invite people to visit it. The location was selected in order to create a rhythm of bridges over the Main. Careful integration of the high and low quays into the embankment walls, a generally filigreed appearance, and thoughtful illumination have contributed to the enrichment of the Main embankment and its repositioning as a central meeting and recreational area in Frankfurt. Its realisation is due to the good cooperation between many disciplines, which is undoubtedly also a reason why political approval and funding could be secured quickly at a convenient time, in advance of Frankfurt's application for the Olympic Games in 2000 or 2004. The political turnaround in 1989 lead to Frankfurt withdrawing its application, but the design for the Main embankment, and with it the bridge, continued on its course.

Spatial development and railways—the Rhine-Alpine corridor Rotterdam-Genoa

Train stations are crystallisation points for inward-orientated settlement development. Higher usage density in their catchment area is justified, because a large proportion of the additional passenger transport can be handled by public transport. ▶4

This basic strategy, called TOD (*Transport-Orientated Development*), only functions, however, if train station areas and the corresponding infrastructures are attractively designed and the tracks are proven to have an adequate capacity. ▶5

Owing to the envisaged significant increase in freight transport along railway corridors of national and European importance,[7] but also in view of the opening of the Gotthard base tunnel in the current year 2016,[8] the required development of the track system needs to be implemented on time. If it is not completed by then, there is the danger that additional public transport facilities cannot be provided, or that existing facilities have to be limited. As this is diametrically opposed to sustainable spatial development, parties responsible for spatial planning took initiatives at the beginning of the 2000s along the main artery of the European railway system, the Rotterdam-Genoa corridor. This ultimately led to the Interreg project CODE 24, referred to as strategic by the EU. Under the leadership of the Rhine-Neckar regional authority, other regional authorities, the ports of Rotterdam and Genoa, and various universities also participated. The chair for Spatial Development at the Swiss Federal Institute of Technology Zurich (ETH), which had provided the impetus, was supported by the Swiss Federal Office for Spatial Planning and the Swiss Gotthard Committee. Fol-

3 *Bridge building over the Main in Frankfurt: Holbeinsteg*
3 *Brückenschlag über den Main in Frankfurt: Holbeinsteg*

bedeutsam. Ein gelungenes Beispiel, an dessen Planung ich Anfang der 1980er Jahre im Rahmen der Frankfurter Museumsuferplanung des Büros AS&P mitwirken durfte, ist der sogenannte Holbeinsteg. Als Fußgängerbrücke konzipiert, entstand mit ihm ein neuer Rundweg zu beiden Seiten des Mainufers und zu den bereits vorhandenen und neu geplanten Museumsbauten. ▶3

Mit dem Brückenschlag wurde auch symbolisiert, dass der Fluss- und Stadtraum des Mains eine neue und lebenswerte Mitte von Frankfurt werden sollte. Die später Holbsteinsteg getaufte Fußgängerbrücke war als modernes Pendant zum Eisernen Steg aus dem 19. Jahrhundert gedacht und verbindet das Nordufer mit dem nahegelegenen Städel Museum. Ihre hochaufragenden Pylone sollten als neue und deutlich wahrnehmbare Zeichen in der Silhouette des Mainufers den bis dahin vernachlässigten Flussraum markieren und zu dessen Besuch einladen. Die Lage wurde so

lowing on from this, the central bottlenecks could be identified over the course of an almost four-year process and a common strategy was worked out for both the spatial and transport development. Its implementation led in 2015 to the founding of the European joint body *Interregional Alliance for the Rhine-Alpine Corridor*.[9]

Felix Günther and Illaria Tosoni, both doctoral students at the first doctoral college, were involved in this large-scale research lab. Their dissertations provide important building blocks for macro regional spatial development in a European context.[10,11]

4 *Inward city development in the catchment area of important European train stations*
4 *Innenentwicklung im Einzugsbereich wichtiger europäischer Bahnhöfe*

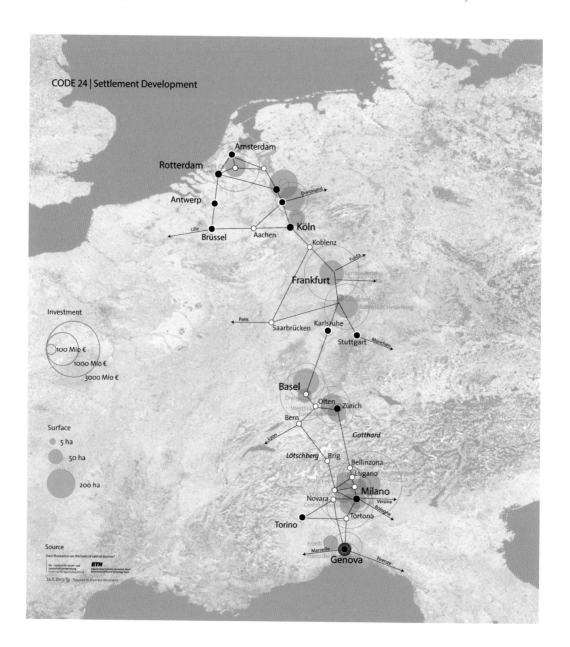

5 Tunnel building site for the new city train at Europagarten in the Europaviertel in Frankfurt am Main. A new district is being created on the former switchyard and in the catchment area of the main train station in which 30,000 people will live and work.
5 Tunnelbaustelle für die neue Stadtbahn im Europagarten des Europaviertels in Frankfurt am Main. Auf dem ehemaligen Rangierbahnhof und im Einzugsbereich des Hauptbahnhofs entsteht ein neues Stadtviertel, auf dem 30.000 Menschen leben und arbeiten werden.

gewählt, dass gleichsam ein Rhythmus der Brücken über den Main entsteht. Sorgsame Einbindung in die Ufermauern des Hoch- und Tiefkais, eine insgesamt filigrane Erscheinung und die überlegte Illumination haben zur Bereicherung des Mainufers und seiner Wiederbelebung als zentralem Frankfurter Begegnungs- und Erholungsraum beigetragen. Seine Entstehung ist der guten Zusammenarbeit vieler Disziplinen zu verdanken. Wohl auch deshalb war die politische Zustimmung und Finanzierung im Vorfeld der Bewerbung Frankfurts zu den Olympischen Spielen für 2000 oder 2004 günstig gewählt und rasch zu erreichen. Die politische Wende 1989 führte zum Rückzug Frankfurts von der Bewerbung, aber die Gestaltung des Mainufers und mit ihr der Brückenschlag nahm weiterhin seinen Lauf.

Raum- und Eisenbahnentwicklung – der Rhein-Alpen-Korridor Rotterdam – Genua

Bahnhöfe sind Kristallisationspunkte für eine nach innen gerichtete Siedlungsentwicklung. Höhere Ausnutzungen in ihrem Einzugsbereich sind gerechtfertigt, weil ein größerer Anteil des zusätzlichen Personenverkehrs durch den öffentlichen Verkehr übernommen werden kann. ▶4

Diese Grundstrategie, im Englischen TOD (*transport oriented development*) genannt, funktioniert aber nur dann, wenn Bahnhofsbereiche und die entsprechenden Infrastrukturen attraktiv gestaltet sind und schienenseitig ausreichende Leistungsfähigkeiten aufweisen. ▶5

Da die Absicht besteht, auf Eisenbahnkorridoren von nationaler und europäischer Bedeutung[7] den Anteil des Güterverkehrs maßgeblich zu steigern, müssen entsprechende Ausbauten des Schienensystems rechtzeitig erfol-

Port development along the Rhine

Over the course of the afore-mentioned corridor project for the Rotterdam-Genoa spatial and infrastructural development, it became clear that the Rhine river waterway could be given a strategic significance. If the freight transport from the "Northern Range" ports increases to the expected extent, then the envisaged delayed development of the central track and road systems along this corridor will lead to considerable overloading and congestion in addition to the already mentioned negative consequences for spatial and settlement development. ▶6

The exploitation of the existing reserves of the Rhine waterway's transport capacity could provide relief, if it is possible to complete the necessary development of relevant ports in the inland areas into multimodal hubs for freight transport.[12] The future design of the ports involved, for example near Mannheim or Cologne, has to take account of the objectives of the respective urban developments, namely an attractive settlement development near the water, on the one hand and, on the other hand, the need for an effective transport infrastructure for one of the most important economic areas in Europe. The dissertation project by Cecilia Braun called "Rhine, Space and Logistics" explores the issues, tasks, and solutions associated with this.[13] Her conclusions can contribute to integrative solutions and give the ports, as spatial structures, new and far-reaching impulses.

Airports and the "Delta" areas in Zurich

Who would deny that airports structure and design space? They are among the most important large-scale "point infrastructures." Frankfurt airport, for example, spans over 2,100 hectares within the fence. More than 80,000 employees work there and, on peak days, over 200,000 passengers pass through it. Airports are therefore quite rightly referred to as airport cities. Reception buildings, terminals, and hangars reflect the respective architectural and urban development spirit of the times, much like at the beginning of the railway era. Because airports and planes change spatiotemporal relationships significantly, much like train stations and trains did in the past, they are driving forces of urban development, not only in the narrower surroundings of the airport, but also along so-called airport axes which develop an autonomous urban development character—similar to rail connections previously. An example of this is the so-called AiRail Terminal, an airport train station built in 2010 with over 200,000 square metres of surface area. The proximity of many European airports to city centres is their advantage and, at the same time, a source of numerous spatial planning conflicts.[14] From the point of view of spatial planning, airport planning is one of the most challenging tasks, because a third dimension (aviation regulations) comes into play to a much greater extent than with conventional planning tasks. The reduction of aircraft noise through suitable take-off and landing procedures, and taking the latest

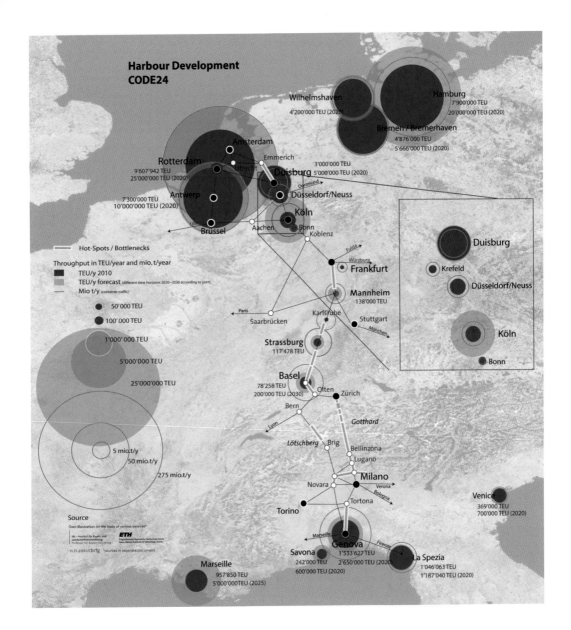

Harbour Development CODE24

Wilhelmshaven
4'200'000 TEU (2020)

Hamburg
7'900'000 TEU
20'000'000 TEU (2020)

Bremen / Bremerhaven
4'876'000 TEU
5'666'000 TEU (2020)

Amsterdam

Emmerich

Rotterdam
9'607'942 TEU
25'000'000 TEU (2020)

Utrecht

Duisburg 3'000'000 TEU
5'000'000 TEU (2020)

Dortmund

Düsseldorf/Neuss

Antwerp
7'300'000 TEU
10'000'000 TEU (2020)

Köln

Lille

Brussel

Aachen

Bonn

Koblenz

Fulda

Würzburg

Frankfurt

Mannheim
138'000 TEU

Paris

Karlsruhe

Stuttgart

Saarbrücken

München

Strassburg
117'478 TEU

Basel
78'258 TEU
200'000 TEU (2030)

Olten

Zürich

Bern

Gotthard

Lyon

Lötschberg   Brig

Bellinzona

Lugano

Milano

Novara

Verona

Bologna

Tortona

Torino

Venice
369'000 TEU
700'000 TEU (2020)

Marseille

Genova
1'533'627 TEU

Savona
242'000 TEU
600'000 TEU (2020)

Firenze

La Spezia
1'046'063 TEU
1'187'040 TEU (2020)

2'650'000 TEU (2020)

Marseille
957'850 TEU
5'000'000TEU (2025)

Duisburg

Krefeld

Düsseldorf/Neuss

Köln

Bonn

Hot-Spots / Bottlenecks

Throughput in TEU/year and mio.t/year
■ TEU/y 2010
■ TEU/y forecast (different time horizons 2020–2030 according to port)
— Mio t/y (container traffic)

● 50'000 TEU
● 100'000 TEU

1'000'000 TEU

5'000'000 TEU

25'000'000 TEU

5 mio.t/y
50 mio.t/y
275 mio.t/y

Source
Own illustration on the basis of various sources*
IRL – Institut für Raum- und Landschaftsentwicklung
Professur für Raumentwicklung
Eidgenössische Technische Hochschule Zürich
Swiss Federal Institute of Technology Zurich
ETH
11.11.2011/cb/fg *sources in separate document

gen, auch im Hinblick auf die Eröffnung des Gotthard-Basis-Tunnels im laufenden Jahr 2016.[8] Gelingt dies nicht, besteht die Gefahr, dass zusätzliche Angebote für den öffentlichen Verkehr nicht bereitgestellt werden können oder sogar bestehende Angebote eingeschränkt werden müssen. Weil dies einer nachhaltigen Raumentwicklung diametral zuwiderläuft, ergriffen für Raumplanung zuständige Akteure Anfang der 2000er Jahre längs der Hauptschlagader des europäischen Eisenbahnsystems, dem Korridor Rotterdam – Genua, die Initiative. Dies führte schließlich zu dem von der EU als strategisch bezeichneten Interreg-Projekt CODE 24. Unter Federführung des Regionalverbandes Rhein-Neckar wirkten weitere Regi-

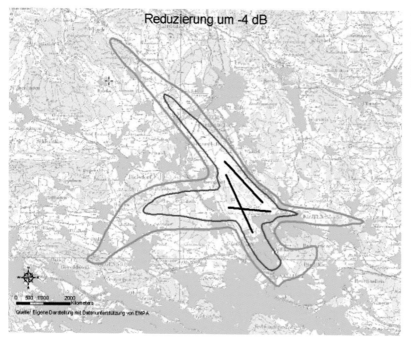

Reduzierung um -4 dB

0 500 1000 2000 Kilometers

Quelle: Eigene Darstellung mit Datenunterstützung von EMPA

7 Aerial photograph of
Zurich airport (view to
the south)
7 Luftbild Flughafen
Zürich (Blick nach
Süden)

technologies and insights from engine research into account, is a central
task in this respect. Yose Kadrin investigated this during the first doctoral
college. Through simulations of air traffic modernised in this way, he was
able to prove that considerable areas could be excluded from the noise
perimeter, which would bring new design potential for airport and spatial
development. Kadrin refers to the areas formerly polluted by noise as "Del-
ta" areas[15] and recommends special customised planning procedures for
their development. ▶7, 8
I became aware of these connections as chairman of an advisory council and test planning procedure for the airport and spatial development
of Zurich airport.[16] As part of this special procedure, all possible runway
configurations were tested, in order to bring the operational requirements
in line with sustainable, long-term spatial development as far as possible.[17]

Power grids

The current changes in the supply of electric power as part of the energy
transition require adaptations of power supply infrastructures. While in
Germany, for example, new and large-scale high-voltage power lines have
to be found for transmitting wind energy from the coasts to the consumer
centres, the focus in Switzerland is on the replacement and bundling of
the existing infrastructures for high-voltage power transmission. As such
power lines' high masts can shape and have a massive influence on the appearance and use of settlement, landscape, and recreational areas, spatial
planning must assume a coordinative role. One of the central challenges is

onalverbände, die Häfen Rotterdam und Genua und verschiedene Universitäten mit. Die Professur für Raumentwicklung der ETH Zürich, die den Anstoß gegeben hatte, wurde vom schweizerischen Bundesamt für Raumplanung und dem Schweizer Gotthard-Komitee unterstützt.

In der Folge konnten in einem fast vierjährigen Prozess die zentralen Flaschenhälse identifiziert und eine gemeinsame Strategie für die Raum- und Verkehrsentwicklung erarbeitet werden. Deren Umsetzung führte 2015 zur Gründung des europäischen Zweckverbands Interregional Alliance for the Rhine-Alpine Corridor.[9]

Felix Günther und Illaria Tosoni, beide Doktorierende des ersten Doktorandenkollegs, wirkten in diesem großräumigen Forschungslabor mit. Ihre Dissertationen schaffen wichtige Bausteine für eine makroregionale Raumentwicklung im europäischen Zusammenhang.[10,11]

Hafenentwicklung am Rhein

Im Rahmen des schon erwähnten Korridorprojektes der Raum- und Infrastrukturentwicklung Rotterdam – Genua wurde deutlich, dass der Wasserstraße des Rheinflusses eine strategische Bedeutung zukommen kann. Sollten die Güterverkehre sich von den „Northern Range"-Seehäfen im erwartenden Ausmaß einstellen, wird der absehbar verzögerte Ausbau der zentralen Schienen- und Straßensysteme in diesem Korridor zu erheblichen Überlastungen – neben den bereits erwähnten negativen Folgewirkungen für die Raum- und Siedlungsentwicklung – führen. ▶6

Das Ausnutzen der vorhandenen Reserven in der Beförderungskapazität der Wasserstraße Rhein könnte Abhilfe schaffen, wenn es gelingt, die dafür erforderliche Entwicklung systemrelevanter Häfen im Hinterland zu multimodalen Drehscheiben des Güterverkehrs voranzubringen.[12] Die zukünftige Gestaltung der infrage kommenden Häfen, beispielsweise im Raum Mannheim oder Köln, vollzieht sich im Spannungsfeld von den Anliegen der jeweiligen Stadtentwicklungen, eine wassernahe und damit an sich attraktive Siedlungsentwicklung zu betreiben und den Erfordernissen einer effektiven Transportinfrastruktur für einen der wichtigsten Wirtschaftsräume Europas. Mit der Erkundung von damit im Zusammenhang stehenden Fragen, Aufgaben und Lösungen beschäftigt sich das Dissertationsvorhaben von Cecilia Braun *Rhein, Raum und Logistik*.[13] Ihre Erkenntnisse können zu integrierenden Lösungen beitragen und den Häfen als Raumgestaltern neue und weitreichende Impulse verleihen.

Flughäfen und die Deltaflächen in Zürich

Wer möchte bestreiten, dass Flughäfen Raumgestalter sind. Sie gehören zu den bedeutsamen und flächenmäßig großen „Punktinfrastrukturen". Der Frankfurter Flughafen beispielsweise belegt, innerhalb des Zauns, über 2100 Hektar. Mehr als 80.000 Beschäftigte arbeiten dort und an Spitzentagen halten sich dort über 200.000 Passagiere auf. Zu Recht wird deshalb von Flughafenstädten oder Airport Cities gesprochen.

8 *Airport and spatial development. Possible reduction of aircraft noise by four decibels.*
8 *Flughafen- und Raumentwicklung. Mögliche Reduktion des Fluglärms bei Reduzierung um vier Dezibel*

recognising which areas require action, in order to identify conflicts at an early stage and to be able to make use of synergies in the interests of an integrated spatial and infrastructural development. ▶9

Within the 2013–2016 doctoral college, Silke Rendigs from the Swiss Federal Institute of Technology Zurich (ETH) is investigating the challenges and tasks for spatial planning in relation to the transformation of the Swiss power transmission grid.[18]

Epilogue

The examples show that intense cooperation is necessary, in order to be able to identify, clarify, and solve conflicts between the various land use interests. This must occur on the basis of the overall context and of an overview of the current and future significant spatial activities. This heralded modern spatial planning in the 1960s and the creation of binding legal foundations.

Spatial planning is, first and foremost, a design task. Its central task is the pre-emptive coordination of spatial interventions, also in order to identify and, if necessary, to preserve or make use of design potential. This task can

Ähnlich wie zu Beginn des Eisenbahnzeitalters spiegeln Empfangsgebäude, Terminalanlagen und Hangars den jeweiligen architektonischen und städtebaulichen Zeitgeist wider. Und weil Flughäfen und Flugzeuge, wie einstmals Bahnhöfe und die Eisenbahn, Raum-Zeit-Verhältnisse markant verändern, sind sie Treiber städtebaulicher Entwicklungen. Dies nicht nur im engeren landseitigen Umfeld des Flughafens, sondern auch längs sogenannter Flughafenachsen, die – ähnlich wie einst Bahnhofsanbindungen – einen eigenständigen städtebaulichen Charakter entwickeln. Ein Beispiel dafür ist das sogenannte AiRail-Terminal, ein seit 2010 überbauter Flughafenbahnhof mit über 200.000 Quadratmetern Geschossfläche. Die nahe Lage vieler europäischer Flughäfen zu den Stadtzentren ist ihr Vorteil und gleichzeitig Quelle zahlreicher raumplanerischer Konflikte.[14] Aus der Sicht der Raumplanung gehört Flughafenplanung zu den extrem anspruchsvollen Aufgaben, weil die dritte Dimension (und damit das Regelwerk der Aviatik) viel stärker ins Spiel kommt als bei den üblichen planerischen Aufgaben. Die Minderung des Fluglärms durch geeignete An- und Ablaufverfahren unter Einbeziehung neuester Techniken und Erkenntnisse aus der Triebwerksforschung ist dabei die zentrale Aufgabe. Im ersten Doktorandenkolleg hat sich Yose Kadrin damit beschäftigt. Er kann durch Simulationen eines auf diese Weise modernisierten Flugverkehrs belegen, das beachtliche Flächen aus dem Lärmperimeter entlassen werden könnten, was neue Gestaltungsspielräume für die Flughafen- und Raumentwicklung mit sich bringen würde. Kadrin bezeichnet die ehemals lärmbelasteten Flächen als Deltaflächen[15] und empfiehlt für ihre Entwicklung besondere, maßzuschneidernde Planungsverfahren. ▶7,8

Auf diese Zusammenhänge wurde ich als Vorsitzender eines Begleitgremiums und Testplanungsverfahrens zur Flughafen- und Raumentwicklung des Flughafens Zürich aufmerksam.[16] Im Rahmen dieses speziellen Verfahrens wurden auch alle möglichen Pistenkonfigurationen getestet, um die Anforderungen des Betriebs und einer nachhaltigen Raumentwicklung bestmöglich in Einklang bringen zu können.[17]

Stromnetze

Die aktuellen Veränderungen in der elektrischen Energieversorgung im Zuge der Energiewende erfordern Anpassungen der Infrastrukturen für die Stromversorgung. Während in Deutschland beispielsweise neue und großräumige Hochspannungstrassen für die Übertragung der Windenergie von den Küsten in die Zentren des Verbrauchs gefunden werden müssen, liegt in der Schweiz der Schwerpunkt auf dem Ersatz und der Bündelung der bestehenden Infrastrukturen für die Stromübertragung im Hochspannungsbereich. Da solche Leitungen mit ihren hohen Masten das Erscheinungsbild und die Nutzung von Siedlungs-, Landschafts- und Erholungsräumen massiv beeinflussen und gestalten können, muss die Raumplanung ihren koordinativen Auftrag wahrnehmen. Eine der zentralen Herausforderungen besteht darin, zu erkennen, in welchen Räumen

9 *Power grids near Kaisten, Switzerland*
9 *Stromnetze bei Kaisten, Schweiz*

be fulfilled effectively if existing design possibilities in conjunction with infrastructures are recognised early on.

An unprejudiced investigation of all possibilities, especially in highly contentious constellations, is not possible by means of conventional, formal processes and consecutive procedural schemata alone. The experiences of recent decades have taught us that informal, temporary, and customised procedures, such as the test planning method, are needed alongside formal procedures, in order to be able to agree on viable solutions. It is basically about identifying the course of spatial development worth pursuing, on the basis of competing ideas. This requires time and money. Compared to the major follow-up investments that are usually involved, however, the costs for pre-emptive planning processes are minuscule and are justified accordingly. The scarcest "resource," however, are enthusiastic and resilient experts, who are prepared to take initiative and to assume responsibility for collaborations that usually last several years.

In the International Doctoral College "Spatial Research Lab," the role of "infrastructure as spatial designer" was discussed and reflected on in numerous dissertation projects. We would be delighted if the results stimulated academic discourse and had an effect on practice.

Handlungsbedarf besteht, um Konflikte frühzeitig identifizieren und Synergien im Sinne einer intergierten Raum- und Infrastrukturentwicklung nutzen zu können. ▶9

Im Rahmen des Doktorandenkollegs 2013–2016 beschäftigt sich Silke Rendigs von der ETH Zürich mit Herausforderungen und Aufgaben für die Raumplanung vor dem Hintergrund der Transformation des Schweizer Stromübertragungsnetzes.[18]

Epilog

Die Beispiele zeigen, dass eine intensive Zusammenarbeit notwendig ist, um Konflikte zwischen den verschiedenen an der Nutzung des Bodens vertretenen Interessen erkennen, klären und lösen zu können. Dies muss aus dem Gesamtzusammenhang heraus und aus der Übersicht der gegenwärtigen und in Zukunft raumbedeutsamen Aktivitäten geschehen. Dafür wurde die moderne Raumplanung in den 1960er Jahren aus der Taufe gehoben und dafür wurden verbindliche rechtliche Grundlagen geschaffen. Raumplanung ist zuvorderst eine Gestaltungsaufgabe. Ihr zentraler Auftrag besteht in der vorausschauenden Koordination raumwirksamer Tätigkeiten, auch um Gestaltungspielräume zu erkennen und wo nötig zu bewahren oder auszunutzen. Dieser Auftrag wird dann wirksam erfüllt, wenn frühzeitig erkannt wird, welche Möglichkeiten der Gestaltung, namentlich im Zusammenspiel mit den Infrastrukturen, überhaupt bestehen. Vorurteilsfreies Erkunden aller infrage kommenden Möglichkeiten, gerade in konfliktreichen Konstellationen, ist mit den üblichen formellen Verfahren und konsekutiven Ablaufschemata alleine nicht möglich. Die Erfahrungen der letzten Jahrzehnte lehren uns, dass als Ergänzung zu den formellen Verfahren informelle, zeitlich begrenzte und maßzuschneidernde Verfahren wie beispielsweise Testplanungen benötigt werden, um tragfähige Lösungen vereinbaren zu können. Im Kern geht es darum, auf der Grundlage konkurrierender Ideen die verfolgenswerte Richtung der räumlichen Entwicklung zu erkennen. Dafür ist Zeit und Geld erforderlich. Im Verhältnis zu den großen Folgeinvestitionen, um die es meistens geht, bewegen sich die Aufwendungen für vorhergehende Planungsprozesse aber im Promillebereich und sind angesichts dessen gerechtfertigt. Die knappste „Ressource" aber sind begeisterungsfähige und belastbare Fachleute, die bereit sind, Initiativen zu ergreifen und Verantwortung für meist viele Jahre dauernde Zusammenarbeiten zu übernehmen.

Im Internationalen Doktorandenkolleg „Forschungslabor Raum" konnte in den letzten Jahren an zahlreichen Dissertationsvorhaben die Rolle der „Infrastrukturen als Raumgestalter" besprochen und reflektiert werden. Wir freuen uns, wenn die Ergebnisse den wissenschaftlichen Diskurs beleben und Wirkung in der Praxis zeigen.

München Munich, 14.08.2013

INFRASTRUCTURE AS SPATIAL DESIGNER ::::: INFRASTRUKTUREN ALS RAUMGESTALTER

Hamburg, 21.11.2013

Belgrad Belgrade, 12.06.2014

Hamburg, 17.11.2013

Stuttgart, 19.03.2014

Belgrad Belgrade, 14.06.2014

Wien Vienna, 13.03.2013

RHINE, SPACE AND LOGISTICS
Integrated development of ports and cities along the Rhine-Alpine-Corridor

CECILIA BRAUN

The rapidly progressing globalisation of the flow of goods is presenting new challenges to the development of logistics and freight transport. Sea ports like Rotterdam and Antwerp are preparing for the increased shipment of containers with massive expansion projects and are striving for the ever more efficient processing of goods for onward transport into inland areas.

The impact of this development on inland transport is especially noticeable along the main north-south transport axis from Rotterdam to Genoa (i.e. the Rhine-Alpine-Corridor). Owing to the increasing transport burden on European rail and road routes, an increasing proportion of the freight will have to be transferred to waterways (Rhine navigation). In order to handle the anticipated volume of containers and prepare for the logistical demands, many inland ports are taking trimodal expansion measures (road – rail – ship), as well as extending container terminals. The logistical requirements and their impact on the environment, as well as the many opportunities to link the development of ports and cities, have not been taken sufficiently into consideration until now. The challenge that presents itself is to assess the various logistical requirements and planning projects of the ports and cities along the Rhine and to coordinate them in advance with the aims of European spatial and transport development.

In order to establish the limitations and capacities of shipping on the Rhine, an overview of port developments along the Rhine axis is required. Based on this overview, one can identify the spatial planning issues and tasks which will be important for integrated spatial and transport development. An intact infrastructure alone does not guarantee the success of international freight transport corridors. It is essential to identify system-relevant inland ports that organise the onward distribution of inland transport and act as a hinterland-hub for the sea ports. In order to ensure the smooth processing of goods and an improved transport flow, a strong cooperation is needed among the actors involved in logistics, port administration, and spatial planning. Sustainable spatial development along the Rhine axis requires a closer study of development options and interrelations between the port authorities and the identification of an integrated overall strategy for the future for significant ports.

Meanwhile, several port cities along the Rhine are planning the mobilisation of potential port areas as extensions of urban residential and transport development. This is leading to competing land-use demands between different parties (port, city, logistics, etc.), which must be addressed early on through cooperative planning procedures. At system-relevant ports in Cologne, Mannheim, Strasbourg, and Basel, conflicts are being explored exemplarily and suggestions for solutions on different planning levels are being sought. The insights gained allow conclusions to be drawn about the overall development of the corridor.

RHEIN, RAUM UND LOGISTIK
Integrierte Hafen- und Stadtentwicklung am Rhein-Alpen-Korridor

CECILIA BRAUN

Die mit hoher Geschwindigkeit voranschreitende Globalisierung der Warenströme stellt die Entwicklung der Logistik und des Güterverkehrs vor neue Herausforderungen. Seehäfen bereiten sich durch gewaltige Ausbauprojekte auf den wachsenden Containerverkehr vor und streben eine schnellstmögliche Abwicklung der Güter für den Weitertransport ins Hinterland an.

Besonders erkennbar sind die Auswirkungen dieser Entwicklung auf den Hinterlandverkehr an der Haupt-Nord-Süd-Verkehrsachse von Rotterdam bis Genua (Rhein-Alpen-Korridor). Aufgrund der steigenden Verkehrsüberlastung auf europäischen Schienen- und Straßenwegen wird ein zunehmender Teil der Güter auf die Wasserstraße (Rheinschifffahrt) verlagert werden müssen. Damit das zu erwartende Containeraufkommen bewältigt werden kann, bereiten sich eine Vielzahl von Binnenhäfen auf die logistischen Anforderungen durch trimodale Ausbaumaßnahmen (Straße-Schiene-Schiff) und Terminalerweiterungen vor. Bislang werden die Anforderungen der Logistik und deren Auswirkungen auf den Raum sowie die vielfältigen Verknüpfungsmöglichkeiten zwischen Hafen- und Stadtentwicklung zu wenig berücksichtigt. Die Herausforderung besteht darin, die unterschiedlichen logistischen Anforderungen und Planvorhaben der Häfen und Städte am Rhein zu erfassen und frühzeitig auf die Ziele der europäischen Raum- und Verkehrsentwicklung abzustimmen.

Um die Engpässe und Kapazitäten der Rheinschifffahrt ausfindig zu machen, ist eine Übersicht der Hafenentwicklungen entlang der Rheinachse notwendig. Anhand dieser Übersicht lassen sich die raumplanerischen Fragestellungen und Aufgaben identifizieren, die für eine integrierte Raum- und Verkehrsentwicklung von Bedeutung sein werden. Eine intakte Infrastruktur allein garantiert nicht den Erfolg der internationalen Güterverkehrskorridore. Unabdingbar sind einige systemrelevante Binnenhäfen, die die Weiterverteilung des Hinterlandverkehrs organisieren und als Binnenhafen-Hub der Seehäfen im Hinterland auftreten. Für die reibungslose Abwicklung der Güter und die Verbesserung des Verkehrsflusses ist daher eine starke Zusammenarbeit zwischen den Akteuren aus den Bereichen Logistik, Hafenwirtschaft und Raumplanung notwendig. Eine nachhaltige Raumentwicklung entlang der Rheinschiene erfordert, die Entwicklungsmöglichkeiten und Wechselbeziehungen der Hafengesellschaften besser zu studieren und eine zukünftige, übergeordnete und integrierte Gesamtstrategie einiger bedeutender Häfen zu erkennen.

Indessen planen mehrere Hafenstädte entlang des Rheins die Mobilisierung von potenziellen Hafenflächen zur Erweiterung der städtischen Siedlungs- und Verkehrsentwicklung. Dabei entstehen konkurrierende Flächennutzungsansprüche zwischen unterschiedlichen Akteuren (Hafen, Stadt, Logistik usw.), die frühzeitig durch kooperative Planungsverfahren angegangen werden müssen. Beispielhaft werden in den systemrelevanten Häfen Köln, Mannheim, Straßburg und Basel Problemstellungen erkundet und Vorschläge zu Lösungen auf lokaler Ebene erarbeitet. Die Erkenntnisse ermöglichen Rückschlüsse auf die gesamtheitliche Korridorentwicklung.

SAVING ENERGY THROUGH INNER DEVELOPMENT?
The contribution of inner urban development to reducing energy consumption

KARIN HOLLENSTEIN

The availability of energy is a significant precondition for the functioning of our society. However, when we produce and use energy, we burden our environment, for example through toxic emissions, non-recyclable waste, or interventions into the landscape. A more economical use of energy is necessary in order to minimise the negative impact of energy consumption and, at the same time, to ensure an adequate energy supply. Spatial development can play a key role in this. Compact, energy-efficient urban development with mixed uses, good public transport connections and short transport routes can make a significant contribution to a more sparing use of energy.

There has been little research so far into how strongly the urban structure can really influence energy consumption. How much energy can be saved by systematic inner development, meaning development within the already existing, settlement area (through new buildings, replacement buildings, adding storeys, extensions, etc.) compared to building on the periphery (outer development)? Initial studies which included assessments of energy consumption for building, mobility, and infrastructure respectively, resulted in a reduction of annual primary energy consumption of up to 20 per cent if available space in the existing settlement area, instead of that on the periphery, was developed. In general, it was shown that inward city development can result in a reduction of per capita energy consumption of up to 30 per cent as compared to development of building zones in the countryside.

A central challenge facing inner development is the transformation of existing buildings. 78 per cent of buildings in Switzerland were built before 1990 and have a rather high energy consumption rate, therefore the modernisation of existing buildings could lead to considerable energy savings. How much energy could be saved through the energetic upgrading of districts, in combination with an increase in user density? What are the greatest difficulties presented by the realisation of such district transformations?

The focus of the research project is to find out, by means of quantitative estimations, what effect various urban development strategies have on the use of energy. Based on the insights gained, it will formulate principles for energy-efficient urban development, especially in Switzerland. The identification of locations to be targeted in the interests of energy-efficient urban development is a central aim in this process.

ENERGIESPAREN DURCH INNENENTWICKLUNG?
Beitrag der Siedlungsentwicklung nach innen zur Senkung der Energieinanspruchnahme

KARIN HOLLENSTEIN

Die Verfügbarkeit von Energie ist eine wesentliche Voraussetzung für das Funktionieren unserer Gesellschaft. Wenn wir Energie gewinnen und nutzen, belasten wir dadurch aber unsere Umwelt, zum Beispiel durch den Ausstoß von Schadstoffen, nicht recycelbare Abfälle oder Eingriffe in die Landschaft. Um die negativen Folgen der Energienutzung möglichst gering zu halten und die Versorgung mit Energie gleichzeitig sicherzustellen, ist ein haushälterischer Umgang mit Energie unumgänglich. Die Raumentwicklung kann dabei eine Schlüsselrolle spielen. Kompakte, energieeffiziente, nutzungsgemischte und gut mit dem öffentlichen Verkehr erschlossene Siedlungen sowie kurze Transportwege können einen wesentlichen Beitrag zum sparsameren Umgang mit Energie leisten.

Wie stark die Siedlungsstruktur die Energieinanspruchnahme tatsächlich beeinflussen kann, ist bisher wenig erforscht. Wie viel Energie lässt sich durch konsequente Innenentwicklung, das heißt Siedlungsentwicklung innerhalb des bereits bestehenden Siedlungsgebiets (durch Neubau, Ersatzneubau, Aufstockung, Anbau etc.) im Vergleich zum Bauen am Siedlungsrand (Außenentwicklung) einsparen? Erste Untersuchungen, bei denen der personenbezogene Energieverbrauch für das Gebäude, die Mobilität und die Infrastruktur abgeschätzt wurde, ergaben einen bis zu 20 Prozent geringeren jährlichen Primärenergieverbrauch, wenn anstelle der Reserven am Siedlungsrand diejenigen im bestehenden Siedlungsgebiet neu bebaut wurden. Generell zeigte sich, dass Innenentwicklung in der Stadt eine bis zu 30 Prozent geringere Energieinanspruchnahme pro Kopf zur Folge haben kann als die Nutzung von Bauzonenreserven auf dem Land.

Eine zentrale Herausforderung der Innenentwicklung ist die Transformation des Gebäudebestands. 78 Prozent der Gebäude in der Schweiz wurden vor 1990 erstellt und haben einen eher hohen Energiebedarf. Dies lässt ein großes Energiesparpotenzial in der Erneuerung bestehender Gebäude vermuten. Wie viel Energie ließe sich durch die energetische Erneuerung von Quartieren in Kombination mit der Erhöhung der Nutzerdichten einsparen? Welches sind die größten Schwierigkeiten bei der Realisierung solcher Quartierstransformationen?

Der Fokus des Forschungsvorhabens liegt darin, anhand quantitativer Abschätzungen herauszufinden, welchen Effekt unterschiedliche Siedlungsentwicklungsstrategien auf die Inanspruchnahme von Energie haben. Auf der Grundlage der gewonnenen Erkenntnisse soll Handlungswissen für die energieeffiziente Siedlungsentwicklung, insbesondere in der Schweiz, gebildet werden. Das Identifizieren von Räumen, die im Sinne einer energieeffizienten Siedlungsentwicklung schwerpunktmäßig zu behandeln sind, ist ein wesentliches Ziel der Arbeit.

TRANSFORMATION OF THE SWISS POWER TRANSMISSION GRID
Challenges and tasks for spatial planning

SILKE RENDIGS

The current changes in electricity supply require the adaptation of power transmission infrastructures, which presents spatial planning with new challenges and tasks. This project analyses which areas require special action in order to achieve integrated spatial and infrastructural development and what tools and procedures are necessary. The planned renunciation of nuclear energy in Switzerland (hitherto 30–40 per cent of national energy generation), the increased use of renewable energies, and the internationalisation of the electricity market necessitate the transformation of power transmission infrastructure. The primary objective of the Swiss confederation remains to ensure a stable, reliable, and lasting power supply. However, the required extension and conversion of power lines presents significant difficulties. The increasing usage demands on limited land resources, a dynamic and disperse settlement development, and strict nature and landscape conservation have restricted the scope for the development of linear structures for years. On the other hand, it is evident on site that power lines shape the space significantly, change the appearance of the landscape, and can also limit planned settlement developments inwardly. The critical examination of existing infrastructures with a view to improvement (such as bundling, relocation, or dismantling) must therefore be an integral aspect of the on-going transformation process.

The clarification of factors that influence spatial design, as well as of spatial conflicts and problems, is an essential precondition for viable development and therefore an urgent task for spatial planning. In Switzerland, clear coordination principles are imposed on spatial planning by the federal constitution and spatial planning law. In accordance with these regulations, spatial planning must participate actively in integrated spatial and infrastructural development in the described transformation process. However, there are still various unanswered questions as to how to fulfil this obligation. What tasks and challenges must spatial planning face? What spatial demands require coordination today and in the future? Which areas are in special need of coordination? Does spatial planning have suitable tools at its disposal to meet the legal task?

In order to solve the power supply issues of the future, it is of key importance for spatial planning to find answers to these questions and provide solution concepts as soon as possible. This project makes a contribution to this by studying the transformation of a strategic infrastructure from the point of view of spatial planning.

TRANSFORMATION DES SCHWEIZER STROMÜBERTRAGUNGSNETZES
Herausforderungen und Aufgaben für die Raumplanung

SILKE RENDIGS

Die aktuellen Veränderungen in der elektrischen Energieversorgung erfordern eine Anpassung der Infrastrukturen für die Stromübertragung und stellen damit die Raumplanung vor neue Herausforderungen und Aufgaben. Das Vorhaben untersucht, welche Räume besondere Handlungserfordernisse für eine integrierte Raum- und Infrastrukturentwicklung aufweisen und welche Instrumente und Verfahren erforderlich sind.

In der Schweiz macht die geplante Abkehr von der Kernenergie (bisher: 30–40 Prozent der Landesproduktion), der vermehrte Einsatz erneuerbarer Energien und die Internationalisierung des Strommarktes die Transformation der Infrastruktur für die Stromübertragung erforderlich. Die oberste Zielvorgabe der Eidgenossenschaft bleibt dabei unverändert der Erhalt einer stabilen dauerhaften Versorgungssicherheit. Der erforderliche Aus- und Umbau der Stromleitungen ist jedoch mit erheblichen Schwierigkeiten verbunden. Die zunehmenden Nutzungsansprüche an die nicht vermehrbare Ressource Boden, eine dynamische und disperse Siedlungsentwicklung und ein strengerer Schutz von Natur und Landschaft lassen seit Jahren die Entwicklungsspielräume für lineare Infrastrukturen schwinden. Auf der anderen Seite zeigt sich vor Ort, dass Übertragungslei-

tungen signifikant den Raum gestalten, das Landschaftsbild verändern und auch planerisch gewollte Siedlungsentwicklungen nach innen einschränken können. Die kritische Prüfung bestehender Infrastrukturen im Hinblick auf Verbesserung (wie Bündelungen, Verlegung oder Rückbau) muss daher Bestandteil des laufenden Transformationsprozesses sein.

Die Klärung von Einflussfaktoren auf die Gestaltung des Raumes sowie von räumlichen Konflikten und Problemen ist eine unabdingbare Voraussetzung für eine zukunftsfähige Entwicklung und daher eine dringliche Aufgabe der Raumplanung. In der Schweiz ist die Raumplanung durch die Bundesverfassung und das Raumplanungsgesetz mit einem klaren Abstimmungs- und Koordinationsauftrag ausgestattet. Sie ist daher gehalten, sich im beschriebenen Transformationsprozess aktiv für eine integrierte Raum- und Infrastrukturentwicklung einzubringen. Allerdings stellen sich bisher noch diverse unbeantwortete Fragen, wie dieser Auftrag zu erfüllen ist: Welchen Aufgaben und Herausforderungen muss sich die räumliche Planung stellen? Welche Raumansprüche sind heute und künftig abstimmungsbedürftig? Welche Räume erfordern einen besonderen Koordinationsbedarf? Und hat die räumliche Planung geeignete Instrumente an der Hand, um ihrem gesetzlichen Auftrag nachzukommen?

Für die Lösung der Zukunftsfragen in der Stromversorgung ist es entscheidend, dass die Raumplanung Antworten auf diese Fragen findet und frühzeitig Lösungskonzepte zur Verfügung stellen kann. Das Vorhaben leistet dafür einen Beitrag, indem es die Transformation einer strategischen Infrastruktur mit der Brille der Raumplanung prüft.

NEW URBAN LANDSCAPE—NETWORK CITY

NEUES STADTLAND – NETZ(WERK)STADT

NEW SPATIAL IMAGES OF THE CULTIVATED LANDSCAPE

UDO WEILACHER

"When dealing with a painting, we are used to the fact that an artist creates it," wrote the Swiss Gustav Ammann in 1941. "But a whole group of people, soldiers, farmers, foresters, soil improvers, etc. work on the picture presented by our landscape. Today, people still have no idea what this undirected work means for the image of our landscape, and how significantly its face will change—certainly not in its favour. [...] For who actually takes responsibility today for these violent interventions and changes of an aesthetic nature, but also related to climate, biology, and hydraulics? The authorities? Is that enough? Is there someone here who is really an authority, who has experience in tending and shaping the image of the landscape, and who does not think only of technical advantages? For what is the nature of these specialists? They are mere technicians, who per-

1 *The "cultivated landscape as a communal asset," here at the Mechtenberg near Gelsenkitchen, is often viewed as a mere side effect and is still subject to rapid change.*
1 *Das „Gemeinschaftsgut Kulturlandschaft", hier am Mechtenberg bei Gelsenkirchen, wird häufig als reines Nebenprodukt betrachtet und unterliegt nach wie vor einem raschen Wandel.*

NEUE RAUMBILDER DER KULTURLANDSCHAFT

UDO WEILACHER

„Bei einem Bilde sind wir gewohnt, dass es von einem Künstler geschaffen wird", schrieb der Schweizer Gustav Ammann 1941. „An unserem Landschaftsbild arbeitet aber eine ganze Gruppe von Personen, Soldaten, Bauern, Förster, Bodenverbesserer u. a. Man macht sich heute noch gar keinen Begriff, was dieses ungeleitete Arbeiten an unserem Landschaftsbild bedeutet und wie bedeutend sich sein Antlitz verändern wird – sicher nicht zu seinen Gunsten. [...] Wer übernimmt denn eigentlich heute die Verantwortung für diese gewaltigen Eingriffe und Veränderungen ästhetischer, aber auch klimatischer, biologischer und wasserbaulicher Art? Die Ämter? Genügt das? Ist hier jemand Massgebender dabei, der wirklich Erfahrung hat auch in Bezug auf Pflege und Gestaltung des Landschaftsbildes und der nicht nur an den technischen Nutzen denkt? Denn welcher Art sind diese Spezialisten? Doch reine Techniker, die das landschaftliche Idyll, ohne es überhaupt zu sehen, mechanisch perfektionieren nur unter dem Gesichtspunkt der Ratio."[1] Ammann, späterer Generalsekretär der International Federation of Landscape Architects IFLA, war einer der ersten Gartenarchitekten im deutschsprachigen Raum, der sich gegen Ende des Zweiten Weltkrieges über „Das Landschaftsbild und die Dringlichkeit seiner Pflege und Gestaltung" weitreichende Gedanken machte. Er forderte damals, dass vorrangig Landschaftsarchitekten die Verantwortung für die Gestaltung des Landschaftsbildes übernehmen sollten, weil nur sie die Landschaft als Gesamtheit im Blick hätten.

Im Internationalen Doktorandenkolleg „Forschungslabor Raum" wird seit Jahren die Erfahrung gemacht, dass die tiefgreifenden Transformationsprozesse in der Landschaft – und die Stadt gilt selbstverständlich als Teil davon – nur in interdisziplinärer Kooperation bewältigt werden können. Keine Einzeldisziplin kann die Folgen dieser Veränderungen im Alleingang meistern, aber an Gustav Ammanns Forderung nach mehr Verantwortungsbewusstsein für die ästhetische Qualität des Landschaftsbildes hat sich dennoch bis heute nichts geändert – im Gegenteil. ▶1

Der Verbrauch der begrenzten „Ressource Landschaft" schreitet mit sichtbaren Folgen ungebremst voran, und die Kulturlandschaft muss noch immer als „institutionell heimatlos" betrachtet werden. „Angesichts der Regelungsdichte in hochentwickelten Gesellschaften ist das Gemeinschaftsgut Kulturlandschaft vielmehr das ‚by-product' [...] unterschiedlicher Institutionen und Institutionensysteme, die auf die heterogenen Kulturlandschaftselemente und -bestandteile wirken."[2] Am aktuellen

fect the landscape idyll mechanically, without seeing it at all, merely from the point of view of reason."[1] Ammann, the later general secretary of the International Federation of Landscape Architects (IFLA), was one of the first garden architects in the German-speaking world who, towards the end of the Second World War, raised significant concerns about "the image of the landscape and the urgency of tending and shaping it." At the time, he called for landscape architects to assume the primary responsibility for shaping the landscape, because it was only they who saw the landscape as a whole.

In the International Doctoral College "Spatial Research Lab," years of experience have shown that the far-reaching transformation processes in the landscape—and urban areas are of course considered part of it—can only be overcome by means of interdisciplinary cooperation. No individual discipline can master the consequences of these changes single-handedly. However, even so, nothing has changed in terms of Gustav Ammann's call for a greater sense of responsibility towards the aesthetic qualities of the landscape—on the contrary. ▶1

The depletion of the limited "resource landscape" is proceeding unchecked, with obvious consequences, and the cultivated landscape must still be regarded as "institutionally homeless." "In view of the regulatory density in highly-developed societies, the cultivated landscape as a communal asset is more of a 'by-product' […] of different institutions and institutional systems that influence the heterogeneous elements and components of the cultivated landscape."[2] The current condition of cultivated landscapes reveals aesthetically, as a sensory perception, what state society is in. "The communal nurturing, cultivation, and use of valuable communal assets forge, even today: solidarity, a community spirit, responsibility, respect," writes the author Rita Bertolini, for example, in her introduction to the book Allmeinde Vorarlberg.[3] Evidently a marked sense of social responsibility for the "cultivated landscape as a communal asset" is reflected clearly in the Austrian region of Vorarlberg in an environment that is still attributed a high ecological and aesthetic quality.[4] ▶2

41 per cent of the land area in Vorarlberg is made up of alpine pastures, whose agricultural use has a very strong influence on the development of the recreational and tourist industry. This is an especially clear example of the significance of the "quality of the landscape as a locational factor." The doctoral student Edgar Hagspiel addresses local supply in rural Vorarlberg in his dissertation and studies how the planned supply structure affects the future settlement development; his research is however also about the preservation of a currently intact social structure which is reflected in the appearance of the landscape. In other regions of Europe, on the other hand, people are much more concerned about the identity of their living environment. They even feel threatened by the foreignness of newly-emerging landscape structures, as these signify a change from the familiar quality of life and accustomed lifestyle. Extensive energy land-

Zustand der Kulturlandschaften lässt sich ästhetisch, also sinnlich wahrnehmbar ablesen, in welcher Verfassung sich die Gesellschaft befindet.

„Die gemeinschaftliche Hege und Pflege, Bewirtschaftung und Nutzung wertvoller Gemeingüter stiftet auch in der heutigen Zeit: Zusammenhalt, Gemeinsinn, Verantwortlichkeit, Respekt", schreibt beispielsweise die Autorin Rita Bertolini in ihrer Einleitung zu dem Buch *Allmeinde Vorarlberg*.[3] Offenbar zeichnet sich das ausgeprägte gesellschaftliche Verantwortungsbewusstsein für das „Gemeinschaftsgut Kulturlandschaft" im österreichischen Bundesland Vorarlberg deutlich sichtbar in einer Umwelt ab, der noch immer eine hohe ökologische und ästhetische Qualität bescheinigt wird.[4] ▶ 2

41 Prozent der Landesfläche Vorarlbergs sind Alpflächen, deren landwirtschaftliche Nutzung die Entwicklung der Freizeit- und Tourismuswirtschaft sehr stark beeinflusst. Hier tritt die Bedeutung der „Landschaftsqualität als Standortfaktor" besonders deutlich zutage. Dieser ist entscheidend für die ökonomische, ökologische und soziale Entwicklung des Bundeslandes. Wenn sich der Doktorand Edgar Hagspiel in seiner Dissertation mit der Nahversorgung im ländlich geprägten Vorarlberg befasst[5] und darauf eingeht, wie sich die geplante Versorgungsstruktur auf die zukünftige Sied-

2 The small community of Mellau in the Austrian region of Vorarlberg is characterised by tourism that is strongly dependent on the preservation of an intact cultivated landscape and therefore on the "locational factor of the landscape."
2 Die kleine Gemeinde Mellau im österreichischen Bundesland Vorarlberg ist geprägt durch einen Tourismus, der vom Erhalt einer intakten Kulturlandschaft und damit vom „Standortfaktor Landschaft" stark abhängig ist.

scapes with wind turbine parks, solar energy fields, or rapeseed and corn monocultures are described as characterless and amorphous, because they no longer correspond to the aesthetic landscape ideals of the pre-industrial era. ▶3

Such judgments, whether they are valid in individual cases or not, have a strong influence on the development of the landscapes and regions in question, as landscapes affect society in turn. "First we shape our environment, then it shapes us," the cultural historian Hermann Glaser stated aptly back in 1968.[5] Both the emotional relationship between people and their living environment and the social structure within a community, even economic developments in a region, are influenced lastingly by the appearance of the landscape. For example, in 2012, in the study "Landscape quality as a locational factor," the Swiss Federal Office for the Environment (BAFU) examined what role the landscape plays in the choice of location for major companies and reached the conclusion: "For some sectors, the quality of the landscape is important, partly so that they can offer employees an attractive residential environment, and in some cases also because the company head office itself should be in a location with an attractive landscape. [...] Business developers are increasingly aware of the importance of the landscape for the attractiveness of a region as a business location, but in the past they were not able to have a significant influence on the corresponding policy-making."[6]

"For this reason, we think it is likely that conscious landscape design will gain significance in future," emphasised the city and regional sociologist

3 *Compared to brown coal mining areas like in Garzweiler, the sourcing of renewable energy has a smaller impact on people and nature, but the population still has a critical view of the interventions.*
3 *Im Vergleich zu Braunkohle-Tagebaugebieten wie in Garzweiler sind die Folgen der Gewinnung erneuerbarer Energien für Mensch und Natur zwar weitaus geringer, doch die Bevölkerung sieht die Eingriffe trotzdem kritisch.*

lungsentwicklung auswirkt, dann geht es dabei zwangsläufig auch um den Erhalt eines aktuell intakten Gesellschaftsgefüges, das im Landschaftsbild seinen angemessenen Ausdruck findet. In anderen Regionen Europas hingegen fürchten die Menschen viel stärker um die Identität ihres Lebensraumes. Sie fühlen sich von der Fremdartigkeit neu entstehender Landschaftsbilder regelrecht bedroht, denn diese signalisieren einen Wandel der gewohnten Lebensqualität und des vertrauten Lebensstils.

Ausgedehnte Energielandschaften mit Windparks, Solarfeldern, Raps- und Maismonokulturen werden als gestalt- und charakterlos beschrieben, weil sie nicht mehr den landschaftsästhetischen Idealbildern aus vorindustrieller Zeit entsprechen. ▶3

Solche Wertungen, ob im Einzelfall zutreffend oder nicht, haben einen starken Einfluss auf die Entwicklung der betroffenen Landschaften und Regionen, denn Landschaftsbilder wirken auf die Gesellschaft zurück. „Erst formen wir unsere Umwelt, und dann formt sie uns", stellte der Kulturhistoriker Hermann Glaser bereits 1968 treffend fest.[6] Sowohl die emotionale Beziehung des Menschen zu seinem Lebensraum als auch das soziale Gefüge in einer Gesellschaft, ja sogar die ökonomischen Entwicklungen in einer Region werden durch das Bild der Landschaft nachhaltig beeinflusst. So untersuchte beispielsweise 2012 das schweizerische Bundesamt für Umwelt BAFU in der Studie *Landschaftsqualität als Standortfaktor*, welche Rolle die Landschaft für die Standortwahl großer Firmen spielt und gelangte zu dem Ergebnis: „Für manche Branchen ist Landschaftsqualität wichtig, teils weil so den Mitarbeitenden ein attraktives Wohnumfeld geboten werden kann, in manchen Fällen aber auch, weil der Firmensitz selbst an landschaftlich attraktiver Lage sein soll. Die [...] Wirtschaftsförderer sind sich der Bedeutung der Landschaft für die Attraktivität einer Region als Wirtschaftsstandort zunehmend bewusst, haben in der Vergangenheit jedoch keinen allzu großen Einfluss auf die entsprechende Politikgestaltung nehmen können."[7]

„Aus diesem Grund halten wir es für wahrscheinlich, dass das bewusste Landschaftsdesign in Zukunft an Bedeutung gewinnt", betonte 2006 der Stadt- und Regionalsoziologe Detlev Ipsen. „Um bei bewussten oder unbewussten Entwicklungen einer Landschaft eingreifen zu können, muss man sie verstehen. Ideen oder gar Leitbilder bewusster Renovierung oder innovativer Entwicklung setzen an dem Bedeutungsgehalt einer Landschaft an. Dazu soll die Theorie der Raumbilder einen Beitrag leisten. Die Theorie der Raumbilder versucht die Gestalt eines Raumes als symbolischen Ausdruck gesellschaftlicher Entwicklungskonzepte zu interpretieren."[8] ▶4

Nach Ipsen sind Raumbilder „Konfigurationen von Dingen, Bedeutungen und Lebensstilen, die alle auf bestimmte gesellschaftliche Entwicklungskonzepte bezogen sind".[9] Raumbilder sind also einerseits das Ergebnis gesellschaftlich-kulturellen Wirkens, haben andererseits aber auch aufgrund ihrer ästhetischen Qualitäten deutliche Rückwirkungen auf das Le-

Detlev Ipsen in 2006. "In order to be able to intervene in conscious or un-conscious developments of a landscape, one must understand it. Ideas or models for conscious regeneration or innovative development are based on the semantic content of a landscape. The theory of spatial images contributes to this, seeking to interpret the features of a space as a symbolic expression of social development concepts."[7] ▶4

According to Ipsen, spatial images are made up of "configurations of things, meanings, and lifestyles, which all refer to certain social development concepts."[8] On the one hand, therefore, spatial images are the result of socio-cultural influences, but, on the other hand, they also have a clear reverse impact on human life due to their aesthetic qualities. "The appearance of a house, a garden, the regional distribution of settlements, the image of a landscape are not random and meaningless for people. On the contrary: through the architecture of their buildings, gardens and landscapes, through the arrangement of objects in space, and through conceptual planning, each society creates its patterns of spatial orientation for a certain period of time. These patterns of space and time are, in turn, orientation frameworks and the basic precondition for targeted action and the development of 'insightful' patterns of behaviour."[9]

The appearance of the landscape is increasingly interspersed with *new* landscape typologies, whose development and diffusion are primarily driven forward by advancing suburbanisation and globalisation processes. Infrastructures for transport, energy, communication, supply and disposal, recreational use, and high-technology agriculture, in particular, have for a long time been integral aspects of cultivated landscapes in the twenty-first century, closely interwoven with historically-shaped landscape fragments. In the wider regional catchment areas of major metropolises, especially where land prices are still affordable, there is an emergence of newly-built settlements on the outskirts, as well as of oversized industrial estates and large logistics centres along motorways and railways. These unusual transitional landscapes do not conform to the usual aesthetic landscape categories. ▶5

"Halls, fields, motorways: the Deggendorf area [135 kilometres to the north-west of Munich] is an example of how inconsiderately the landscape is currently being dealt with. [...] Regional and landscape plans are gradually losing their significance, because communities and companies are constantly seeking to undermine these hindrances to them," was stated in the newspaper *Süddeutsche Zeitung* in January 2016 under the title "Concrete world." Everywhere in Europe, the question is arising as to who will assume responsibility in future for the aesthetic development of cultivated landscapes.

In her dissertation,[10] Katrin Rismont addresses modern agricultural industry, whose intensive farming methods and functional but aesthetically unappealing production landscapes are the target of increasing public criticism, especially in urban development regions. ▶6

4 Spatial images, according to Detlev Ipsen, are "configurations of things, meanings, and lifestyles, which all refer to certain social development concepts." This also applies to the north of Munich.

4 Raumbilder, so Detlev Ipsen, sind „Konfigurationen von Dingen, Bedeutungen und Lebensstilen, die alle auf bestimmte gesellschaftliche Entwicklungskonzepte bezogen sind". Das gilt auch für den Münchner Norden.

ben der Menschen. „Die Gestalt eines Hauses, eines Gartens, die regionale Verteilung von Siedlungen, das Bild der Landschaft sind nicht zufällig und bedeutungslos für den Menschen. Im Gegenteil: Durch die Architektur ihrer Gebäude, Gärten und Landschaften, durch das Arrangement der Dinge im Raum und durch konzeptionelle Planung schafft sich jede Gesellschaft für eine bestimmte Zeit ihre Muster der räumlichen Orientierung. Diese Muster von Raum und Zeit sind dann wiederum Orientierungsrahmen und grundlegende Voraussetzung für gezieltes Handeln und die Entstehung ‚einsichtiger' Verhaltensmuster."[10]

Das Landschaftsbild wird heute zunehmend von *neuen* Landschaftstypologien durchsetzt, deren Entstehung und Ausbreitung vorwiegend durch fortschreitende Suburbanisierungs- und Globalisierungsprozesse gefördert wird. Vor allem Infrastrukturen für Verkehr, Energie, Kommunikation, Ver- und Entsorgung, Freizeitnutzung und hochtechnisierte Landwirtschaft sind längst integrale Bestandteile der Kulturlandschaften im 21. Jahrhundert, eng verwoben mit historisch geprägten Landschaftsfragmenten. Im weiten regionalen Einzugsbereich großer Metropolen, bevorzugt dort, wo die Bodenpreise noch erschwinglich sind, entstehen Neu-

Whether we like it or not, the high-tech agricultural industry is responsible to a large extent for the shaping of a "product" that people are forced to face daily: an industrially-shaped agricultural landscape. It contributes to determining the appearance of urban areas worldwide and, according to the theories of Ipsen and Glaser, it also has a clear reverse impact on the behavioural patterns of people, owing to its aesthetic qualities. With the increasing inward city development within urban areas, there is also an increasing recreational pressure on agricultural areas surrounding major cities, which must soon provide more than just food production. The agricultural areas will therefore be qualified as attractive parts of recreational landscapes near urban areas in the future. This does not necessarily mean that the productivity of agricultural areas must be restricted in favour of a recreational purposes, but rather it can be combined with an aesthetic upgrading of the functional landscape. New planning and design strategies need to be worked out, in order to integrate the highly technological intensive agricultural industry better into the urban context – both functionally and aesthetically. Back in 1973, Umberto Eco pointed out that "all cultural phenomena are, in reality, systems of signs, which means that

5 *Infrastructure landscapes, like here to the north of the Vienna metropolitan region, do not conform to standard aesthetic landscape categories, but nevertheless shape the landscape.*
5 *Infrastrukturlandschaften, wie hier im Norden der Metropolregion Wien, entziehen sich den üblichen landschaftsästhetischen Kategorisierungsversuchen und prägen dennoch das Raumbild.*

6 *In an urban envi-
ronment, like here in
the densely populated
Ruhr area, agricultural
landscapes play a key
role as recreational and
leisure areas close to the
urban area. Aesthetics
is considered a central
purpose of these produc-
tion landscapes.*
6 *Im urbanen Um-
feld, wie hier im dicht
besiedelten Ruhrgebiet,
spielen Landwirtschafts-
flächen eine Schlüssel-
rolle als stadtnahe
Erholungs- und Freizeit-
areale. Ästhetik gilt als
eine zentrale Funktion
dieser Produktionsland-
schaften.*

besiedlungen in Ortsrandlagen sowie überdimensionierte Gewerbegebiete und große Logistikzentren entlang von Autobahnen und Bahnstrecken. Diese eigenartigen Übergangslandschaften entziehen sich den üblichen landschaftsästhetischen Kategorisierungsversuchen. ▶5

„Hallen, Äcker, Autobahnen: Der Raum Deggendorf [135 Kilometer nord-westlich von München] ist ein Beispiel dafür, wie rücksichtslos inzwischen mit der Landschaft umgegangen wird. […] Regional- und Landschaftsplä-ne verlieren langsam ihre Wirkung, weil Gemeinden und Unternehmen ständig bemüht sind, diese für sie hinderlichen Instrumente auszuhebeln", war im Januar 2016 unter der Überschrift „Betonwelt"[11] in der *Süddeutschen Zeitung* zu lesen. Überall in Europa drängt sich inzwischen die Frage auf, wer in Zukunft für die ästhetische Entwicklung der Kulturlandschaften die Verantwortung tragen wird.

Katrin Rismont nimmt in ihrer Dissertation[12] die moderne Agrarindustrie ins Visier, deren intensive Bewirtschaftungsmethoden und zweckmäßige, aber ästhetisch reizlose Produktionslandschaften gerade in urbanen Ent-wicklungsregionen immer stärker in die öffentliche Kritik geraten. ▶6

culture can be understood as communication."[11] From a semiotic point of view, cultivated landscapes can be viewed as communication structures in which spatial images play a central role, especially for conveying location-specific information, such as about the local or regional quality of life. The emergence of a large-scale "total landscape without regional identity" is explained by Rolf Peter Sieferle as "a residual product of a multitude of actions that each pursue their own purposes, as a result of work, transport, residence, recreation, consumption, landscape planning, and nature preservation [...]."[12] The resulting urban landscape transformation, in his understanding, is the unintentional result of an array of well-intentioned individual plans and development policy decisions of an almost opaque complexity. However, the appearance of urban landscape transformation, its aesthetic, is by no means incidental or meaningless for people. "Environmental design is a political issue insofar as a particular policy, a certain fundamental political attitude 'produces' a certain environment and, vice versa, a certain environment also prompts a certain policy."[13]

Whatever objective is being pursued when intervening in urban landscape transformation, one of the keys evidently lies in the structuralist view of the landscape. The notion that the landscape is a spatial total work of art that one can preserve in a static ideal state has long been obsolete. Instead the landscape, as a complex organism, must be able to change constantly to retain vitality, without losing its structural integrity in the process. A central characteristic of complex organisms is the existence of interlinked structures that ensure a certain stability and enable the permanent flow of energy, material, and information. Many of these structural networks, such as water systems, transport systems, energy systems, green systems, or communication systems, ensure the vitality of the landscape today, as well as its ability to change, grow, and transform. They are usually so closely interlinked that it is risky to view them as sectoral and to seek to develop them purely functionally and rationally. Owing to their interrelationships, layering, and interpenetration, the structural systems strengthen and complement each other in the everyday environment.

When addressing "Green Infrastructure" as a strategic planning concept in an urban context, Sonja Gantioler[14] makes use of the structuralist point of view. What does "Green Infrastructure" actually mean? The American environment and city planners Mark Benedict and Edward McMahon answer this question in their 2002 publication Green Infrastructure: Smart Conservation for the 21st Century: "Whereas green space is often viewed as something that is nice to have, the term green infrastructure implies something that we must have. Protecting and restoring our nation's natural life support system is a necessity, not an amenity. [...] Green infrastructure is a new term, but it's not a new idea," state the experts.[15] The notion emerged in the USA in the mid-1990s, but Benedict and McMahon attribute the invention of the idea to none other than Frederick Law Olmsted, the designer and builder of Central Park in New York. ▶7

Die hochtechnisierte Agrarindustrie ist nolens volens in maßgeblichem Umfang für die Gestaltung eines „Produkts" verantwortlich, welches die Menschen unvermeidlich täglich vor Augen haben: die industriell geprägte Agrarlandschaft. Sie bestimmt das (Raum-)Bild der Städte weltweit mit und hat gemäß den Theorien von Ipsen und Glaser auch aufgrund ihrer ästhetischen Qualitäten deutliche Rückwirkungen auf die Verhaltensmuster der Menschen. Mit zunehmender Innenentwicklung wächst zudem im Umland großer Städte der Erholungs- und Freizeitdruck auf die landwirtschaftlichen Nutzflächen, die bald mehr leisten müssen als reine Nahrungsmittelproduktion. Die landwirtschaftlichen Nutzflächen sind daher so zu qualifizieren, dass sie zukünftig attraktive Teile stadtnaher Erholungslandschaften werden. Das muss nicht unbedingt bedeuten, dass man die Produktivität der Landwirtschaftsflächen zugunsten der Erholungsfunktion einschränkt, sondern kann mit einer ästhetischen Aufwertung der Nutzlandschaft verbunden sein. Es gilt, neue Planungs- und Entwurfsstrategien zur erarbeiten, um die hochtechnisierte, intensive Agrarindustrie besser in den urbanen Kontext zu integrieren – sowohl funktional als auch ästhetisch.

Umberto Eco wies bereits 1976 darauf hin, dass „alle Kulturphänomene Zeichensysteme sind, d.h. dass Kultur im wesentlichen Kommunikation ist".[13] Kulturlandschaften sind in semiotischer Hinsicht als Kommunikationsstrukturen aufzufassen, in der die Raumbilder eine zentrale Rolle spielen, insbesondere bei der Vermittlung von ortsspezifischen Informationen, zum Beispiel über die lokale oder regionale Lebensqualität. Die Ausbildung einer weiträumigen „totalen Landschaft ohne regionale Identität", erklärt Rolf Peter Sieferle als „Residualprodukt einer Vielzahl von Handlungen, die jeweils ihren eigenen Zweck verfolgen, als Ergebnis von Arbeit, Verkehr, Wohnen, Freizeit, Konsum, Landschaftsplanung und Naturschutz [...]."[14] Die entstehende „Transformationslandschaft" ist seinem Verständnis nach das unbeabsichtigte Resultat einer Vielzahl von gut gemeinten Einzelplanungen und entwicklungspolitischen Entscheidungen von fast unüberschaubarer Komplexität. Das Bild der urbanen Transformationslandschaft, ihre Ästhetik ist jedoch keineswegs zufällig oder bedeutungslos für den Menschen. „Umweltgestaltung ist insofern ein Politikum, als eine bestimmte Politik, eine bestimmte politische Grundauffassung und Haltung eine bestimmte Umwelt ‚produziert' und umgekehrt eine bestimmte Umwelt auch eine bestimmte Politik evoziert."[15]

Welches Ziel auch immer man beim Eingriff in urbane Transformationslandschaften verfolgt – ein Schlüssel liegt offenbar in der strukturalistischen Betrachtungsweise von Landschaft. Die Vorstellung, dass Landschaft ein räumliches Gesamtkunstwerk sei, das man in einem statischen Idealzustand konservieren kann, ist längst überholt. Vielmehr muss sich die Landschaft als komplexer Organismus ständig wandeln können, um lebendig zu bleiben, darf dabei aber ihre strukturelle Integrität nicht verlieren. Zentrales Merkmal komplexer Organismen ist die Existenz ver-

netzter Strukturen, die für eine gewisse Stabilität sorgen und den permanenten Fluss von Energie, Materie und Information ermöglichen. Eine Vielzahl solcher strukturellen Geflechte, zum Beispiel Wassersysteme, Verkehrssysteme, Energiesysteme, Grünsysteme oder Kommunikationssysteme gewährleisten heute die Lebendigkeit von Landschaft als auch ihre Veränderungs-, Wachstums- und Wandlungsfähigkeit. Sie sind in der Regel derart eng miteinander verflochten, dass es riskant ist, sie sektoral betrachten und rein zweckrational gestalten zu wollen. Gerade durch ihre Verflechtung, Überlagerung und gegenseitige Durchdringung stärken und ergänzen sich die Struktursysteme in der alltäglichen Umwelt.

Bei der Auseinandersetzung mit „Grüner Infrastruktur" als strategischem Planungskonzept im urbanen Kontext macht sich Sonja Gantioler[16] die strukturalistische Betrachtungsweise zunutze. Was bedeutet „Grüne Infrastruktur" überhaupt? Diese Frage beantworteten die amerikanischen Umwelt- und Stadtplaner Mark Benedict und Edward McMahon 2002 in ihrer Publikation *Green Infrastructure: Smart Conservation for the 21st Century*: „Während Grünräume häufig als etwas Schönes betrachtet werden, das man gerne hätte [nice to have], signalisiert der Begriff ‚green infrastructure' etwas, das wir unbedingt benötigen [must have]. Der Schutz und der Wiederaufbau des natürlichen Lebenserhaltungssystems unserer Nation ist eine Notwendigkeit und keine Annehmlichkeit. […] Grüne Infrastruktur ist ein neuer Begriff, aber es ist keine neue Idee", räumen die Experten ein.[17] Mitte der 1990er Jahre tauchte der Begriff in den USA auf, aber als Erfinder der Idee würdigen Benedict und McMahon keinen Geringeren als Frederick Law Olmsted, den Entwerfer und Erbauer des Central Parks in New York. ►7

Olmsted propagierte bereits 1903 die umfassende Vernetzung urbaner Grünanlagen zur Verbesserung der Lebensqualität in den Städten. Mit Blick auf die Geschichte des Stadtgrüns in Europa könnte man gewiss noch andere „Erfinder" identifizieren und das Geburtsdatum der Idee vom grünen Netzwerk sicher etwas vordatieren. Entscheidend ist jedoch, dass diese grünen Netzwerke nie an der Stadtgrenze endeten, sondern sich weit ins Umland ausdehnten und damit zur Strukturierung der Stadt-Landschafts-Netzwerke beitrugen.

Die Erfolgsgeschichten vom Bau der Donauinsel im Wien der 1970er Jahre, von der IBA Emscher Park in den 1990er Jahren oder der aktuellen Transformation der Mülldeponie Fresh Kills in New York zeigen beispielhaft die Stärken der strukturalistischen Entwurfs- und Planungsansätze. In solchen Projekten zur Gestaltung großer urbaner Transformationslandschaften wird nicht zwischen grünen, grauen oder blauen Strukturen unterschieden, auch nicht zwischen gegenwärtigen oder vergangenen, sozialen oder technischen, natürlichen oder künstlichen, städtischen oder ländlichen. In der intelligenten Verknüpfung all dieser Netze liegt die Stärke dieser Projekte ebenso wie in der Schaffung vielfältiger, polyvalenter Räume, die sich Mensch und Natur auf ihre individuelle Weise aktiv aneignen können.

Already back in 1903, Olmsted propagated the comprehensive interlinking of urban green areas to improve the quality of life in cities. Looking back at the history of urban greenery in Europe, one could undoubtedly identify further "inventors" and set the birthdate of the idea of a green network further in the past. What is decisive, however, is that these green networks never ended at the city border, but extended far out into the surrounding area and therefore contributed to the structuring of the city and landscape networks.

The success stories of the building of the Danube Island in Vienna in the 1970s, the IBA Emscher Park in the 1990s, or the current transformation of the Fresh Kills waste disposal site in New York exemplarily show the strengths of structuralist design and planning approaches. In such projects for designing large-scale urban landscape transformation, there is no distinction between green, grey, or blue structures, nor between contemporary or past, social or technical, natural or artificial, or urban or rural structures. The strength of these projects lies in the intelligent amalgamation of all these networks, as well as in the creation of varied and polyvalent spaces that people and nature can appropriate actively in their own individual way. It is only in this way that a urban landscape transformation can change its face without losing it. The new images with their specific aesthetic play key roles, as they help to communicate environmental qualities in a universally-understandable, non-verbal manner.

8 Can this industrial wasteland in Lisbon change its face without losing it? The transformed landscape will neither become Arcadia nor remain residual space.
8 Kann diese Industriebrache in Lissabon ihr Gesicht verändern, ohne ihr Gesicht zu verlieren? Die transformierte Landschaft wird weder Arkadien noch Restfläche bleiben.

Nur so kann eine Landschaft im Wandel, eine Transformationslandschaft ihr Gesicht verändern, ohne ihr Gesicht zu verlieren. Den neuen Raumbildern mit ihrer spezifischen Ästhetik kommen dabei durchaus Schlüsselrollen zu, weil mit ihrer Hilfe auf universell verständliche, nonverbale Art über die Qualitäten von Umwelt kommuniziert wird.

Wien Vienna, 01.05.2016

Wien Vienna, 05.05.2016

Wien Vienna, 05.05.2016

München Munich, 14.08.2013

München Munich, 14.08.2013

Stuttgart, 16.03.2014

WHOSE URBAN NATURE?
Modelling the operationalisation of "Green Infrastructure" as a strategic planning concept, in order to address dynamics of economic and socio-ecological inequality

SONJA GANTIOLER

In recent years, a series of economic and financial crises have drawn increasing attention to inequality in the distribution of income, capital and wealth, and its potential impact on the economy and society as a whole, in particular with regard to residential property and housing. At the same time, expanding urban sprawl has contributed to the deterioration of ecosystems and the loss of biological diversity. In the city, but also elsewhere in the landscape, natural and semi-natural features are often dispersed and isolated elements, which are concentrated in a few areas and are largely absent in others. On-going urban transformation processes, such as the development of new residential areas or greater urban densities, can potentially exacerbate ecological and economic inequalities.

One of the targets of the biodiversity strategy of the European Union is to counter the potential isolation of areas of high value for the conservation of biological diversity, both at the wider landscape and urban level, by implementing "Green Infrastructures" (GI). The term refers to the protection and renaturation of a network of natural and semi-natural areas, and of environmental features and open spaces that contribute to the conservation of biological diversity and are responsible for providing a series of functions and benefits for the well-being of the local population. Its aim is to ensure wider availability and to improve access to these areas, and to the services created, by conserving, restoring, and especially connecting the remaining patches on a variety of scales. However, what the concept means concretely in

practice and whether it delivers what it promises are still the subject of on-going discussions among researchers and practitioners.

This dissertation therefore focuses on the question of how and to what extent the concept of "Green Infrastructure," when implemented as a strategic planning approach, can counter ecological inequalities and the potentially resulting social inequalities. This requires, first of all, a comprehensive analysis of the principles and characteristics of the concept, in order to evaluate how it might differ from previously applied design and planning approaches. This is followed by a definition of normative terms such as inequality and justice, in order to set out the ethical basis of the dissertation and translate it into a potential model. Based on case studies about the effectiveness of existing approaches in cities such as Vienna and Milan, the conceptual and action model will be finalised and concluding guidelines be provided on how to take the potential dynamics of economical and socio-ecological inequality into account when applying the concept of "Green Infrastructure" or when developing its principles and key characteristics.

WESSEN NATUR IN DER STADT?
Ein Modell zur Anwendung von „Grüner Infrastruktur" als strategisches Planungskonzept, um Dynamiken von ökonomischer und sozio-ökologischer Ungleichheit zu begegnen

SONJA GANTIOLER

Eine Reihe von Wirtschafts- und Finanzkrisen haben in den letzten Jahren vermehrt Ungleichheiten in der Verteilung von Einkommen, Kapital und Vermögen und ihre möglichen Auswirkungen auf die Wirtschaft und die Gesellschaft insgesamt in den Mittelpunkt gerückt. Dies gilt in besonderem Maße für die Rolle von Wohneigentum. Gleichzeitig hat die weitergehende städtische Zersiedelung zur Zerstörung von Ökosystemen und zum Verlust biologischer Vielfalt beigetragen. Natürliche und naturnahe Lebensräume sind nicht nur in der Stadt häufig zerstreute und isolierte Flächen, die sich auf einige wenige Gebiete konzentrieren und in anderen weitgehend fehlen. Laufende urbane Transformationsprozesse wie die Entwicklung neuer Wohngebiete oder die erhöhte Innenverdichtung bergen dabei das Potenzial, mögliche ökologische Ungleichheiten auch durch ökonomische Ungleichheiten zu verschärfen.

Die Biodiversitätsstrategie der Europäischen Union beinhaltet unter anderem das Ziel, bis 2020 der möglichen Isolierung von Gebieten mit hohem Wert für die Erhaltung biologischer Vielfalt auch in der Stadt durch die Umsetzung „Grüner Infrastrukturen" (GI) zu begegnen. Der Begriff bezieht sich dabei auf den Schutz und die Renaturierung eines Netzwerks von natürlichen und naturnahen Flächen, Umwelteigenschaften und Freiflächen, die zum Erhalt der biologischen Vielfalt beitragen und für die Bereitstellung einer Reihe von Funktionen und Leistungen verantwortlich sind, die dem Wohl des Menschen dienen. Über die Erhaltung, Wiederherstellung und vor allem Verbindung verbleibender Flächen auf verschiedenen Maßstabsebenen soll eine ausgeglichene Verfügbarkeit und ein verbesserter Zugang zu den Räumen, aber auch zu dem geschaffenen Nutzen gewährleistet werden. Doch was das Konzept konkret in der Praxis bedeutet und ob es hält, was es verspricht, wird noch ausgiebig unter Forschern und Praktikern diskutiert und verhandelt.

Die Dissertation konzentriert sich daher auf die Frage, auf welche Weise und in welchem Umfang das Konzept der „Grünen Infrastruktur", sofern als strategischer Planungsansatz umgesetzt, den ökologischen und daraus möglicherweise resultierenden sozialen Ungleichheiten entgegenwirken kann. Dies erfordert zunächst eine umfassende Analyse der Prinzipien und Eigenschaften des Konzepts, um zu evaluieren, wie es sich möglicherweise von zuvor verwendeten Design- und Planungsansätzen unterscheidet. Es folgt die grundsätzliche Aufarbeitung normativer Begriffe wie Ungleichheit und Gerechtigkeit, um die ethische Grundlinie der Dissertation zu bestimmen und in ein mögliches Modell zu übersetzen. Basierend auf Fallstudien zur Wirksamkeit der bestehenden Ansätze in Städten wie Wien und Mailand, soll abschließend ein konzeptionelles Handlungsmodell entstehen und eine Anleitung für die Berücksichtigung von potenziellen Dynamiken der ökonomischen und sozio-ökologischen Ungleichheit bei Anwendung des Konzepts „Grüne Infrastruktur" oder seiner Prinzipien und wesentlichen Eigenschaften entwickelt werden.

DISTRICT-ORIENTATED LOCAL SUPPLY AND CENTRE-ORIENTATED REGIONAL SUPPLY

Spatial planning conditions in rural areas, based on the example of Vorarlberg

EDGAR HAGSPIEL

Ten points about district-orientated local supply and the role of the retail sector for viable centres, based on preliminary orientation in Vorarlberg:

1. The supply of consumer goods from local sources is an indicator of qualitative residential development and a high quality of life. This applies in particular to the local supply of food products.

2. A qualitative and quantitative view of supply structures is necessary to clarify the question of a suitable retail supply structure, enabling framework conditions and situations to be identified and evaluated. The relevant influencing factors with regard to the "circumstances affecting spatial planning" are illuminated.

3. Settlement development in the main settlement valley in Vorarlberg can in principle be characterised as having a polycentric structure. A consideration of the settlement hubs according to the system of central localities is lacking. Well-functioning and attractive village and town centres are a possible consequence of a well-functioning and attractive retail sector.

4. The population is changing. It is getting older and more heterogeneous. Requirements are changing. The future requirements of our grandchildren are to a certain extent foreseeable.

5. The so-called "shopping centre regulation" put forward by Austrian commercial code was annulled in 2010, with the aim of avoiding dual approaches as far as possible. Until then, regional authorities had not issued any directives based on this regulation to clarify the relevant parameters and assessment standards. Regions had already demanded the annulment of this "shopping centre regulation" back in 2003, stating that the regional planning policies were appropriate and adequate. The aim of this work is to clarify this.

6. The spatial planning options for targeted spatial intervention are restricted due to the constitution. The "safeguarding of local supply" is an example of this. The scope for spatial planning should be widened again.

7. Several foreseeable futures should be taken into account when considering the centres from the point of view of viable development.

8. Examples of the supply and settlement structure form a link between theory and practice.

9. The research is taking place in Vorarlberg by means of a preliminary orientation for spatial planning.

10. The objective is a good coordination of the settlement and retail supply structure, insofar as this is possible in terms of spatial planning, along with the greatest possible transferability of the insights to comparable regions.

QUARTIERORIENTIERTE NAHVERSORGUNG UND ZENTRENORIENTIERTE REGIONALVERSORGUNG
Raumplanerische Voraussetzungen im ländlichen Raum am Beispiel Vorarlberg

EDGAR HAGSPIEL

Zehn Punkte zur quartierorientierten Nahversorgung und zur Rolle des Einzelhandels betreffend enkeltauglicher Zentren; Vororientierung Vorarlberg:

1. Die Versorgung mit Konsumgütern in der Nähe ist Indikator einer qualitativen Siedlungsentwicklung und hohen Lebensqualität. Dies trifft insbesondere auf die Nahversorgung (Lebensmittel) zu.

2. Für die Klärung der Frage nach einer angemessenen Einzelhandelsversorgungsstruktur ist eine qualitative und quantitative Betrachtung von Versorgungsstrukturen erforderlich. Damit können sensible Rahmenbedingungen und Situationen identifiziert und bewertet werden. Im Hinblick auf die für „die Raumplanung maßgeblichen Verhältnisse" werden die wesentlichen Hebel im Wirkungsgefüge beleuchtet.

3. Die Siedlungsentwicklung in Vorarlberg kann im Hauptsiedlungstal grundsätzlich mit einer polyzentrischen Schwerpunktbildung charakterisiert werden. Gleichzeitig fehlt eine Betrachtung der Siedlungsschwerpunkte nach dem System der zentralen Orte. Gut funktionierende und attraktive Dorf- und Stadtzentren sind mögliche Folge eines gut funktionierenden und attraktiven Einzelhandels.

4. Die Bevölkerung verändert sich. Sie wird älter und heterogener. Die Bedürfnisse ändern sich. Die künftigen Bedürfnisse unserer Enkel sind zum Teil absehbar.

5. Die sogenannte „Einkaufszentrenregelung" in der österreichischen Gewerbeordnung wurde im Jahr 2010 mit dem Ziel einer weitestgehenden Vermeidung von Doppelgleisigkeiten aufgehoben. Bis dahin haben die Landeshauptleute keine auf dieser Regelung gestützte Verordnung zur Klärung der entsprechenden Kenngrößen und Beurteilungsmaßstäbe erlassen. Bereits 2003 forderten die Länder den Entfall dieser „Einkaufszentrenregelung" mit der Begründung, dass die raumordnungsrechtlichen Bestimmungen als geeignet und ausreichend erachtet werden. Ziel dieser Arbeit ist es, dies zu klären.

6. Die Möglichkeiten der Raumplanung zur zielgerichteten räumlichen Intervention sind aufgrund der Verfassung begrenzt. Ein Beispiel ist der „Schutz der Nahversorgung" und hier die Klärung der Schutzbedürftigkeit. Die Möglichkeiten der räumlichen Planung sollen wieder geweitet werden.

7. Für eine Betrachtung der Zentren nach den Gesichtspunkten einer enkeltauglichen Entwicklung sind mehrere absehbare Zukünfte zu berücksichtigen.

8. Beispiele der Versorgungs- und Siedlungsstruktur bilden das Bindeglied zwischen Theorie und Praxis.

9. Die Erprobung erfolgt in Vorarlberg mittels einer raumplanerischen Vororientierung.

10. Ziel ist eine gute Abstimmung der Siedlungs- mit der Einzelhandelsversorgungsstruktur, soweit dies aus Sicht der Raumplanung möglich ist; weiters eine größtmögliche Übertragbarkeit der Erkenntnis auf vergleichbare Regionen.

BEAUTY FROM FUNCTION AND AS FUNCTION

The aesthetic of modern agriculture in urban regions

KATRIN RISMONT

Agricultural structures have changed significantly in recent decades and the landscape has been shaped by the processes of modern agricultural industry. The cultivated landscape, characterised by small-scale farming on the urban periphery, and which people are so fond of, is obsolete and can only be preserved from the point of view of historical interest. Today, the landscape in industrial regions is largely farmed using the latest high-tech agricultural engineering. A growing urban population is increasing the usage pressure on agricultural spaces in the surrounding area. At the same time, modern agriculture is facing more significant intensification and mechanisation pressure from a global point of view. As a consequence, cities will be confronted with new and unfamiliar images of the landscape. Therefore, new identities have to be created for the cultivated landscapes and open spaces in the urban periphery, in order to keep them equally attractive both as a residential environment for urban dwellers seeking recreation and, at the same time, as agricultural land to be farmed. What form must the modern production landscape of the future take in order to be compatible with urban space? In order to create new and viable landscape structures for urban regions, it is necessary to develop and convey aesthetic categories and design qualities that move away from the ideals of the traditional pre-industrial landscape. What are the elementary conditions today for beauty in the landscape and what in-sights can be gained from this for the valorisation of a modern agricultural landscape?

It requires a "beauty resulting from function and as a function in itself," referring to the design theory of the Swiss industrial designer Max Bill from the mid-twentieth century. In accordance with this, experiments in landscape aesthetics directed by Professor Udo Weilacher were carried out in 2008-2010 on the fields at Mechtenberg in Essen. The project aimed to allow an aesthetic quality to emerge automatically from the agricultural working process and was based on a cooperation between the landscape architect Professor Paolo Bürgi and the local farmer Hubertus Budde. The resulting questions and insights serve as a starting point for the dissertation. What is the present-day dialogue between aesthetics and function? What practicable symbioses between functionality and beauty are conceivable now and in the future with the latest agricultural technology? As a planner, how does one communicate with a farmer about design matters?

The aim is to develop recommendations for design initiatives when dealing with modern agricultural areas. The focus is on the large-scale agricultural corridor on the urban periphery. This task requires a thorough study of the requirements placed on the modern agricultural landscape by urban society, of the contemporary understanding of landscape, and of the processes and techniques of modern agriculture.

SCHÖNHEIT AUS FUNKTION UND ALS FUNKTION
Ästhetik moderner Agrarbewirtschaftung in der Stadtregion

KATRIN RISMONT

Die Strukturen der Agrarwirtschaft haben sich in den letzten Jahrzehnten stark gewandelt und die Kulturlandschaft durch moderne agrarindustrielle Prozesse geprägt. Das am Stadtrand geschätzte und lieb gewonnene Landschaftsbild einer kleinbäuerlich geprägten Kulturlandschaft ist obsolet und kann nur unter musealen Gesichtspunkten aufrechterhalten werden. Heute wird Landschaft in Industrieregionen größtenteils unter Anwendung modernster Landtechnik auf Hightech-Niveau bewirtschaftet. Eine Zunahme der Bevölkerung in Städten erhöht gleichzeitig den Nutzungsdruck auf die landschaftlichen Freiräume im Umland. Demgegenüber steht die moderne Landwirtschaft, die aus globaler Sicht einem hohen Intensivierungs- und Mechanisierungsdruck ausgesetzt ist. Das konfrontiert den Städter mit ungewohnten und wenig vertrauten Bildern im Landschaftsraum. Für die Freiräume im urbanen Umfeld müssen neue kulturlandschaftliche Identitäten geschaffen werden, um sie als Wohnumfeld für den erholungsuchenden Städter und als zu bewirtschaftendes Agrarland gleichermaßen attraktiv zu halten. Wie muss die moderne Produktionslandschaft der Zukunft gestaltet werden, um stadtverträglich zu sein? Um neue Landschaftsbilder zu schaffen, die tragfähig für urbane Regionen sind, müssen ästhetische Kategorien und gestalterische Qualitäten entwickelt und vermittelt werden, die sich von den Idealen einer überkommenen vorindustri-ellen Landschaft lösen. Was sind dann heute die Elementarbedingungen des landschaftlich Schönen und welche Erkenntnisse lassen sich daraus für die In-Wertsetzung von moderner Agrarlandschaft gewinnen?

Es bedarf einer „Schönheit aus Funktion und als Funktion", angelehnt an die Gestaltungstheorie des Schweizer Industriedesigners Max Bill aus der Mitte des 20. Jahrhunderts. Ganz in diesem Sinne wurden 2008–2010 auf den Feldern des Mechtenbergs in Essen landschaftsästhetische Experimente unter der Leitung von Professor Udo Weilacher durchgeführt. Mit dem Anspruch, eine ästhetische Qualität im landwirtschaftlichen Arbeitsprozess automatisch entstehen zu lassen, basierte das Projekt auf der Zusammenarbeit zwischen dem Landschaftsarchitekten Professor Paolo Bürgi und dem ansässigen Landwirt Hubertus Budde. Daraus resultierende Fragen und Erkenntnisse dienen als Ausgangspunkt für die Dissertation. Wie sieht heute Ästhetik und Funktion im Dialog aus? Welche praktikablen Symbiosen zwischen Nützlichkeit und Schönheit sind jetzt und in Zukunft mit modernster Landtechnik denkbar? Wie kommuniziert man als Planer mit dem Landwirt über Gestaltungsfragen?

Ziel ist, gestalterische Handlungsempfehlungen im Umgang mit den Flächen moderner Erwerbslandwirtschaft zu entwickeln. Im Fokus steht die großflächig betriebene, stadtnahe Agrarflur. Diese Aufgabe erfordert es, sowohl die Anforderungen einer städtischen Gesellschaft an die moderne Agrarlandschaft und das zeitgenössische Landschaftsverständnis zu untersuchen als auch die Prozesse moderner Landbewirtschaftung intensiv zu studieren.

APPENDIX
ANHANG

BIOGRAPHIES

Milica Bajić-Brković

Prof. Milica Bajić-Brković (*1947) is an architect and urban planner with a focus on the built environment. Her specialist area is sustainable urban and spatial development. After a full professorship at Belgrade University, she held a BPTT professorship for Planning and Development at the University of the West Indies. From 2012 to 2015, Bajić-Brković was president of ISOCARP. She is a member of the consulting group for Sustainable Transport for the UN General Secretary.

Giovanna Fossa

Prof. Ing. Giovanna Fossa (*1958) holds a professorship for Urban Design and Planning at the School of Building and Environmental Engineering, Department of Architecture and Urbanism, at the Politechnico di Milano. She has many years of international experience (teaching, research, and projects) in the fields of urban regeneration and planning, regional and landscape planning, tourism and place branding, with a special focus on metropolitan regions. Her publications include: *An Atlas for Milan*, Skira 2006.

Michael Heller

Dip.-Ing. Michael Heller (*1953) has been project coordinator at AS&P, Albert Speer & Partner GmbH in Frankfurt am Main, and an associate lecturer in design in spatial planning design in the Institute of Spatial and Landscape Development (IRL) at the Swiss Federal Institute of Technology Zurich (ETH) since 2007. From 1985 to 1991, and also in 1994, he worked for AS&P, Albert Speer & Partner GmbH; in 1994, he also worked at Fischer + Heller, Architekten/Planer in Brühl. From 1998 to 2007, he was associate lecturer in urban-developmental building theory and design in urban development at the Institute for Urban Development and Regional Planning (ISL), University Fridericiana in Karlsruhe. In 1991, he was an academic associate at the Institut for Local, Regional and National Planning (ORL), Swiss Federal Institute of Technology Zurich (ETH).

Michael Koch

Prof. Dr. Michael Koch (*1950) is Professor of Urban Development and District Planning in the Department of Urban Planning at the HafenCity University Hamburg. Until 2004, he was Professor of Urban Development at

Milica Bajić-Brković

Prof. Milica Bajić-Brković (*1947) ist Architektin und Stadtplanerin mit Fokus auf die gebaute Umwelt. Ihr Spezialgebiet ist die nachhaltige Stadt- und Raumentwicklung. Nach einer ordentlichen Professur an der Universität Belgrad hatte sie einen BPTT-Lehrstuhl für Planung und Entwicklung an der University of the West Indies inne. Von 2012 bis 2015 war Brković Präsidentin der ISOCARP. Sie ist Mitglied der Beratergruppe für nachhaltigen Transport des UN-Generalsekretärs.

Giovanna Fossa

Prof. Ing. Giovanni Fossa (*1958) hat einen Lehrstuhl für Stadtgestaltung und -planung an der Schule für Bau- und Umweltingenieurwesen, Fachbereich Architektur und Urbanistik, am Poiltecnico di Milano inne. Sie verfügt über langjährige, internationale Erfahrungen (Lehre, Forschung und Projekte) in den Bereichen Stadterneuerung und -planung, Regional- und Landschaftsplanung, Tourismus und Place Branding, mit besonderem Fokus auf Metropolregionen. Zu ihren Publikationen gehört: *An Atlas for Milan*, Skira 2006.

Michael Heller

Dipl.-Ing. Michael Heller (*1953) ist seit 2007 Projektkoordinator der AS&P, Albert Speer & Partner GmbH in Frankfurt am Main und Lehrbeauftragter für Raumplanerisches Entwerfen an der Eidgenössischen Technischen Hochschule Zürich (ETH) am Institut für Raum- und Landschaftsentwicklung (IRL). Von 1985 bis 1991 war er bei AS&P, Albert Speer & Partner GmbH tätig, ebenso seit 1994, wie auch bei Fischer + Heller, Architekten/Planer in Brühl. 1998 bis 2007 war er Lehrbeauftragter für Städtebaubezogene Gebäudelehre und Städtebauliches Entwerfen an der Universität Fridericiana Karlsruhe am Institut für Städtebau- und Landesplanung (ISL), 1991 wissenschaftlicher Mitarbeiter der Eidgenössischen Technischen Hochschule Zürich (ETH) am Institut für Orts-, Regional- und Landesplanung (ORL).

Michael Koch

Prof. Dr. Michael Koch (*1950) ist Professor für Städtebau und Quartierplanung im Studiengang Stadtplanung an der HafenCity Universität Hamburg. Bis 2004 war er Professor für Städtebau am Fachbereich Architektur

the Department of Architecture at Bergische University Wuppertal. Before that, he taught and researched at various universities in Germany and Switzerland. Michael Koch is a member of numerous professional associations and advisory councils in both countries. As an architect and urban planner, he is a partner at the office yellow z urbanism architecture, Zurich/Berlin.

Markus Neppl

Prof. Markus Neppl (*1962) studied architecture at RWTH in Aachen and was a co-founder there of the student planning group ARTECTA. In 1990, he founded the firm ASTOC architects & planners in Cologne, together with Peter Berner, Oliver Hall and Kees Christiaanse, which has 50 employees and works on numerous urban-developmental projects and buildings of various sizes. In 1999, he was called to the chair of Urban Development at the University of Kaiserslautern. This was followed in 2004 by a call to the chair of Urban District Development and Design at Karlsruhe Institute for Technology (KIT) in Karlsruhe. From 2008 to 2012, he was Dean at the Faculty of Architecture and, since 2012, he is Dean of Studies at the Faculty of Architecture.

Eva Ritter

Dr. Eva Ritter (*1955) is a doctor and behavioural therapist; since 1995, she has specialised in empowerment coaching and systemic organisational consultancy. She cooperates with the health service and works in companies as an external lecturer in further education (presentation and communication training, conflict management), also running in-house seminars in personal development for managers and teams. Since 2000, she has been a lecturer at Karlsruhe University and at the Swiss Federal Institute of Technology Zurich (ETH).

Walter L. Schönwandt

Univ. Prof. em. Dr.-Ing. Walter L. Schönwandt (*1950), Dipl-Ing. Dipl-Psych, was Director of the Institute for the Foundations of Planning at Stuttgart University from 1993 to 2016. He has held guest professorships in Oxford, Vienna, and Zurich, and is a member of the Chamber of Architects Baden-Württemberg, the Academy for Spatial Research and Planning (ARL), the Association for Urban, Regional and National Planning (SRL), the Association of European Schools of Planning (AESOP), the International Association for People-Environment Studies (IAPS), the International Society of City and Regional Planners (ISOCARP), and the Association of Collegiate Schools of Planning (ACSP). In addition, he is also assessor, consultant and author.

der Bergischen Universität Wuppertal. Zuvor hat er an mehreren Hochschulen in Deutschland und der Schweiz unterrichtet und geforscht. Michael Koch ist Mitglied zahlreicher Berufsverbände und Beiräte in beiden Ländern. Als Architekt und Stadtplaner ist er Teilhaber des Büros yellow z urbanism architecture, Zürich/Berlin.

Markus Neppl

Prof. Markus Neppl (*1962) hat Architektur an der RWTH in Aachen studiert und war dort Mitbegründer der studentischen Planungsgruppe ARTECTA. 1990 gründete er zusammen mit Peter Berner, Oliver Hall und Kees Christiaanse das Büro ASTOC architects & planners in Köln, welches mit 50 Mitarbeitern zahlreiche städtebauliche Projekte und Gebäude in unterschiedlichen Größenordnungen bearbeitet. 1999 wurde er auf den Lehrstuhl für Städtebau an die Universität Kaiserslautern berufen. 2004 erfolgte der Ruf auf den Lehrstuhl für Stadtquartiersplanung und Entwerfen an das Karlsruher Institut für Technologie (KIT) in Karlsruhe. 2008 bis 2012 war er Dekan der Fakultät für Architektur und seit 2012 ist er Studiendekan der Fakultät für Architektur.

Eva Ritter

Dr. Eva Ritter (*1955) ist Ärztin und Verhaltenstherapeutin, seit 1995 spezialisiert auf Empowerment-Coaching und systemische Organisationsberatung. Sie kooperiert im Gesundheitswesen und in Unternehmen als externe Dozentin in der Weiterbildung (Präsentations- und Kommunikationstraining, Konfliktmanagement) und leitet Inhouse-Seminare in der Personalentwicklung für Führungskräfte und Teams. Seit 2000 ist sie als Lehrbeauftragte an der Universität Karlsruhe und an der Eidgenössischen Technischen Hochschule Zürich (ETH) tätig.

Walter L. Schönwandt

Univ. Prof. em. Dr.-Ing. Walter L. Schönwandt (*1950), Dipl.-Ing. Dipl.-Psych., war von 1993 bis 2016 Direktor des Instituts für Grundlagen der Planung an der Universität Stuttgart. Er hatte Gastprofessuren in Oxford, Wien und Zürich inne, ist unter anderem Mitglied der Architektenkammer Baden-Württemberg, der Akademie für Raumforschung und Landesplanung (ARL), der Vereinigung für Stadt-, Regional- und Landesplanung (SRL), der Association of European Schools of Planning (AESOP), der International Association for People-Environment Studies (IAPS), der International Society of City and Regional Planners (ISOCARP), der Association of Collegiate Schools of Planning (ACSP) sowie Gutachter, Berater und Autor.

Bernd Scholl

Prof. Dr. Bernd Scholl (*1953) has held a full professorship for Spatial Development at the Swiss Federal Institute of Technology Zurich (ETH) since 2006. He is a delegate there for the Master of Advanced Studies in Spatial Planning course and, from 2011 to 2013, he was Chairman of the Network City and Landscape (NSL) at ETH Zurich. As a co-owner of a planning bureau with its head office in Zurich, he has contributed to numerous urban and regional development projects nationally and internationally since 1987 and has been Chairman of many international competition juries, test planning procedures, and expert commissions. From 1997 to 2006, he was Director of the Institute for Urban Development and Regional Planning at Karlsruhe University and a tenured professor in the same faculty.

Rolf Signer

Dr. Rolf Signer (*1948) first completed a diploma in cultural engineering at the Swiss Federal Institute of Technology Zurich (ETH). Subsequently, he completed post-graduate studies in spatial planning at the same university and was awarded a doctorate (Dr. Sc. Techn.). He works as a planning expert in Switzerland and is partner in an office for urban and regional planning in Zurich. Their projects encompass works on an urban and regional scale, both nationally and internationally. As a member of the International Society of City and Regional Planners (ISCARP), he was head of the national Swiss delegation from 2000 to 2006. From 2009 to 2016, he was president of the Zurich Study Society for Planning, Architecture and Mobility (ZBV).

Werner Tschirk

Dr. Werner Tschirk (*1981) studied spatial planning at TU Wien (Vienna University of Technology). From 2007 to 2012, he completed his thesis as part of the International Doctoral College "Spatial Research Lab" on the subject of "Planning as a Learning Process." Since 2005, Tschirk has been a research associate at the Department of Spatial Planning at Vienna University of Technology. He is an initiator and developer of the "Spatial Planning Network," a communication platform for planners. He also works in the field of Local Spatial Planning in planning practice.

Nicole Uhrig

Prof. Dr. Nicole Uhrig (*1970) studied landscape architecture and planning in Berlin and Barcelona. She worked for the planning firms G. Kiefer an STrauma in Berlin and as a freelance landscape architect. She was a research associate at the faculty run by Prof. Dr. Udo Weilacher at Leibniz

Bernd Scholl

Prof. Dr. Bernd Scholl (*1953) ist seit 2006 ordentlicher Professor für Raumentwicklung an der Eidgenössischen Technischen Hochschule Zürich (ETH). Er ist dort Delegierter für den Studiengang Master of Advanced Studies in Raumplanung und war von 2011 bis 2013 Vorsitzender des Netzwerks Stadt und Landschaft (NSL) der ETH Zürich. Als Mitinhaber eines Planungsbüros mit Sitz in Zürich wirkt er seit 1987 in zahlreichen Vorhaben der Stadt- und Regionalentwicklung im In- und Ausland mit und war Vorsitzender zahlreicher international besetzter Wettbewerbsjurys, Testplanungsverfahren und Expertenkommissionen. Von 1997 bis 2006 war er Direktor des Instituts für Städtebau und Landesplanung an der Universität Karlsruhe und Ordinarius für den gleichnamigen Lehrstuhl.

Rolf Signer

Dr. Rolf Signer (*1948) erwarb zunächst an der Eidgenössischen Technischen Hochschule Zürich (ETH) das Diplom eines Kultur-Ingenieurs. Darauf absolvierte er an derselben Schule das Nachdiplomstudium in Raumplanung und erwarb den Doktortitel (Dr. sc. techn.). Er arbeitet als Planungsfachmann in der Schweiz und ist Mitinhaber eines Büros für Stadt- und Regionalplanung in Zürich. Die Projekte umfassen Arbeiten im städtischen und regionalen Maßstab im In- und Ausland. Als Mitglied der Internationalen Gesellschaft für Stadt- und Regionalplaner (ISOCARP) war er von 2000 bis 2006 Leiter der nationalen Delegation Schweiz. Von 2009 bis 2016 war er Präsident der Zürcher Studiengesellschaft für Bau- und Verkehrsfragen ZBV.

Werner Tschirk

Dr. Werner Tschirk (*1981) studierte Raumplanung an der Technischen Universität Wien. Von 2007 bis 2012 promovierte er im Rahmen des Internationalen Doktorandenkollegs „Forschungslabor Raum" zum Thema „Planung als Lernprozess". Seit 2005 ist Tschirk wissenschaftlicher Mitarbeiter am Department für Raumplanung an der TU Wien. Er ist Initiator und Entwickler des „Netzwerks Raumplanung", einer Kommunikationsplattform für Planerinnen und Planer. Zudem ist er im Bereich der Örtlichen Raumplanung in der Planungspraxis tätig.

Nicole Uhrig

Prof. Dr. Nicole Uhrig (*1970) studierte Landschaftsarchitektur und -planung in Berlin und Barcelona. Sie war in den Planungsbüros G. Kiefer und STrauma in Berlin und als freiberufliche Landschaftsarchitektin tätig. Sie war wissenschaftliche Mitarbeiterin am Lehrstuhl von Prof. Dr. Udo Weila-

University Hannover, and later a lecturer at TU Munich and the School of Architecture at Bremen University. Since May 2016, she has been Professor for the International Masters in Landscape Architecture at Anhalt University.

Andreas Voigt

Prof. Dr. techn. Andreas Voigt (*1962) is a spatial planner, and associate university professor for Local Planning at the Department of Spatial Planning at TU Wien (Vienna University of Technology). His research and teaching focuses are sustainable urban and spatial development and spatial simulation on the basis of the spatial simulation laboratory at TU Wien (SimLab).

Udo Weilacher

Prof. Dr. Udo Weilacher (*1963) is a landscape architect. Before studying landscape architecture in 1986 at the Technical University of Munich, he learned landscape gardening. From 1989 to 1990, he was a student at the California State Polytechnic University, Pomona/Los Angeles and completed his landscape architecture studies at TU Munich in 1993. After that, he worked as a research assistant and associate lecturer at Karlsruhe University and the Swiss Federal Institute of Technology Zurich (ETH), where he completed his dissertation with distinction in 2002. In 2002, he was appointed as full professor of landscape architecture and design at Hannover University and, from 2006 to 2008, he served there as the Dean of the Faculty of Architecture and Landscape Sciences. Since April 2009, Weilacher is full professor of landscape architecture and industrial landscape at TU Munich.

cher an der Leibniz Universität Hannover, später Lehrbeauftragte der TU München und der School of Architecture der Hochschule Bremen. Seit Mai 2016 ist sie Professorin des internationalen Masterstudiengangs Landscape Architecture der Hochschule Anhalt.

Andreas Voigt

Prof. Dr. techn. Andreas Voigt (*1962) ist Raumplaner, außerordentlicher Universitätsprofessor für Örtliche Raumplanung am Department für Raumplanung der Technischen Universität Wien. Die Forschungs- und Lehrschwerpunkte konzentrieren sich auf nachhaltige Stadt- und Raumentwicklung und raumbezogene Simulation auf Basis des Stadtraum-Simulationslabors TU Wien (SimLab).

Udo Weilacher

Prof. Dr. Udo Weilacher (*1963) ist Landschaftsarchitekt mit Ausbildung im Garten- und Landschaftsbau, bevor er 1986 Landespflege an der Technischen Universität München studierte. Von 1989 bis 1990 war er an der California State Polytechnic University, Pomona/Los Angeles und schloss sein Landschaftsarchitekturstudium an der TU München 1993 ab. Danach war er als wissenschaftlicher Angestellter und Lehrbeauftragter an der Universität Karlsruhe und an der Eidgenössischen Technischen Hochschule Zürich (ETH) tätig, wo er 2002 seine Dissertation mit Auszeichnung fertigstellte. 2002 wurde er als Professor für Landschaftsarchitektur an die Universität Hannover berufen und leitete dort von 2006 bis 2008 als Dekan die Fakultät für Architektur und Landschaft. Seit April 2009 ist Weilacher Professor für Landschaftsarchitektur und industrielle Landschaft an der TU München.

NOTES

Werner Tschirk, p. 18

1 At the time of publication of this volume, two thirds of the participants in the first curriculum have completed their dissertation successfully.

2 Cf. preface, page 10 in this book

3 10.03.–15.03.2013 | UT Vienna, opening week; 12.08.–16.08.2013 | TU Munich; 18.11.–22.11.2013 | HCU Hamburg; 17.03.–21.03.2014 | University of Stuttgart; 09.06.–13.06.2014 | University of Belgrade; 09.11.–14.11.2014 | Swiss Federal Institute of Technology Zurich (ETH); 15.03.–20.03.2015 | Politecnico di Milano (Milan Polytechnic); 21.06.–26.06.2015 | Karlsruher Institut für Technologie (Karlsruhe Technology Institute); 29.11.–04.12.2015 | Villa Vigoni, Italy and 01.05.–06.05.2016 | UT Vienna, concluding week

4 The "limbic system" is a closely networked group of areas of the brain involved with processing emotions and with memory processes. Apart from regulating emotions, it also influences memory or drive. It plays an important role in learning and memory.

5 Cf. Rogers, Carl R.: *Lernen in Freiheit. Zur Bildungsreform in Schule und Universität.* Munich 1969

6 Further information about the accompanying coaching: Ritter, Eva: "Kommunikation und Prozessgestaltung im Kolleg". In: Internationales Doktorandenkolleg Forschungslabor Raum (ed.): *Spatial Research Lab. The Logbook.* Berlin 2012, p. 42–49

Rolf Signer, p. 30

1 Cf. International Doctoral College (ed.): *Spatial Resarch Lab. The Logbook.* Berlin 2012, p. 42–49

2 Cf. Bunge, Mario Augusto: "Treatise on Basic Philosophy". In: Bunge, Mario Augusto (ed.): *Epistemology & Methodology I, Exploring the World.* Vol. 5, Dordrecht 1983, p. 72f.

3 Cf. Signer, Rolf: *Argumentieren in der Raumplanung.* Dissertation ETH Zurich 1994, p. 141

4 Cf. ibid., p. 141f

5 For the significance of inspections cf. Scholl, Bernd: *Aktionsplanung. Zur Behandlung komplexer Schwerpunktaufgaben in der Raumplanung.* Zurich 1995, p. 178. "Do not forget anything important" is an important maxim for clarifying problems in spatial planning. This maxim is also called "requirement of total evidence" and goes back to Carnap. Quoted according to Scholl (1995), p. 96f. "Those who know maxims and do not need them are better off than those who need them and do not know them," quoted according to Maurer, Jakob: *Maximen für Planer.* Zurich 1995

6 Cf. Bunge, Mario Augusto: "Treatise on Basic Philosophy". In: Bunge, Mario Augusto (ed.): *Epistemology & Methodology I, Exploring the World.* Vol. 5, Dordrecht 1983, p. 72f. "Memory, traditionally regarded as a source of knowledge—about the past—can at most distort acquired knowledge, never generate it."

7 Cf. ibid., p. 199

8 In relation to the opening of the Gotthard base tunnel in December 2016, a trial operation and then a pilot operation were carried out before it opened for everyday use.
Cf. Schneeberger, Paul: "Bald erste Güterzüge im Basistunnel". In: *Neue Zürcher Zeitung.* 01.03.16, p. 14

9 Neisser, Ulric: *Kognition und Wirklichkeit: Prinzipien und Implikationen der kognitiven Psychologie.* Stuttgart 1979, p. 19 (Original: *Cognition and Reality: Principles and Implications of Cognitive Psychology.* San Francisco 1976)

10 "A schema is the part of the whole perception cycle that is within the perceiver, can be modified through experience, and is somehow specific to what is perceived. The schema absorbs information made available by the sensory organs and is changed by this information. It guides movement and exploratory activities, which make further information available, and is changed once again by this." Quoted according to Neisser, Ulric: *Cognition and Reality: Principles and Implications of Cognitive Psychology.* San Francisco 1976, p. 54

11 Cf. ibid., p. 21

12 Guski, Rainer: *Wahrnehmung. Eine Einführung in die Psychologie der menschlichen Informationsaufnahme.* Stuttgart 2000, p. 76

13 Neisser, Ulric: *Kognition und Wirklichkeit: Prinzipien und Implikationen der kognitiven Psychologie.* Stuttgart 1979, p. 26

14 Cf. Signer, Rolf: *Argumentieren in der Raumplanung.* Dissertation ETH Zurich 1994, p. 207. The expression "You can't help recognising it!" comes from Potter in connection with understanding a written word: Potter, Mary C.: "Remembering". In: Osherson, Daniel N./Smith Edward E. (ed.): *Thinking. An Invitation to Cognitive Science.* 3rd edition, Cambridge 1990, p. 27: "If you look at a written word, you can't help recognizing it."— assuming of course that one is not illiterate.

15 Cf. Scholl, Bernd: *Aktionsplanung. Zur Behandlung komplexer Schwerpunktaufgaben in der Raumplanung.* Zurich 1995, p. 105f. or cf. Maurer, Jakob: *Maximen für Planer.* Zurich, 1995, p. 16

16 "Whatever is seen has been looked upon from some viewpoint or other: there is no vision from nowhe-

Vorwort, S. 10

1 Da die deutsche Sprache keine adäquate Möglichkeit für die gleichberechtigte Darstellung sowohl der maskulinen als auch der femininen Form bietet, wird in diesem Buch im Folgenden aufgrund der besseren Lesbarkeit überwiegend die maskuline Form verwendet.

Werner Tschirk, S. 19

1 Zum Zeitpunkt der Veröffentlichung der vorliegenden Publikation haben zwei Drittel der Teilnehmer des ersten Curriculums ihre Dissertation erfolgreich abgeschlossen.

2 Vgl. Vorwort, Seite 11 in diesem Buch

3 10.03.–15.03.2013 | TU Wien, Auftaktwoche; 12.08.–16.08.2013 | TU München; 18.11.–22.11.2013 | HCU Hamburg; 17.03.–21.03.2014 | Universität Stuttgart; 09.06.–13.06.2014 | University of Belgrade; 09.11.–14.11.2014 | ETH Zürich; 15.03.–20.03.2015 | Politecnico di Milano; 21.06.–26.06.2015 | Karlsruher Institut für Technologie; 29.11.–04.12.2015 | Villa Vigoni, Italien und 01.05.–06.05.2016 | TU Wien, Abschlusswoche

4 Das „limbische System" ist eine eng vernetzte Gruppe von Hirnarealen, die mit der Verarbeitung von Emotionen und mit Gedächtnisprozessen befasst sind. Es beeinflusst neben der Steuerung von Emotionen auch das Gedächtnis oder den Antrieb. Es spielt für Lernen und Erinnerung eine große Rolle.

5 Vgl. Rogers, Carl R.: *Lernen in Freiheit. Zur Bildungsreform in Schule und Universität.* München 1969

6 Weitere Informationen zum begleitenden Coaching: Ritter, Eva: „Kommunikation und Prozessgestaltung im Kolleg." In: Internationales Doktorandenkolleg Forschungslabor Raum (Hg.): *Forschungslabor Raum. Das Logbuch.* Berlin 2012, S. 42–49

Rolf Signer, S. 31

1 Vgl. Internationales Doktorandenkolleg „Forschungslabor Raum" (Hg.): *Forschungslabor Raum. Das Logbuch.* Berlin 2012, S. 42–49

2 Vgl. Bunge, Mario Augusto: „Treatise on Basic Philosophy". In: Bunge, Mario Augusto (Hg.): *Epistemology & Methodology I, Exploring the World.* Band 5, Dordrecht 1983, S. 72f.

3 Vgl. Signer, Rolf: *Argumentieren in der Raumplanung.* Dissertation ETH Zürich, Zürich 1994, S. 141

4 Vgl. ebd., S. 141f.

5 Zur Bedeutung des Augenscheins vgl. Scholl, Bernd: *Aktionsplanung. Zur Behandlung komplexer Schwerpunktaufgaben in der Raumplanung.* Zürich 1995, S. 178. „Nichts Wichtiges vergessen" ist eine wichtige Maxime für das Klären von Problemen in der Raumplanung; diese Maxime heißt auch Regel vom Gesamtdatum und geht auf Carnap zurück. Zitiert nach Scholl, Bernd: *Aktionsplanung. Zur Behandlung komplexer Schwerpunktaufgaben in der Raumplanung.* Zürich 1995, S. 96f. „Wer Maximen kennt und sie nicht braucht, ist besser dran, als wer sie braucht und sie nicht kennt", zitiert nach Maurer, Jakob: *Maximen für Planer.* Zürich 1995

6 Vgl. Bunge, Mario Augusto: „Treatise on Basic Philosophy". In: Bunge, Mario Augusto (Hg.): *Epistemology & Methodology I, Exploring the World.* Band 5, Dordrecht 1983, S. 72f. Das Gedächtnis, das häufig als Quelle des Wissens – über die Vergangenheit – betrachtet wird, kann höchstens erworbenes Wissen verdrehen, nie erzeugen.

7 Vgl. ebd., S. 199

8 Im Zusammenhang mit der Eröffnung des Gotthard-Basistunnels im Dezember 2016 folgt auf den Probebetrieb der Versuchsbetrieb, ehe dann der Alltagsbetrieb startet. Vgl. Schneeberger, Paul: „Bald erste Güterzüge im Basistunnel". In: *Neue Zürcher Zeitung.* 01.03.16, S. 14

9 Neisser, Ulric: *Kognition und Wirklichkeit: Prinzipien und Implikationen der kognitiven Psychologie.* Stuttgart 1979, S. 19 (Original: *Cognition and Reality: Principles and Implications of Cognitive Psychology.* San Francisco 1976)

10 „Ein Schema ist jener Teil des ganzen Wahrnehmungszyklus, der im Inneren des Wahrnehmenden ist, durch Erfahrung veränderbar und irgendwie spezifisch für das, was wahrgenommen wird. Das Schema nimmt Information auf, wenn sie bei den Sinnesorganen verfügbar wird, und es wird durch diese Information verändert. Es leitet Bewegungen und Erkundungsaktivitäten, die weitere Information verfügbar machen, und wird durch diese wiederum verändert." Zitiert nach Neisser, Ulric: *Kognition und Wirklichkeit: Prinzipien und Implikationen der kognitiven Psychologie.* Stuttgart 1979, S. 50

11 Vgl. ebd., S. 26 ff.

12 Guski, Rainer: *Wahrnehmung. Eine Einführung in die Psychologie der menschlichen Informationsaufnahme.* Stuttgart 2000, S. 76

13 Neisser, Ulric: *Kognition und Wirklichkeit: Prinzipien und Implikationen der kognitiven Psychologie.* Stuttgart 1979, S. 26

14 Vgl. Signer, Rolf: *Argumentieren in der Raumplanung.* Dissertation ETH Zürich, Zürich 1994, S. 207. Der Ausdruck „You can't help recognizing it!" stammt von Potter in Zusammenhang mit der Erfassung eines ge-

re." Quoted according to Bunge, Mario Augusto: *The Sociology-Philosophy Connection*. New York 1999, p. 4

17 Cf. Signer, Rolf: *Planungstheorie und -methodik – Ansätze oder die Art des Denkens*. Lecture as part of the International Doctoral College, TU Vienna, March 2013.

18 "Approach" is understood here according to Bunge: "Way of looking at things or handling them. Manner in which a problem (cognitive, practical, or moral) is tackled." Quoted according to Bunge, Mario Augusto: *Dictionary of Philosophy*. New York 1999, p. 21. "In general, an approach may be construed as a body B of *background knowledge* together with a set P of problems (*problematics*), a set A of *aims*, and a set M of methods (*methodics*)." Quoted according to Bunge, Mario Augusto (Ed.): *Epistemology & Methodology I, Exploring the World*. Vol. 5, Dordrecht 1983, p. 259. Cf. Also Signer, Rolf: *Planungstheorie und -methodik – Ansätze oder die Art des Denkens*. Lecture as part of the International Doctoral College, TU Vienna, March 2013.

19 In Belgrade there were the groups *Planning Methodology* (Communication, involved parties, process development), *Planning Methodology* (Design methods and planning instruments), *Surface potentials in (urban) space* (Interior development, density, constructional transformation, conversion), *Infrastructure systems and the city; mobility* (Transport, supply, energy, logistics, innovation, efficiency) and *Reinterpreting the urban landscape* (Aesthetics, urban qualities, perception).

20 Cf. Burckhardt, Lucius: *Warum ist Landschaft schön? Die Spaziergangswissenschaft*. Berlin 2006, p. 263

21 For the role of the image cf. Signer, Rolf: "'The Image Precedes the Idea' Images in Spatial Planning". In: International Doctoral College (ed.): *Spatial Research Lab. The Logbook*. Berlin 2012, p. 50ff.

22 These notes come from Nicole Uhrig.

23 Such were the circumstances. Ideally, of course, forays ashore would have been ideal to have been able to study parts of the Spatial Research Labs closer as examples.

24 In Zurich, the five thematic groups bore the following names: 1. Integrated development concept Dietikon—Spreitenbach/Killwangen, 2. How will the Limmat Valley railway yard develop further in future? 3. What public spaces do the new development hubs in the Limmat Valley need? 4. Interior development and the regeneration of existing settlements, and 5. Connections and networks in the Limmat Valley—waterways as an opportunity?

25 Cf. Daum, Matthias/Schneeberger, Paul: *Daheim. Eine Reise durch die Agglomeration*. Zurich 2013. The readings: "Stadt statt Güterwagen?" (p. 129ff.), "Jenseits des Shoppingcenters" (p. 145ff.) and "So tickt dieses Land" (p. 202ff.)

26 Cf. Fossa, Giovanna on p. 218 in this book

27 As stated by Ilaria Tosoni.

Nicole Uhrig, p. 54

1 Schlögel, Karl: *Im Raume lesen wir die Zeit*. Frankfurt a. M. 2006, p. 287

2 Febvre, Lucien: *Annales d'histoire sociale* 1940, 12, p. 49. Quoted in Vercelloni, Matteo/Virgilio Vercelloni: *The Invention of the Western Garden*. Milan 2010, p. 13

3 Langenscheidt dictionary Latin-German/German-Latin. Berlin/Munich 1973

4 Further information about the project: http://klima-metropole-ruhr-2022.rag.de, 25.02.2016

5 Schöbel, Sören: Infrastruktur in der Landschaft. Lecture at the specialist congress "Bundesnetzagentur meets Science" in Berlin on 25.06.2013

6 Kühne, Olaf/Spellerberg, Annette: *Heimat und Heimatbewusstsein in Zeiten erhöhter Flexibilitätsanforderungen. Empirische Untersuchungen im Saarland*. Wiesbaden 2010. Quoted in Kühne, Olaf et al.: *Transformation und Landschaft: Die Folgen sozialer Wandlungsprozesse auf Landschaft*. Wiesbaden 2015, p. 10

7 Cf. Kühne, Olaf et al.: *Transformation und Landschaft: Die Folgen sozialer Wandlungsprozesse auf Landschaft*. Wiesbaden 2015

Michael Koch, Markus Neppl, Walter Schönwandt, Bernd Scholl, Andreas Voigt, Udo Weilacher: Urban Landscape Transformation, p. 70

1 International Doctoral College (ed.): *Spatial Resarch Lab. The Logbook*. Berlin 2012, p. 14

2 Ibid.

3 Ibid.

4 Ibid.

5 Ibid., p. 13

6 In detail on this subject: Schönwandt, Walter/Wasel, Peter: "Das semiotische Dreieck – ein gedankliches Werkzeug beim Planen. Teil 1". In: *Bauwelt*. Vol. 19, 1997 (88), p. 1028–1042 and "Das semiotische Dreieck – ein gedankliches Werkzeug beim Planen. Teil 2". In: *Bauwelt*. Vol. 20, 1997 (88), p. 1118–1132

7 The ensuing comments with a focus on "landscape" are based on a previously unpublished manuscript by Udo Weilacher as a basis for a presentation (2013).

8 Cf. Bossel, Hartmut: *Modellbildung und Simulation*. Wiesbaden 1994

9 Cf. Ricica, Kurt/Voigt, Andreas (eds.) et al.: *Raumverträglichkeit als Beitrag zur nachhaltigen Raumnutzung*. Vienna 1998

10 Cf. Schönwandt, Walter/Voigt, Andreas: "Planungsansätze". In: Akademie für Raumforschung und Landesplanung (ARL) (ed): *Handwörterbuch der Raumordnung*. Hannover 2005, p. 769–776

11 Ritter, Joachim: "Landschaft. Zur Funktion des Ästhetischen in der modernen Gesellschaft". (1963) In:

schriebenen Wortes: Potter, Mary C.: „Remembering". In: Osherson, Daniel N./Smith Edward E. (Hg.): *Thinking. An Invitation to Cognitive Science*. Ausgabe 3, Cambridge 1990, S. 27: „If you look at a written word, you can't help recognizing it." – vorausgesetzt allerdings, man ist kein Analphabet.

15 Vgl. Scholl, Bernd: *Aktionsplanung. Zur Behandlung komplexer Schwerpunktaufgaben in der Raumplanung.* Zürich 1995, S. 105f. oder vgl. Maurer, Jakob: *Maximen für Planer.* Zürich, 1995, S. 16

16 „Whatever is seen, has been locked upon from some viewpoint or other: there is no vision from nowhere." Zitiert nach Bunge, Mario Augusto: *The Sociology-Philosophy Connection.* New York 1999, S. 4

17 Vgl. Signer, Rolf: *Planungstheorie und -methodik – Ansätze oder die Art des Denkens.* Vorlesung im Rahmen des Doktorandenkollegs, TU Wien März 2013

18 „Approach" wird hier im Sinne von Bunge folgendermaßen verstanden: „Way of looking at things or handling them. Manner in which a problem (cognitive, practical, or moral) is tackled." Zitiert nach Bunge, Mario Augusto: *Dictionary of Philosophy.* New York 1999, S. 21. „In general, an approach may be construed as a body B of *background knowledge* together with a set P of problems (*problematics*), a set A of *aims*, and a set M of methods (*methodics*)." Zitiert nach Bunge, Mario Augusto (Hg.): *Epistemology & Methodology I, Exploring the World.* Band 5, Dordrecht 1983, S. 259. Vgl. auch Signer, Rolf: *Planungstheorie und -methodik – Ansätze oder die Art des Denkens.* Vorlesung im Rahmen des Doktorandenkollegs, TU Wien März 2013

19 In Belgrad handelte es sich um die Gruppen *Planungsmethodik* (Kommunikation, Akteure, Prozessgestaltung), *Planungsmethodik* (Entwurfsmethoden und Planungsinstrumente), *Flächenpotentiale im (urbanen) Raum* (Innenentwicklung, Dichte, bauliche Transformation, Konversion), *Infrastruktursysteme und Stadt, Mobilität* (Transport, Versorgung, Energie, Logistik, Innovation, Effizienz), *Umdeutung der StadtLandSchaft* (Ästhetik, urbane Qualitäten, Wahrnehmung).

20 Vgl. Burckhardt, Lucius: *Warum ist Landschaft schön? Die Spaziergangswissenschaft.* Berlin 2006, S. 263

21 Zur Rolle des Bildes vgl. Signer, Rolf: „Das Bild geht der Idee voraus – Von Bildern in der Raumplanung". In: Internationales Doktorandenkolleg Forschungslabor Raum (Hg.): *Forschungslabor Raum. Das Logbuch.* Berlin 2012, S. 50ff.

22 Diese Hinweise stammen von Nicole Uhrig.

23 Das war als Umstand hinzunehmen. Idealerweise wären natürlich „Fischzüge" ans Land ideal gewesen, um exemplarisch Teile des Laborraums näher unter die Lupe nehmen zu können.

24 In Zürich trugen die fünf thematisch orientierten Gruppen die folgenden Namen: 1. Integriertes Entwicklungskonzept Dietikon – Spreitenbach/Killwangen, 2. Wie entwickelt sich der Rangierbahnhof Limmattal in der Zukunft weiter?, 3. Welche öffentlichen Räume brauchen die neuen Entwicklungsschwerpunkte im Limmattal?, 4. Innenentwicklung und Siedlungserneuerung im Bestand, 5. Verbindungen und Vernetzung im Limmattal – Gewässer als Chance?

25 Vgl. Daum, Matthias/Schneeberger, Paul: *Daheim. Eine Reise durch die Agglomeration.* Zürich 2013. Die Lesungen: „Stadt statt Güterwagen?" (S. 129ff.), „Jenseits des Shoppingcenters"(S. 145ff.) und „So tickt dieses Land" (S. 202ff.)

26 Vgl. Fossa, Giovanna auf S. 219 in diesem Buch

27 Aus den Ausführungen von Ilaria Tosoni.

Nicole Uhrig, S. 55

1 Schlögel, Karl: *Im Raume lesen wir die Zeit.* Frankfurt a. M. 2006, S. 287

2 Febvre, Lucien: *Annales d'histoire sociale* 1940, 12, S. 49. Zitiert in Vercelloni, Matteo/Virgilio Vercelloni: *The Invention of the Western Garden.* Milan 2010, S. 13

3 Langenscheidt Wörterbuch Lateinisch-Deutsch/ Deutsch Lateinisch. Berlin/München 1973

4 Mehr Information zum Projekt: http://klimametropole-ruhr-2022.rag.de, 25.02.2016

5 Schöbel, Sören: Infrastruktur in der Landschaft. Vortrag am Fachkongress „Bundesnetzagentur meets Science" in Berlin vom 25.06.2013

6 Kühne, Olaf/Spellerberg, Annette: *Heimat und Heimatbewusstsein in Zeiten erhöhter Flexibilitätsanforderungen. Empirische Untersuchungen im Saarland.* Wiesbaden 2010. Zitiert in Kühne, Olaf et al.: *Transformation und Landschaft: Die Folgen sozialer Wandlungsprozesse auf Landschaft.* Wiesbaden 2015, S. 10

7 Vgl. Kühne, Olaf et al.: Transformation und Landschaft: Die Folgen sozialer Wandlungsprozesse auf Landschaft. Wiesbaden 2015

Michael Koch, Markus Neppl, Walter Schönwandt, Bernd Scholl, Andreas Voigt, Udo Weilacher: Urbane Transformationslandschaften, S. 71

1 Internationales Doktorandenkolleg Forschungslabor Raum (Hg.): *Forschungslabor Raum. Das Logbuch.* Berlin 2012, S. 15

2 Ebd.

3 Ebd.

4 Ebd.

5 Ebd., S. 13

6 Ausführlich dazu: Schönwandt, Walter/Wasel, Peter: „Das semiotische Dreieck – ein gedankliches Werkzeug beim Planen. Teil 1". In: *Bauwelt*. Heft 19, 1997 (88), S. 1028–1042 und „Das semiotische Dreieck – ein gedankliches Werkzeug beim Planen. Teil 2". In: *Bauwelt*. Heft 20, 1997 (88), S. 1118–1132

Ibid.: *Subjektivität*. Six essays, Frankfurt a. M. 1989, p. 150–151

12 Jackson, John Brinckerhoff/Horowitz, Helen L. (eds.): *Landscape in Sight. Looking at America*. New Haven 1997, p. 304–305

13 Jackson, John Brinckerhoff: "Landschaften. Ein Resümee (1984)". In: Franzen, Brigitte/Krebs Stefanie (eds.): *Landschaftstheorie. Texte der Cultural Landscape Studies*. Cologne 2005; p. 43

Original: Jackson, John Brinckerhoff: "Concluding with Landscapes". In: Ibid.: *Discovering the Vernacular Landscape*. New Haven/London 1984, p. 145–157

Walter Schönwandt, p. 82

1 Mandelbaum, Seymour J.: "A complete general theory of planning is impossible." In: *Policy Sciences*. Ausgabe 11, Amsterdam 1979, p. 59–71

2 Cf. Schönwandt, Walter: *Planung in der Krise?* Stuttgart 2002, p. 62ff.

3 Sennett, Richard: *Handwerk*. Berlin 2009, p. 243

4 Lindblom, Charles E.: "The Science of 'Muddling Through.'" In: Stein, Jay M. (ed.): *Classic Readings in Urban Planning*. New York 1995, p. 35–48. Original in: *Public Administration Review*, Edition 19, 1959, p. 78–88

5 For a detailed representation of the rational planning concept and the criticism thereof, see for example Schönwandt, Walter: *Planung in der Krise?* Stuttgart 2002, p. 13ff and p. 30ff.

6 Cf. ibid., p. 34

7 Bunge, Mario: *Finding Philosophy in Social Science*. London 1996, p. 249

8 Mazza, Luigi: "If Strategic 'Planning Is Everything, Maybe It's Nothing.' Comments on Albrecht's and Balducci's article: 'Practicing Strategic Planning.'" In: *disP – The Planning Review*. Edition 49.3, 3/2013, p. 40–42

9 It should be emphasised explicitly that the authors are highly valued colleagues, but even they cannot simply disregard basic methodological principles.

10 Albrechts, L./Balducci, A./Hillier, J. (eds.): *Strategic Planning. An International Perspective*. London 2016 (in preparation). In which: Part 1: *Situated practices of strategic planning*; Aims and Rationale of the Book

11 Ibid., p. 1ff.

Markus Neppl. p. 112

1 Neppl, Markus (ed.) et al.: *Auf dem Weg zum Räumlichen Leitbild Karlsruhe*. Karlsruhe KIT 2015, p. 3–4

2 VINEX ("Vierde Nota Ruimtelijke Ordening Extra," English: "Fourth Special Memorandum on Spatial Planning") is a Dutch housing programme launched in 1993 by the Dutch Housing Ministry (Ministerie van Volkshuisvesting, Ruimtelijke Ordening en Milieubeheer) with the aim of building around 750,000 new housing units nationwide between 1995 and 2015 (wikipedia.org/vinex); vgl. Boeijenga, Jelte/Mensink Jeroen: *Vinex Atlas*. Rotterdam 2008

3 Cf. Lootsma, Bart: *SuperDutch: Neue niederländische Architektur*. Translated by Marlene Müller-Haas. Munich 2002

4 The cooperative planning procedure "Die Parkstadt Süd" in the city of Cologne is being developed in a cooperative urban development and open space planning procedure. The planning procedure of the five teams is therefore embedded within an intensive participatory programme with the public. City of Cologne: http://www.stadt-koeln.de/leben-in-koeln/koeln-heute-fuer-morgen/parkstadt-sued-ein-neues-stadtquartier-zwischen-rhein-und-universitaet, 08.04.2016

5 The master plan "Innenstadt Köln" (Cologne City Centre) by the firm AS&P (Frankfurt) shows how the city centre of Cologne can and should be developed further in forthcoming years. The master plan is understood as a development concept that sets out the functional and design qualities of the city centre. Concrete measures, divided according to so-called intervention areas, are proposed and show what steps are required to achieve a qualitative improvement of this important urban area. Companies for the Cologne region: http://www.masterplan-koeln.de/Masterplan-Koeln-Startseite.start_masterplan_koeln.0.html, 08.04.2016

6 Fingerhuth, Carl: "Die spezifische Aufgabe eines Beirates in Aspern Seestadt". In: aspern, Die Seestadt Wiens (ed.): *Positionen zur Stadtproduktion*. Vienna 2015, p.20

7 Weißmüller, Laura: "Klötzchenspiel." In: *Süddeutsche Zeitung*. No. 20, 26.01.2016

8 In the university city of Tübingen, disused spaces are to be reactivated not only for housing development. The aim is to create varied and vibrant districts with a high identification value and residential qualities for a wide range of users. The model of building cooperatives is at the centre of this: families, single persons, trade professionals, or investors collaborate to build a townhouse according to their own requirements. The building groups receive an option on a site from the municipal authorities, which they can purchase after the reservation by the city has expired. City of Tübingen: https://www.tuebingen.de/98.html, 08.04.16

9 Janson, Alban/Tigges, Florian: *Grundbegriffe der Architektur*. Basel 2013, p. 338–339

Anita Grams, p. 136

1 The dissertation was sponsored by the Swiss National Fund (SNF).

7   Die nachfolgenden Ausführungen zum Fokus „Landschaft" basieren auf einem bislang unveröffentlichten Manuskript von Udo Weilacher als Grundlage eines Vortrages (2013).

8   Vgl. Bossel, Hartmut: *Modellbildung und Simulation*. Wiesbaden 1994

9   Vgl. Ricica, Kurt/Voigt, Andreas (Hg.) et al.: *Raumverträglichkeit als Beitrag zur nachhaltigen Raumnutzung*. Wien 1998

10 Vgl. Schönwandt, Walter/Voigt, Andreas: „Planungsansätze". In: Akademie für Raumforschung und Landesplanung (ARL) (Hg.): *Handwörterbuch der Raumordnung*. Hannover 2005, S. 769–776

11 Ritter, Joachim: „Landschaft. Zur Funktion des Ästhetischen in der modernen Gesellschaft". (1963) In: Ders.: *Subjektivität. Sechs Aufsätze*, Frankfurt a. M. 1989, S. 150–151

12 Jackson, John Brinckerhoff/Horowitz, Helen L. (Hg.): *Landscape in Sight. Looking at America*. New Haven 1997, S. 304–305

13 Jackson, John Brinckerhoff: „Landschaften. Ein Resümee (1984)". In: Franzen, Brigitte/Krebs Stefanie (Hg.): *Landschaftstheorie. Texte der Cultural Landscape Studies*. Köln 2005; S. 43
    Original: Jackson, John Brinckerhoff: „Concluding with Landscapes". In: Ders.: *Discovering the Vernacular Landscape*. New Haven/London 1984, S. 145–157: „Landscape is not a scenery, it is not a political unit; it is really no more than a collection, a system of man-made spaces on the surface of the earth. Whatever its shape or size, it is never simply a natural space, a feature of the natural environment; it is always artificial, always synthetic, always subject to sudden or unpredictable change."

Walter Schönwandt, S. 83

1   Mandelbaum, Seymour J.: „A complete general theory of planning is impossible". In: *Policy Sciences*. Ausgabe 11, Amsterdam 1979, S. 59–71

2   Vgl. Schönwandt, Walter: *Planung in der Krise?* Stuttgart 2002, S. 62ff.

3   Sennett, Richard: *Handwerk*. Berlin 2009, S. 243

4   Lindblom, Charles E.: „The Science of ‚Muddling Through'". In: Stein, Jay M. (Hg.): *Classic Readings in Urban Planning*. New York 1995, S. 35–48. Original in: *Public Administration Review*, Ausgabe 19, 1959, S. 78–88

5   Für eine detaillierte Darstellung des rationalen Planungsbegriffs sowie der Kritik daran siehe zum Beispiel Schönwandt, Walter: *Planung in der Krise?* Stuttgart 2002, S. 13ff. und S. 30ff.

6   Vgl. ebd., S. 34

7   Bunge, Mario: *Finding Philosophy in Social Science*. London 1996, S. 249

8   Mazza, Luigi: „If Strategic ‚Planning Is Everything, Maybe It's Nothing'. Comments on Albrechts and Balducci's article: ‚Practicing Strategic Planning'". In: disP – *The Planning Review*. Ausgabe 49.3, 3/2013, S. 40–42

9   Es sei ausdrücklich betont, dass es sich bei den Autoren um hochgeschätzte Kolleginnen und Kollegen handelt, aber auch sie können methodische Grundprinzipien nicht so ohne weiteres außer Kraft setzen.

10 Albrechts, L./Balducci, A./Hillier, J. (Hg.): *Strategic Planning. An International Perspective*. London 2016 (in Vorbereitung). Darin: Part 1: *Situated practices of strategic planning*; Aims and Rationale of the Book

11 Ebd., S. 1ff. Anmerkungen

Markus Neppl, S. 113

1   Neppl, Markus (Hg.) et al.: *Auf dem Weg zum Räumlichen Leitbild Karlsruhe*. Karlsruhe KIT 2015, S. 3–4

2   VINEX („Vierde Nota Ruimtelijke Ordening Extra", deutsch: vierte außerordentliche Note zur Raumordnung) ist ein 1993 ins Leben gerufenes niederländisches Wohnungsbauprogramm des niederländischen Wohnbauministeriums (Ministerie van Volkshuisvesting, Ruimtelijke Ordening en Milieubeheer) mit dem Ziel, zwischen 1995 und 2015 landesweit rund 750.000 neue Wohnungen zu bauen (wikipedia.org/vinex); vgl. Boeijenga, Jelte/Mensink Jeroen: *Vinex Atlas*. Rotterdam 2008

3   Vgl. Lootsma, Bart: *SuperDutch: Neue niederländische Architektur*. Übersetzt von Marlene Müller-Haas, München 2002

4   Das kooperative Planungsverfahren „Die Parkstadt Süd" der Stadt Köln wird in einem kooperativen, städtebaulich-freiraumplanerischen Verfahren entwickelt. Der Planungsprozess der fünf Teams ist daher in ein intensives Beteiligungsprogramm mit der Öffentlichkeit eingebettet. Stadt Köln: http://www.stadt-koeln.de/leben-in-koeln/koeln-heute-fuer-morgen/parkstadt-sued-ein-neues-stadtquartier-zwischen-rhein-und-universitaet, 08.04.2016

5   Der Masterplan Innenstadt Köln des Büros AS&P (Frankfurt) zeigt auf, in welcher Weise die Kölner Innenstadt in den kommenden Jahren städtebaulich weiterentwickelt werden kann und sollte. Der Masterplan versteht sich als Entwicklungskonzept, das die funktionalen und gestalterischen Qualitäten der Innenstadt herausarbeitet. Konkrete Maßnahmen, gegliedert nach sogenannten Interventionsräumen, werden vorgeschlagen und zeigen auf, in welchen Schritten die qualitätsvolle Weiterentwicklung dieses wichtigen Stadtraums erfolgen kann. Unternehmer für die Region Köln e. V.: http://www.masterplan-koeln.de/Masterplan-Koeln-Startseite.start_masterplan_koeln.0.html, 08.04.2016

6   Fingerhuth, Carl: „Die spezifische Aufgabe eines Beirates in Aspern Seestadt". In: aspern, Die Seestadt Wiens (Hg.): *Positionen zur Stadtproduktion*. Wien 2015, S.20

Franzikas Drasdo, p. 140

1 Cf. Altman, Irwin/Low, Setha M.: *Place Attachment – Human Behavior and Environment – Advances in Theory and Research*. New York 1992, p. 7

2 Manzo, Lynne C./Perkins, Douglas D.: "Finding common ground: the importance of place attachment to community participation and planning." In: *Journal of Planning Literature*. Vol. 20, 2006, p. 347

3 Cf. Devine-Wright, Patrick/Howes, Yuko: "Disruption of place attachment and the protection of restorative environments: A wind energy case study." In: *Journal of Environmental Psychology*. Vol. 30, 2010, p. 271

4 Cf. von Wirth, Timo: *Places in Transformation: Integrating Residents' Perspectives and Spatial Characteristics into the Assessment of Urban Quality of Life*. Dissertation No. 22162. Swiss Federal Institute of Technology Zurich (ETH), 2014

Andreas Voigt, p. 156

1 Cf. Scholl, Bernd (ed.): *Stadtgespräche*. Zurich 2007

2 Cf. Grams, Anita: *Spielräume für Dichte*. Dissertation ETH Zurich 2015

3 Cf. Sieverts, Thomas: "Vitality, Sense, Fit, Access, Control – Beobachtungen und Anmerkungen einer China-Reise." In: *Gestalteter Lebensraum, Gedanken zur öffentlichen Raumplanung*, Festschrift für Friedrich Moser. Vienna1987

4 Calvino, Italo: Invisible Cities. Vintage Books, London 1997, p.9

5 Cf. Schönwandt, Walter/Voigt, Andreas: "Planungsansätze," in: Akademie für Raumforschung und Landesplanung (ARL) (ed.): *Handwörterbuch der Raumordnung*. Hannover 2005, p. 769–776

6 Blotevogel, Hans H.: Raum. Dortmund 2005, p. 831–841

7 ibid., p. 840

8 ibid.

9 This train of thought is based on an exchange with Bernd Scholl, reinforced by a corresponding presentation as part of the International Doctoral College on the occasion of the doctoral symposium in Zurich in 2014, as well as an exchange with Konstantinos Fisoglou, Vienna, and Katharina Tyran, Vienna-Berlin.

10 Cf. International Doctoral College (ed.): *Forschungslabor Raum. Das Logbuch*. Berlin 2012, p. 13

11 Viennese term for café gardens or pavement cafés in public space

12 Cf. Bertolini, Rita: *Allmeinde Vorarlberg – Von der Kraft des gemeinsamen Tuns*. Bregenz 2012: Dellenbaugh, Mary et al (eds.): Urban Commons: Moving Beyond State and Market. Basel 2015

13 Cf. Bertolini, Rita: *Allmeinde Vorarlberg – Von der Kraft des gemeinsamen Tuns*. Bregenz 2012, p. 8

14 Cf. Franck, Georg: *Ökonomie der Aufmerksamkeit*. München 1998; cf. Knierbein, Sabine: *Die Produktion zentra-ler öffentlicher Räume in der Aufmerksamkeitsökonomie*. Wiesbaden 2010

15 Moser, Friedrich: *Gesehen. Aquarelle – Ölbilder – Computerversionen 1973 bis 2001*. Vienna 2001

16 Cf. Franck, Georg: "Künstliche Raumzeit. Zur ökonomischen Interdependenz von Raum und Zeit." In: *Merkur – Deutsche Zeitschrift für europäisches Denken*. Vol. 582, 9/1997, p. 902–913

17 This selection is based on an exchange with Sabine Knierbein, director of the research group "Urban Culture and Public Space," TU Vienna.

18 Urban development Vienna: https://www.wien.gv.at/stadtentwicklung/studien/oeffentlicherraum.html, 27.02.16

19 Konstantinos Fisoglou, Chairman of the Association of Hellenic Societies in Austria (OESA) via e-mail, 27.02.2016

20 Katharina Tyran, Slavicist, independent researcher, working i.e. on language history, identity construction and border studies, via e-mail, 29.02.2016

Michael Koch, p. 188

1 An international graduate programme at the HafenCity University (HCU) based on this research initiative is investigating these questions under the title "Urban Metamorphoses."

2 Cf. Dell, Christopher: *Das Urbane – Wohnen. Leben. Produzieren*. Berlin 2014

3 Bassand, Michel: "Métropoles et métropolisation." In: Koch, Michael/Schmid, Willy: *Die Stadt in der Schweizer Raumplanung: Ein Lesebuch*. Zurich 1999, p. 106ff.

4 Cf. Oswald, Franz/Schüller, Nicola et al. (eds.): *Neue Urbanität – das Verschmelzen von Stadt und Landschaft*. Zurich 2004

5 *Stadtaspekte* is a relatively new magazine with its head office in Berlin, whose team comprises journalists, urban developers, sociologists, and ethnologists. The citizens of the city determine the topics. http://www.stadtaspekte.de, 30.03.16

6 Stadtaspekte e. V. (ed.): *Stadtaspekte. Special edition: Neue Räume – Baukultur in Deutschlands Städten*. Berlin 2015

7 Cf. Albers, Gerd: *Entwicklungslinien im Städtebau*. Bauwelt Fundamente, Vol. 46, Gütersloh 1975; cf. Posener, Julius/Schäche, Wolfgang (eds.): *Vorlesungen zur Geschichte der neuen Architektur. 1750–1933*. Five special editions of *ARCH+*, magazine for architects, urban planners, and community policy groups No. 48, 53, 59, 63/64, 69/70. Aachen 1979

8 Cf. Baumeister, Reinhard: *Stadt-Erweiterungen in technischer, baupolizeilicher und wirtschaftlicher Beziehung*. Berlin 1876

9 Cf. Sitte, Camillo: *Der Städtebau nach seinen künstlerischen Grundsätzen*. Vienna 1889

7 Weißmüller, Laura: „Klötzchenspiel". In: *Süddeutsche Zeitung*. Nr. 20, 26.01.2016

8 In der Universitätsstadt Tübingen sollen brachliegende Flächen nicht nur für den Wohnungsbau reaktiviert werden. Ziel ist es, vielfältige und lebendige Quartiere mit hohem Lebens- und Identifikationswert für ganz unterschiedliche Nutzerinnen und Nutzer zu schaffen. Im Zentrum steht das Modell der Baugemeinschaften: Familien, Alleinstehende, Gewerbetreibende oder Investoren schließen sich zusammen, um nach ihren eigenen Vorstellungen ein Stadthaus zu errichten. Die Baugruppen erhalten von der Stadt eine Option auf ein Grundstück, das sie nach Ablauf der Reservierung von der Stadt erwerben können. Stadt Tübingen: https://www.tuebingen.de/98.html, 08.04.16

9 Janson, Alban/Tigges, Florian: *Grundbegriffe der Architektur*. Basel 2013, S. 338–339

Anita Grams, S. 136

1 Die Dissertation wurde vom Schweizerischen Nationalfonds SNF gefördert.

Franziska Drasdo, S. 140

1 Vgl. Altman, Irwin/Low, Setha M.: *Place Attachment – Human Behavior and Environment – Advances in Theory and Research*. New York 1992, S. 7

2 Manzo, Lynne C./Perkins, Douglas D.: „Finding common ground: the importance of place attachment to community participation and planning". In: *Journal of Planning Literature*. Heft 20, 2006, S. 347

3 Vgl. Devine-Wright, Patrick/Howes, Yuko: „Disruption of place attachment and the protection of restorative environments: A wind energy case study". In: *Journal of Environmental Psychology*. Heft 30, 2010, S. 271

4 Vgl. von Wirth, Timo: *Places in Transformation: Integrating Residents' Perspectives and Spatial Characteristics into the Assessment of Urban Quality of Life*. Dissertation Nr. 22162. Eidgenössische Technische Hochschule ETH Zürich, 2014

Andreas Voigt, S. 157

1 Im Englischen: „Urban Landscape Transformation"

2 Vgl. Scholl, Bernd (Hg.): *Stadtgespräche*. Zürich 2007

3 Vgl. Grams, Anita: *Spielräume für Dichte*. Dissertation ETH Zürich 2015

4 Vgl. Sieverts, Thomas: „Vitality, Sense, Fit, Access, Control – Beobachtungen und Anmerkungen einer China-Reise". In: *Gestalteter Lebensraum, Gedanken zur öffentlichen Raumplanung, Festschrift für Friedrich Moser*. Wien 1987

5 Calvino, Italo: *Die unsichtbaren Städte*. München 1985, S. 13

6 Vgl. Schönwandt, Walter/Voigt, Andreas: „Planungsansätze". In: Akademie für Raumforschung und Landesplanung (ARL) (Hg.): *Handwörterbuch der Raumordnung*. Hannover 2005, S. 769–776

7 Blotevogel, Hans H.: *Raum*. Dortmund 2005, S. 831–841

8 Ebd., S. 840

9 Ebd.

10 Diesem Gedankengang liegt der Austausch mit Bernd Scholl, verstärkt durch einen entsprechenden Vortrag im Rahmen des Internationalen Doktorandenkollegs anlässlich der Doktorandenwoche Zürich 2014, sowie der Austausch mit Konstantinos Fisoglou, Wien und Katharina Tyran, Wien-Berlin zugrunde.

11 Vgl. Internationales Doktorandenkolleg „Forschungslabor Raum" (Hg.): *Forschungslabor Raum. Das Logbuch*. Berlin 2012, S. 13

12 Wiener Begriff für Gastgarten im öffentlichen Raum

13 Vgl. Bertolini, Rita: *Allmeinde Vorarlberg – Von der Kraft des gemeinsamen Tuns*. Bregenz 2012; weiterführend: Dellenbaugh, Mary (Hg.) et al.: *Urban Commons: Moving Beyond State and Market*. Basel 2015

14 Vgl. Bertolini, Rita: *Allmeinde Vorarlberg – Von der Kraft des gemeinsamen Tuns*. Bregenz 2012, S. 8

15 Vgl. Franck, Georg: *Ökonomie der Aufmerksamkeit*. München 1998; vgl. Knierbein, Sabine: *Die Produktion zentraler öffentlicher Räume in der Aufmerksamkeitsökonomie*. Wiesbaden 2010

16 Moser, Friedrich: *Gesehen. Aquarelle – Ölbilder – Computerversionen 1973 bis 2001*. Wien 2001

17 Vgl. Franck, Georg: „Künstliche Raumzeit. Zur ökonomischen Interdependenz von Raum und Zeit". In: *Merkur – Deutsche Zeitschrift für europäisches Denken*. Heft 582, 9/1997, S. 902–913

18 Diese Auswahl basiert auf einem Austausch mit Sabine Knierbein, Leiterin der Forschungsgruppe „Stadtkultur und Öffentlicher Raum", TU Wien.

19 Stadtentwicklung Wien: https://www.wien.gv.at/stadtentwicklung/studien/oeffentlicherraum.html, 27.02.16

20 Konstantinos Fisoglou, Obmann des Verbands Hellenischer Vereine in Österreich (OESA) via E-Mail, 27.02.2016

21 Katharina Tyran, Slawistin, freie Wissenschaftlerin, forscht u.a. zu Sprachgeschichte, Identitätskonstruktionen und Border Studies, via E-Mail, 29.02.2016

Michael Koch, S. 189

1 Ein auf einer Forschungsinitiative basierendes Internationales Promotionsprogramm an der HafenCity Universität (HCU) geht diesen Fragen unter dem Titel „Urbane Metamorphosen" nach.

2 Vgl. Dell, Christopher: *Das Urbane – Wohnen. Leben. Produzieren*. Berlin 2014

3 Bassand, Michel: „Métropoles et métropolisation". In: Koch, Michael/Schmid, Willy: *Die Stadt in der Schweizer Raumplanung: Ein Lesebuch*. Zürich 1999, S. 106ff.

10 Klaus Selle from RWTH Aachen is representative here of the longstanding debate about a reorientation or widening of planning. Compare the platform: PND Planung Neu Denken. http://www.planung-neu-denken.de, 08.04.16

11 Cf. Weiner, Hendrik: "Mit kollaborativen Design-Projekten urbane Räume ortsspezifisch entwickeln und erforschen." In: Lange, Jan/Müller, Jonas (eds.): *Wie plant die Planung? Kultur- und planungswissenschaftliche Perspektiven auf die Praxis der räumlichen Planung.* Series of works "Berliner Blätter. Ethnographische und ethnologische Beiträge," Vol. 71, Berlin 2016.
On the basis of many years of practice, Hendrik Weiner is working on a dissertation with the title: "Der Ort als Akteur: Kollaboratives Design als Methode ortsspezifischer Stadtentwicklung – urbane Transformation mit Kindern und Jugendlichen" (working title) at HafenCity University Hamburg.

12 Lorch, Catrin: "Assemble gelingt, woran Städteplaner scheitern". Sueddeutsche online: http://www.sueddeutsche.de/kultur/britischer-kunstpreis-assemble-gelingt-woran-staedteplaner-scheitern-1.2766027, 08.12.15

13 Cf. Wainwright, Oliver: "Die Straße, die den Turner Prize gewann." In: Bund deutscher Architekten BDA (ed.): *Der Architekt.* Edition 1/ 2016, p. 56ff.

14 Cf. Eccli, Manfred et al.: "Kreativquartier: Eine andere Art der Transformation." In: Bund deutscher Architekten BDA (ed.): *Der Architekt.* Edition 2/2014, p. 48–51;
And cf. Kasparek, David: "Ein entschleunigtes Stück Stadt. Teleinternetcafe im Gespräch mit David Kasparek." In: Bund deutscher Architekten BDA (ed.): *Der Architekt.* Edition 1/2016, p. 43ff.

15 Ring, Kristien/AA PROJECTS/Senatsverwaltung für Stadtentwicklung und Umwelt (eds.): *Selfmade City. Berlin: Stadtgestaltung und Wohnprojekte in Eigeninitiative.* Berlin 2013

16 Rosa, Marcos/Weiland, Ute (eds.): *Handmade Urbanism: Mumbai – São Paulo – Istanbul – Mexico City – Cape Town: From Community Initiatives to Participatory Models.* Berlin 2013

17 From 20.07.–23.07.2016, a symposium sponsored by the VW Foundation is being held on this subject: *Disziplinäre Grenzgänge – Ein Perspektivenwechsel,* organised by Michael Koch, Yvonne Siegmund, Renée Tribble, Amelie Rost, HafenCity University Hamburg.

18 Cf. Franck, Georg: "Architektur als Mannschaftssport." In: *Neue Zürcher Zeitung.* http://www.nzz.ch/architektur-als-mannschaftssport-1.14171583, 07.01.12; cf. Franck, Georg: "Die urbane Allmende, Zur Herausforderung der Baukultur durch die nachhaltige Stadt." In: *Merkur – Deutsche Zeitschrift für europäisches Denken.* Vol.746, 7/2011, p. 567–582

19 Cf. page 136 in this book

20 Cf. page 260 in this book

21 Cf. page 106 in this book

22 Cf. page 102 in this book

23 Cf. page 214 in this book

24 Cf. page 212 in this book

25 Cf. page 184 in this book

26 Cf. page 210 in this book

27 Cf. page 104 in this book

28 Cf. Schneidewind, Uwe/Singer-Brodowski, Mandy: *Transformative Wissenschaft. Klimawandel im deutschen Wissenschaft- und Hochschulsystem.* Marburg 2014, p. 69

29 Cf. ibid., p. 20ff.

30 The "University of Neighbourhoods," an educational and research project initiated by Professor Bernd Kniess and the team at HCU (www.udn.hcu-hamburg.de), successfully addressed many of the aspects mentioned in this article in the years 2008-2013, despite difficult working conditions, as a cooperative project between the HCU, IBA Hamburg, and Kulturfabrik Kampnagel.

Bettina Wyss, p. 214

1 Dinter, Stefan: *Karlsruhe. Eine Stadt erleben.* Karlsruhe 2015

Bernd Scholl, p. 230

1 Nollert, Markus: "Zur Bedeutung des Entwerfens in Klärungsprozessen der Raumentwicklung. Möglichkeiten und Anforderungen an ein ‚raumplanerisches Entwerfen' im regionalen Maßstab." In: International Doctoral College "Spatial Research Lab" (ed.): *Spatial Research Lab. The Logbook.* Berlin 2012, p. 112f.

2 Freisitzer, Kurt/Maurer, Jakob (eds.) et al.: *Das Wiener Modell. Erfahrungen mit innovativer Stadtplanung – Empirische Befunde aus einem Grossprojekt.* Vienna 1987

3 Scholl, Bernd: "Die Methode der Testplanung – Exemplarische Veranschaulichung für die Auswahl und den Einsatz von Methoden in Klärungsprozessen" In: Akademie für Raumforschung und Landesplanung ARL (ed.): *Grundriss der Raumordnung und Raumentwicklung.* Hannover 2011

4 Cf. Scholl, Bernd: *Aktionsplanung. Zur Behandlung komplexer Schwerpunktaufgaben in der Raumplanung.* Zurich 1995

5 Gesellschaft für Ingenieurbaukunst (ed.): *Robert Maillart – Betonvirtuose.* Zurich 1996

6 Gesellschaft für Ingenieurbaukunst (ed.): *Christian Menn – Brückenbauer.* Basel 1997

7 Scholl, Bernd/Günther, Felix: "Corridor 24: Spatial Development along the North-South Railway Link from Rotterdam to Genoa." In: Scholl, Bernd (ed.): *SAPONI, Spaces and Projects of National Importance.* Zurich 2011

4 Vgl. Oswald, Franz/Schüller, Nicola et al. (Hg.): *Neue Urbanität – das Verschmelzen von Stadt und Landschaft.* Zürich 2004

5 *Stadtaspekte* ist ein relativ neues Magazin mit Sitz in Berlin, dessen Team sich aus Journalisten, Stadtentwicklern, Soziologen und Ethnologen zusammensetzt. Die Themen bestimmen die Bewohner der Stadt. http://www.stadtaspekte.de, 30.03.16

6 Stadtaspekte e. V. (Hg.): *Stadtaspekte. Sonderausgabe: Neue Räume – Baukultur in Deutschlands Städten.* Berlin 2015

7 Vgl. Albers, Gerd: *Entwicklungslinien im Städtebau.* Bauwelt Fundamente, Band 46, Gütersloh 1975; vgl. Posener, Julius/Schäche, Wolfgang (Hg.): *Vorlesungen zur Geschichte der neuen Architektur. 1750–1933.* Fünf Sonderhefte von ARCH+, Zeitschrift für Architekten, Stadtplaner und kommunalpolitische Gruppen Nr. 48, 53, 59, 63/64, 69/70. Aachen 1979

8 Vgl. Baumeister, Reinhard: *Stadt-Erweiterungen in technischer, baupolizeilicher und wirtschaftlicher Beziehung.* Berlin 1876

9 Vgl. Sitte, Camillo: *Der Städtebau nach seinen künstlerischen Grundsätzen.* Wien 1889

10 Klaus Selle der RWTH Aachen sei hier stellvertretend für die schon lange während Debatte um eine Neuausrichtung oder Erweiterung der Planung genannt. Vergleiche hierzu die Plattform: PND Planung Neu Denken. http://www.planung-neu-denken.de, 08.04.16

11 Vgl. Weiner, Hendrik: „Mit kollaborativen Design-Projekten urbane Räume ortsspezifisch entwickeln und erforschen“. In: Lange, Jan/Müller, Jonas (Hg.): *Wie plant die Planung? Kultur- und planungswissenschaftliche Perspektiven auf die Praxis der räumlichen Planung.* Schriftenreihe „Berliner Blätter. Ethnographische und ethnologische Beiträge“. Band 71, Berlin 2016.
Hendrik Weiner arbeitet vor dem Hintergrund einer jahrelangen Praxis an der Dissertation mit dem Titel: „Der Ort als Akteur: Kollaboratives Design als Methode ortsspezifischer Stadtentwicklung – urbane Transformation mit Kindern und Jugendlichen“ (Arbeitstitel) an der HafenCity Universität Hamburg.

12 Lorch, Catrin: „Assemble gelingt, woran Städteplaner scheitern“. Sueddeutsche online: http://www.sueddeutsche.de/kultur/britischer-kunstpreis-assemble-gelingt-woran-staedtplaner-scheitern-1.2766027, 08.12.15

13 Vgl. Wainwright, Oliver: „Die Straße, die den Turner Prize gewann“. In: Bund deutscher Architekten BDA (Hg.): *Der Architekt.* Ausgabe 1/ 2016, S. 56ff.

14 Vgl. Eccli, Manfred et al.: „Kreativquartier: Eine andere Art der Transformation“. In: Bund deutscher Architekten BDA (Hg.): *Der Architekt.* Ausgabe 2/2014, S. 48–51; vgl. Kasparek, David: „Ein entschleunigtes Stück Stadt. Teleinternetcafe im Gespräch mit David Kasparek“. In: Bund deutscher Architekten BDA (Hg.): *Der Architekt.* Ausgabe 1/2016, S. 43ff.

15 Ring, Kristien/AA PROJECTS/Senatsverwaltung für Stadtentwicklung und Umwelt (Hg.): *Selfmade City. Berlin: Stadtgestaltung und Wohnprojekte in Eigeninitiative.* Berlin 2013

16 Rosa, Marcos/Weiland, Ute (Hg.): *Handmade Urbanism: Mumbai – São Paulo – Istanbul – Mexico City – Cape Town: From Community Initiatives to Participatory Models.* Berlin 2013

17 Vom 20.07.–23.07.2016 findet in Hamburg dazu ein von der VW-Stiftung gefördertes Symposium statt: *Disziplinäre Grenzgänge – Ein Perspektivenwechsel,* organisiert von Michael Koch, Yvonne Siegmund, Renée Tribble, Amelie Rost, HafenCity Universität Hamburg.

18 Vgl. Franck, Georg: „Architektur als Mannschaftssport“. In: *Neue Zürcher Zeitung.* http://www.nzz.ch/architektur-als-mannschaftssport-1.14171583, 07.01.12; vgl. Franck, Georg: „Die urbane Allmende, Zur Herausforderung der Baukultur durch die nachhaltige Stadt“. In: *Merkur – Deutsche Zeitschrift für europäisches Denken.* Heft 746, 7/2011, S. 567–582

19 Vgl. Seite 137 in diesem Buch

20 Vgl. Seite 261 in diesem Buch

21 Vgl. Seite 107 in diesem Buch

22 Vgl. Seite 103 in diesem Buch

23 Vgl. Seite 215 in diesem Buch

24 Vgl. Seite 213 in diesem Buch

25 Vgl. Seite 185 in diesem Buch

26 Vgl. Seite 211 in diesem Buch

27 Vgl. Seite 105 in diesem Buch

28 Vgl. Schneidewind, Uwe/Singer-Brodowski, Mandy: *Transformative Wissenschaft. Klimawandel im deutschen Wissenschaft- und Hochschulsystem.* Marburg 2014, S. 69

29 Vgl. ebd., S. 20ff.

30 Die „Universität der Nachbarschaften“, ein von Professor Bernd Kniess und Team an der HCU initiiertes Ausbildungs- und Forschungsprojekt (www.udn.hcu-hamburg.de), thematisierte in den Jahren 2008–2013 erfolgreich, trotz schwieriger Arbeitsbedingungen als Kooperationsprojekt von HCU, IBA Hamburg und der Kulturfabrik Kampnagel viele der in diesem Artikel genannten Aspekte.

Bettina Wyss, S. 214

1 Dinter, Stefan: *Karlsruhe. Eine Stadt erleben.* Karlsruhe 2015

Bernd Scholl, S. 231

1 Nollert, Markus: „Zur Bedeutung des Entwerfens in Klärungsprozessen der Raumentwicklung. Möglichkeiten und Anforderungen an ein ‚raumplanerisches Entwerfen‘ im regionalen Maßstab“. In: Internationa-

8   Scholl, Bernd: "Der Gotthardbasistunnel – Folgen für die Raumentwicklung." In: Rheinkolleg: *Welterbe zwischen Strom und Schiene.* p. 28–32, 14. Internationale Jahrestagung des Rheinkollegs 3.–4.11.2006 in Bacharach, Speyer 2007

9   Scholl, Bernd: "Spatial Planning and Development in a European and Macro Regional Context." In: Drewello, Hansjörg/Scholl, Bernd (ed.): *Integrated Spatial and Transport Infrastructure Development – The Case of the European North-South Corridor Rotterdam-Genoa.* London 2015

10   Günther, Felix: *Grossräumige Erkundung – Eine Methode zur Vorbereitung raumplanerischer Interventionen in Räumen nationaler und europäischer Bedeutung.* Dissertation ETH Zurich 2015

11   Tosoni, Ilaria: *Shared spatial strategies and actions design: Approaches and instruments enabling collaborative design processes at the large, regional and macro-regional scale.* Dissertation ETH Zurich 2015

12   Braun, Cecilia: *Integrierte Hafen- und Stadtentwicklung am Rhein-Alpen-Korridor – Vor dem Hintergrund der logistischen Anforderungen und den Potenzialen der Stadtentwicklung am Beispiel der Hafenstädte Mannheim und Straßburg.* Masters thesis as part of the MAS Spatial Planning at ETH Zurich 2015

13   Cf. p. 258 in this book

14   Scholl, Bernd: *The Interrelationships of Airport and Spatial Development: Zurich Airport – Experiences from a Test Planning Process.* Series of papers at the ORL Institute at Karlsruhe University, Karlsruhe 2010

15   Kadrin, Yose: *Langfristperspektiven für die Raum- und Flughafenentwicklung in europäischen Metropolregionen – Am Beispiel der Flughafenregion Zürich.* Dissertation ETH Zurich 2012

16   Scholl, Bernd: *The Interrelationships of Airport and Spatial Development: Zurich Airport – Experiences from a Test Planning Process.* Series of papers at the ORL Institute at Karlsruhe University, Karlsruhe 2010

17   Scholl, Bernd/Nebel, Reto: "Urban Transformation in Airport Regions." In: *disP – The Planning Review.* No. 197 2/2014 (50th volume). Zurich 2014, p. 65–75

18   Rendigs, Silke: "Handlungserfordernisse einer integrierten Raum- und Infrastrukturentwicklung. Eine Untersuchung vor dem Hintergrund der Stromversorgung und der beabsichtigten Energiewende". Project with the support of the Schweizerischer Nationalfonds SNF (Swiss National Foundation). Zurich/Bern 2015. Cf. p. 262 in this book.

Udo Weilacher, p. 266

1   Ammann, Gustav: "Das Landschaftsbild und die Dringlichkeit seiner Pflege und Gestaltung." In: *Schweizerische Bauzeitung.* No.15/1941; p. 172–174

2   Apolinarski, Ingrid/Gailing, Ludger/Röhring, Andreas: "Institutionelle Aspekte und Pfadabhängigkeiten des regionalen Gemeinschaftsgutes Kulturlandschaft" (Working Paper). Erkner 2004, p. 18

3   Bertolini, Rita: *Allmeinde Vorarlberg – Von der Kraft des gemeinsamen Tuns.* Bregenz 2012, p. 8

4   Cf. Naturschutzrat Vorarlberg: annual report 2014 (PDF). http://www.naturschutzrat.at, 30.01.16

5   Cf. page 290 in this book

6   Glaser, Hermann: "Umweltgestaltung und Gesellschaft." In: *Bauen + Wohnen.* Vol. 22/1968, p. I 6

7   B,S,S. Volkswirtschaftliche Beratung AG: *Landschaftsqualität als Standortfaktor: Stand des Wissens und Forschungsempfehlung. Schlussbericht.* Basel 2012, p. 4

8   Ipsen, Detlev: *Ort und Landschaft.* Wiesbaden 2006, p. 92

9   Ipsen, Detlev: *Raumbilder. Kultur und Ökonomie räumlicher Entwicklung.* Pfaffenweiler 1997, p. 6

10   Ibid., S. 37/39

11   Kartzer, Hans: "Betonwelt". In: *Süddeutsche Zeitung.* No. 12, Saturday/Sunday 16./17. January 2016; p. R13

12   Cf. p. 292 in this book

13   Eco, Umberto: "Function and Sign: Semiotics of Architecture" (1973) in: Leach, Neil (Ed.): Rethinking Architecture. A Reader in Cultural Theory. London, New York 1997, p. 173/174

14   Sieferle, Rolf P.: "Die totale Landschaft" in: Oswald, Franz/Schüller, Nicola (eds.): *Neue Urbanität – das Verschmelzen von Stadt und Landschaft.* Zurich 2003, p. 74f.

15   Glaser, Hermann: "Umweltgestaltung und Gesellschaft." In: *Bauen + Wohnen.* Vol.22/1968, p. I 6

16   Cf. p. 288 in this book

17   Benedict, Mark A./McMahon, Edward T.: *Green Infrastructure: Smart Conservation for the 21st Century.* Washington D.C. 2002, p. 7/8

les Doktorandenkolleg Forschungslabor Raum (Hg.): *Forschungslabor Raum. Das Logbuch.* Berlin 2012, S. 112f.

2 Freisitzer, Kurt/Maurer, Jakob (Hg.) et al.: *Das Wiener Modell. Erfahrungen mit innovativer Stadtplanung – Empirische Befunde aus einem Grossprojekt.* Wien 1987

3 Scholl, Bernd: „Die Methode der Testplanung – Exemplarische Veranschaulichung für die Auswahl und den Einsatz von Methoden in Klärungsprozessen". In: Akademie für Raumforschung und Landesplanung ARL (Hg.): *Grundriss der Raumordnung und Raumentwicklung.* Hannover 2011

4 Vgl. Scholl, Bernd: *Aktionsplanung. Zur Behandlung komplexer Schwerpunktaufgaben in der Raumplanung.* Zürich 1995

5 Gesellschaft für Ingenieurbaukunst (Hg.): *Robert Maillart – Betonvirtuose.* Zürich 1996

6 Gesellschaft für Ingenieurbaukunst (Hg.): *Christian Menn – Brückenbauer.* Basel 1997

7 Scholl, Bernd/Günther, Felix: „Corridor 24: Spatial Development along the North-South Railway Link from Rotterdam to Genua". In: Scholl, Bernd (Hg.): *SAPONI, Spaces and Projects of National Importance.* Zürich 2011

8 Scholl, Bernd: „Der Gotthardbasistunnel – Folgen für die Raumentwicklung". In: Rheinkolleg: *Welterbe zwischen Strom und Schiene.* S. 28–32, 14. Internationale Jahrestagung des Rheinkollegs 3.–4.11.2006 in Bacharach, Speyer 2007

9 Scholl, Bernd: „Spatial Planning and Development in an European and Macro Regional Context". In: Drewello, Hansjörg/ Scholl, Bernd (Hg.): *Integrated Spatial and Transport Infrastructure Development – The Case of the European North-South Corridor Rotterdam-Genoa.* London 2015

10 Günther, Felix: *Grossräumige Erkundung – Eine Methode zur Vorbereitung raumplanerischer Interventionen in Räumen nationaler und europäischer Bedeutung.* Dissertation ETH Zürich 2015

11 Tosoni, Ilaria: *Shared spatial strategies and actions design: Approaches and instruments enabling collaborative design processes at the large, regional and macro-regional scale.* Dissertation ETH Zürich 2015

12 Braun, Cecilia: *Integrierte Hafen- und Stadtentwicklung am Rhein-Alpen-Korridor – Vor dem Hintergrund der logistischen Anforderungen und den Potenzialen der Stadtentwicklung am Beispiel der Hafenstädte Mannheim und Straßburg.* Masterarbeit im Rahmen des MAS Raumplanung an der ETH Zürich 2015

13 Vgl. S. 259 in diesem Buch

14 Scholl, Bernd: *The Interrelationships of Airport and Spatial Development: Zurich Airport – Experiences from a Test Planning Process.* Schriftenreihe des ORL-Institutes der Universität Karlsruhe, Karlsruhe 2010

15 Kadrin, Yose: *Langfristperspektiven für die Raum- und Flughafenentwicklung in europäischen Metropolregionen – Am Beispiel der Flughafenregion Zürich.* Dissertation ETH Zürich 2012

16 Scholl, Bernd: *The Interrelationships of Airport and Spatial Development: Zurich Airport – Experiences from a Test Planning Process.* Schriftenreihe des ORL-Institutes der Universität Karlsruhe, Karlsruhe 2010

17 Scholl, Bernd/Nebel, Reto: „Urban Transformation in Airport Regions". In: *disP – The Planning Review.* Nr. 197 2/2014 (50. Jahrgang). Zürich 2014, S. 65–75

18 Rendigs, Silke: *Handlungserfordernisse einer integrierten Raum- und Infrastrukturentwicklung. Eine Untersuchung vor dem Hintergrund der Stromversorgung und der beabsichtigten Energiewende.* Projekt mit Unterstützung des schweizerischen Nationalfonds SNF. Zürich/Bern 2015. Vgl. S. 263 in diesem Buch

Udo Weilacher, S. 267

1 Ammann, Gustav: „Das Landschaftsbild und die Dringlichkeit seiner Pflege und Gestaltung". In: *Schweizerische Bauzeitung.* Nr. 15/1941, S. 172–174

2 Apolinarski, Ingrid/Gailing, Ludger/Röhring, Andreas: „Institutionelle Aspekte und Pfadabhängigkeiten des regionalen Gemeinschaftsgutes Kulturlandschaft" (Working Paper). Erkner 2004, S. 18

3 Bertolini, Rita: *Allmeinde Vorarlberg – Von der Kraft des gemeinsamen Tuns.* Bregenz 2012, S. 8

4 Vgl. Naturschutzrat Vorarlberg: Jahresbericht 2014 (PDF). http://www.naturschutzrat.at, 30.01.16

5 Vgl. Seite 291 in diesem Buch

6 Glaser, Hermann: „Umweltgestaltung und Gesellschaft". In: *Bauen + Wohnen.* Band 22/1968, S. I 6

7 B,S,S. Volkswirtschaftliche Beratung AG: *Landschaftsqualität als Standortfaktor: Stand des Wissens und Forschungsempfehlung.* Schlussbericht. Basel 2012, S. 4

8 Ipsen, Detlev: *Ort und Landschaft.* Wiesbaden 2006, S. 92

9 Ipsen, Detlev: *Raumbilder. Kultur und Ökonomie räumlicher Entwicklung.* Pfaffenweiler 1997, S. 6

10 Ebd., S. 37/39

11 Kratzer, Hans: „Betonwelt". In: *Süddeutsche Zeitung.* Nr. 12, Samstag/Sonntag 16./17.Januar 2016; S. R13

12 Vgl. S. 293 in diesem Buch

13 Eco, Umberto: *Einführung in die Semiotik.* München 1988, S. 295

14 Sieferle, Rolf P.: „Die totale Landschaft". In: Oswald, Franz/Schüller, Nicola (Hg.): *Neue Urbanität – das Verschmelzen von Stadt und Landschaft.* Zürich 2003, S. 74f.

15 Glaser, Hermann: „Umweltgestaltung und Gesellschaft". In: *Bauen + Wohnen.* Band 22/1968, S. I 6

16 Vgl. S. 289 in diesem Buch

17 Benedict, Mark A./McMahon, Edward T.: *Green Infrastructure: Smart Conservation for the 21st Century.* Washington D.C. 2002, S. 7/8 (Übersetzung: U. Weilacher)

ACKNOWLEDGEMENTS DANK

The editors would like to thank the following for contributing to the content and financing of this publication:
Für die inhaltlichen sowie finanziellen Beiträge bedanken sich die Herausgeber herzlichst bei:

Milica Bajić-Brković
Alessandro Balducci
Gabriele Berauschek
Reinhard Breit
Sabrina Brenner
Gerd Buziek
Simona Casaulta-Meyer
Heike Dederer
Wolfgang Dickhaut
Kai Michael Dietrich
Vladan Đjokić
Jesko Fezer
Konstaninos Fisoglou
Giovanna Fossa
Tim Geilenkeuser
Maria Teresa Genoni
Michael Getzner
Ingrid und Richard Giefing
Anita Grams
Oliver Hager
Jasper Haubensack
Michael Heller
Christoph Hemberger
Sigrun Hüger
Ulrich Illing
Anke Karmann-Woessner
Andreas Kipar
Birgit Kögler
Martina Koll-Schretzenmayr
Bodo Krumwiede
Richard Macho

Thomas Madreiter
Armin Marty
Kurt Matyas
Doris Mayer
Viviane Meer
Elisabeth Merk
Valentina Miskovic
Vesna Mulic
Hanspeter Müller
Philipp Neff
Andrea Neuhaus
Markus Nollert
Manuel Peer
Adalbert Prechtl
Silke Rendigs
Alexander Rieck
Eva Ritter
Caterina Sala Vitale
Heimo Schedl
Rudolf Scheuvens
Hape Schneider
Mario Schneider
Bernd Scholl
Guido Sempell
Antonella Sgobba
Rolf Signer
Klaus Sill
Michael Sittard
Werner Steinke
Antje Stokmann
Gabriele Sturm
Giancarlo Tancredi
Ilaria Tosoni
Werner Tschirk
Filip Tyran

Katharina Tyran
Nicole Uhrig
Sonja Weber
Simona Weisleder
Isabel Wieshofer
Gesa Ziemer
Renate Zuckerstätter-Semela

ESRI Deutschland (Environmental Systems Research Institute)
ETH Zürich
HafenCity University Hamburg
Karlsruher Institut für Technologie (KIT)
Technische Universität München
Technische Universität Wien
Universität Stuttgart
HafenCity Hamburg GmbH
Referat für Stadtplanung und Bauordnung (Stadt München)
Fraunhofer IAO
Planzer Logistik AG
SBB Cargo AG
Bauverwaltung Spreitenbach
Stadtplanungsamt (Stadt Karlsruhe)
Stadt Wien
Albert Speer Stiftung

PICTURE CREDITS BILDNACHWEIS

18, 21: Internationales Doktorandenkolleg
Forschungslabor Raum

28/29, 90/91, 128/129, 162/163, 194/195, 250/251
Collages Collagen „Erinnerungsstücke und Treibgut"
assembled by erstellt von Sonja Weber. (Thanks to the
professors, teachers, and doctoral students for kindly
providing the images for the collages. Dank gilt den
Professoren, Lehrbeauftragten und Doktoranden, die
freundlicherweise das Bildmaterial für die Collagen
zur Verfügung gestellt haben.)

34: Rolf Signer

35: Rolf Signer after nach Ulric Neisser

44: Anita Grams

45 top oben: Edgar Hagspiel

45 bottom unten: Google Maps, 6.6.2014

46: Silke Rendigs

47: Anita Grams

48 top oben: Rolf Signer

48 bottom unten: Katarina Bajc

49 top oben: Udo Weilacher

49 bottom unten: Katarina Bajc

50: Anita Grams

51 top oben Giovanna Fossa

51 bottom left unten links: Anita Grams

51 bottom right unten rechts: Andreas Voigt

52 top oben: Anita Grams

52 bottom unten: Andreas Voigt

53: Anita Grams

56, 57: Nicole Uhrig

63: lohrberg stadtlandschaftsarchitektur

64: Nicole Uhrig

96: Jonas Bellingrodt

97: Sabrina Brenner

98/99, 100, 101: Silke Rendigs

102/103: Sabrina Brenner

104/105: Martin Storz/GRAFFITTI

106/107: Mario Schneider

108/109: Florian Stadtschreiber

114, 118, 119, 120, 122, 123: ASTOC Architects and
Planners, Köln

130, 131: Jonas Bellingrodt

132: Udo Weilacher

133: Jonas Bellingrodt

134: Sabrina Brenner

135: Jonas Bellingrodt

136/137: Timon Furrer (ETH Zürich)

138/139: Janna Hohn

140/141: Franziska Drasdo

144/145: Jonas Bellingrodt

148 bottom unten: Silke Rendigs

148/149 top oben: Anita Grams

150/151 top oben: Sabrina Brenner

151 right rechts: Anita Grams

152/153: Silke Rendigs

166 top oben: Integration 2012, Sebastian Zeddel,
diploma thesis Diplomarbeit TU Wien, adviser
Betreuerin: Claudia Yamu

166 bottom unten: Fabian Dembski

169, 170: Andreas Voigt

174/175: Sabrina Brenner

176 top oben: Nicole Uhrig

176 bottom unten, 177, 178, 179: Jonas Bellingrodt

180/181: Katarina Bajc

182/183: Jonas Bellingrodt

184/185: Renée Tribble

204: Jonas Bellingrodt

205, 206/207: Silke Rendigs

208, 209: Jonas Bellingrodt

210/211: LAVA / Fraunhofer IAO

212/213: Anna Kirstgen

214/215: Bettina Wyss

218/219: Metrogramma, Milan for the Milan City Plan

220, 221: S. Topuntoli, Milan

222/223 top oben: Sabrina Brenner

223 bottom unten: Jonas Bellingrodt

224: Sabrina Brenner

225, 226, 227: Jonas Bellingrodt

236, 237: K. Freisitzer, J. Maurer

239: Bernd Scholl

240: ETH Zürich, IRL, F. Günther

241: Bernd Scholl

243: ETH Zürich, IRL, F. Günther, C. Braun

244: Bilddatenbank ETH Zürich, LBS_R1-920923

246: Yose Kadrin

248, 252, 253: Silke Rendigs

254/255: Sabrina Brenner

256 top oben: Nicole Uhrig

256 bottom unten: Sabrina Brenner

257: Nicole Uhrig

258/259: Cecilia Braun

260/261: Karin Hollenstein

262/263: Timon Furrer (ETH Zürich)

266: Udo Weilacher

269: Land Vorarlberg

270, 273, 274, 275, 278: Udo Weilacher

281: Udo Weilacher

282 top oben: Udo Weilacher

282 bottom unten, 283: Sabrina Brenner

284, 285, 286: Sonja Gantioler

287: Mario Schneider

288/289: Sonja Gantioler

290/291: Land Vorarlberg, 2006

292/293: CLAAS KGaA mbH

316: Sonja Weber

IMPRINT IMPRESSUM

© 2016 by jovis Verlag GmbH
Texts by kind permission of the authors.
Pictures by kind permission of the photographers/holders of the picture rights.
Das Copyright für die Texte liegt bei den AutorInnen.
Das Copyright für die Abbildungen liegt bei den FotografInnen/InhaberInnen der Bildrechte.

Universities participating in the Doctoral College:
Am Doktorandenkolleg beteiligte Universitäten:
ETH Zürich
HafenCity Universität Hamburg
Karlsruher Institut für Technologie (KIT)
TU München
TU Wien
Universität Stuttgart

Cover Umschlagmotiv: Udo Weilacher
Editor Redaktion: Sonja Weber M.A.
Collagen Seiten pages: 28/29, 90/91, 128/129, 162/163, 194/195, 250/251: Sonja Weber M.A.

Translation Übersetzung: Lynne Kolar-Thompson
Proofreading Korrektur: Mary Dellenbaugh, Berlin / Jana Pippel, Berlin
Design and setting Gestaltung und Satz: jovis Verlag: Susanne Rösler, Samuel Zwerger
Lithography Lithografie: Bild1Druck, Berlin
Printing and binding Druck und Bindung: Graspo CZ a.s., Zlín

Bibliographic information published by the Deutsche Nationalbibliothek
The Deutsche Nationalbibliothek lists this publication in the Deutsche Nationalbibliografie;
detailed bibliographic data are available on the Internet at http://dnb.d-nb.de
Bibliografische Information der Deutschen Nationalbibliothek
Die Deutsche Nationalbibliothek verzeichnet diese Publikation in der Deutschen Nationalbibliografie; detaillierte bibliografische Daten sind im Internet über http://dnb.d-nb.de abrufbar.

jovis Verlag GmbH
Kurfürstenstraße 15/16
10785 Berlin

www.jovis.de

ISBN 978-3-86859-385-3